[X____]
[Fact_]

[reign_of_x]

[proof_X]
[death_X]

X-FACTOR BY LEAH WILLIAMS VOL. 2. Contains material originally published in magazine form as X-FACTOR (2020) #6-10. First printing 2021. ISBN 978-1-302-92185-9. Published by MARVEL WORLDWIDE, INC., a subsidiary of MARVEL ENTERTAINMENT, LLC. OFFICE OF PUBLICATION: 1290 Avenue of the Americas, New York, NY 10104. © 2021 MARVEL No similarity between any of the names, characters, persons, and/or institutions in this magazine with those of any living or dead person or institution is intended, and any such similarity which may exist is purely coincidental. **Printed in Canada.** KEVIN FEIGE, Chief Creative Officer; DAN BUCKLEY, President, Marvel Entertainment; JOE QUESADA, EVP & Creative Director; DAVID BOGART, Associate Publisher & SVP of Talent Affairs; TOM BREVOORT, VP, Executive Editor; NICK LOWE, Executive Editor, VP of Content, Digital Publishing; DAVID GABRIEL, VP of Print & Digital Publishing; JEFF YOUNGQUIST, VP of Production & Special Projects; ALEX MORALES, Director of Publishing Operations; DAN EDINGTON, Managing Editor; RICKEY PURDIN, Director of Talent Relations; JENNIFER GRÜNWALD, Senior Editor, Special Projects; SUSAN CRESPI, Production Manager; STAN LEE, Chairman Emeritus. For information regarding advertising in Marvel Comics or on Marvel.com, please contact Vit DeBellis, Custom Solutions & Integrated Advertising Manager, at vdebellis@marvel.com. For Marvel subscription inquiries, please call 888-511-5480. **Manufactured between 7/16/2021 and 8/17/2021 by SOLISCO PRINTERS, SCOTT, QC, CANADA.**

10 9 8 7 6 5 4 3 2 1

Vol. 2

Writer:	**Leah Williams** **with David Baldeón** (#10)
Artist:	**David Baldeón** **with David Messina** (#10) **& Lucas Werneck** (#10)
Color Artist:	**Israel Silva**
Letterer:	**VC's Joe Caramagna**
Cover Art:	**Ivan Shavrin**

Head of X:	**Jonathan Hickman**
Design:	**Tom Muller**
Assistant Editors:	**Annalise Bissa** **& Shannon Andrews** **Ballesteros**
Editor:	**Jake Thomas**
Senior Editor:	**Jordan D. White**

Collection Editor:	**Jennifer Grünwald**
Assistant Editor:	**Daniel Kirchhoffer**
Assistant Managing Editor:	**Maia Loy**
Assistant Managing Editor:	**Lisa Montalbano**
VP Production & Special Projects:	**Jeff Youngquist**
SVP Print, Sales & Marketing:	**David Gabriel**
Editor in Chief:	**C.B. Cebulski**

[xfac_[0.6]
[tor__[0.6]

Death is an awakening from the dream
of life. Burrow in sleep, down, down...

--THERESA CASSIDY*

*

[xfac_[0.6]
[tor__[0.6]

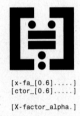

[x-fa_[0.6].....]
[ctor_[0.6].....]

[X-factor_alpha.]

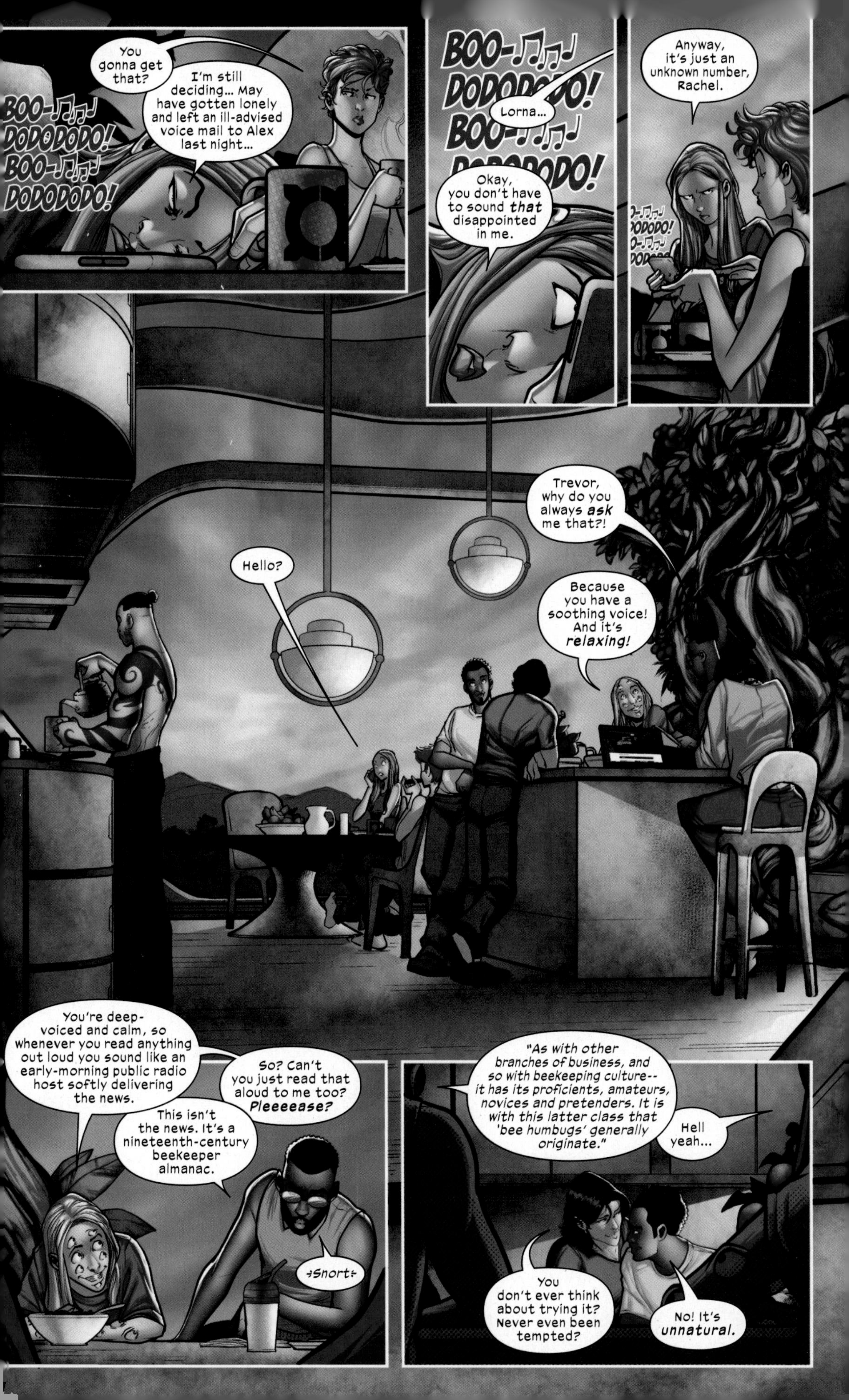

BOO-♫♫♩ DODODODO! BOO-♫♫♩ DODODODO!
You gonna get that?
I'm still deciding... May have gotten lonely and left an ill-advised voice mail to Alex last night...
BOO-♫♫♩ DODODODO! BOO-♫♫♩ DODODODO!
Lorna...
Okay, you don't have to sound *that* disappointed in me.
Anyway, it's just an unknown number, Rachel.
Hello?
Trevor, why do you always *ask* me that?!
Because you have a soothing voice! And it's *relaxing!*
You're deep-voiced and calm, so whenever you read anything out loud you sound like an early-morning public radio host softly delivering the news.
So? Can't you just read that aloud to me too? *Pleeeease?*
This isn't the news. It's a nineteenth-century beekeeper almanac.
Snort
"As with other branches of business, and so with beekeeping culture-- it has its proficients, amateurs, novices and pretenders. It is with this latter class that 'bee humbugs' generally originate."
Hell yeah...
You don't ever think about trying it? Never even been tempted?
No! It's *unnatural.*

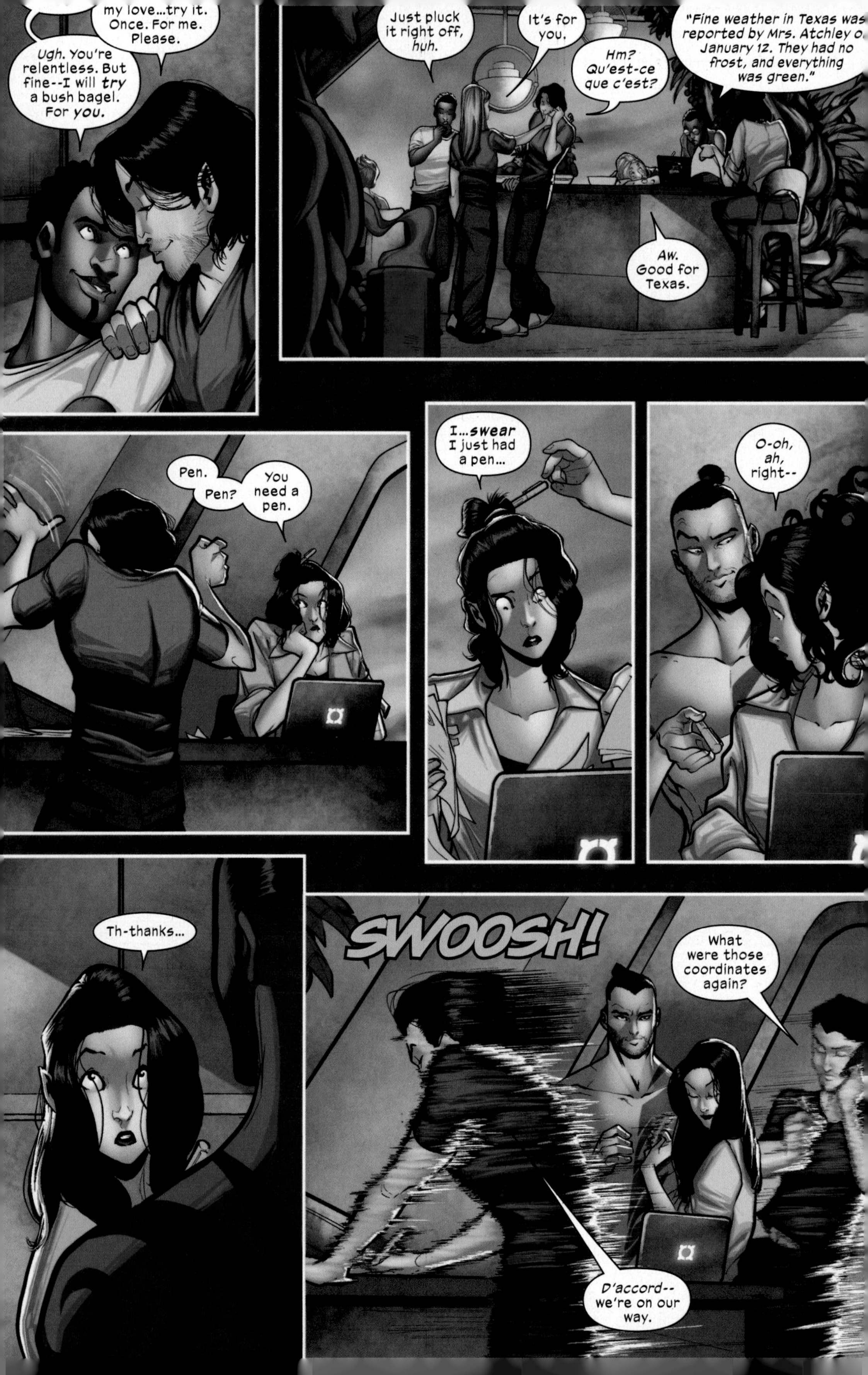
my love...try it. Once. For me. Please.
Ugh. You're relentless. But fine--I will try a bush bagel. For you.
Just pluck it right off, huh.
It's for you.
Hm? Qu'est-ce que c'est?
"Fine weather in Texas was reported by Mrs. Atchley o January 12. They had no frost, and everything was green."
Aw. Good for Texas.
Pen.
Pen?
You need a pen.
I...swear I just had a pen...
O-oh, ah, right--
Th-thanks...
SWOOSH!
What were those coordinates again?
D'accord-- we're on our way.

[00_proof_X]
[00_death_X]

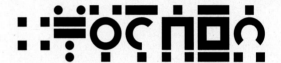

DEATHS TOO CLOSE FOR COMFORT

X-FACTOR has been investigating dead and missing mutants, thus ensuring their resurrections. More recently, that applied to Siryn after her cliffside fall.

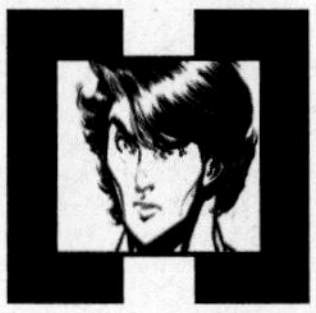
Northstar

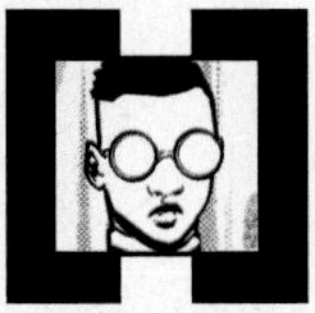
Prodigy

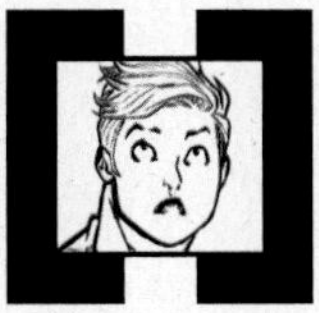
Prestige

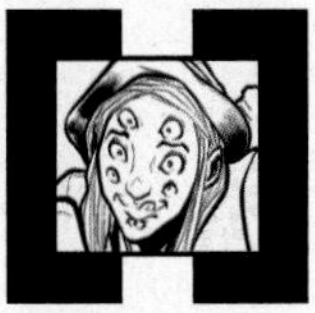
Eye-Boy

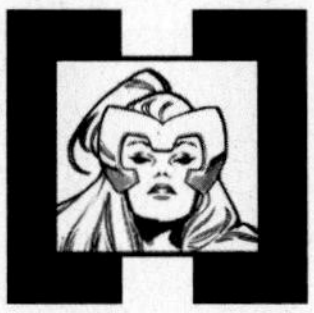
Polaris

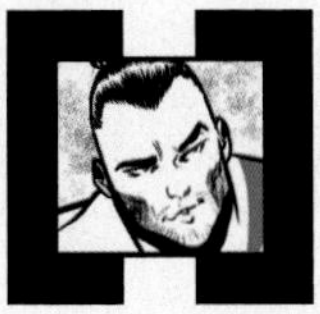
Daken

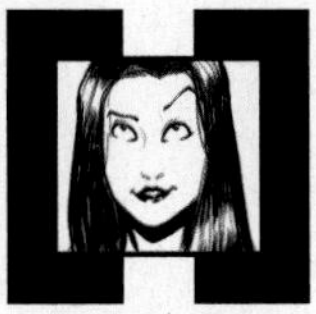
Aurora

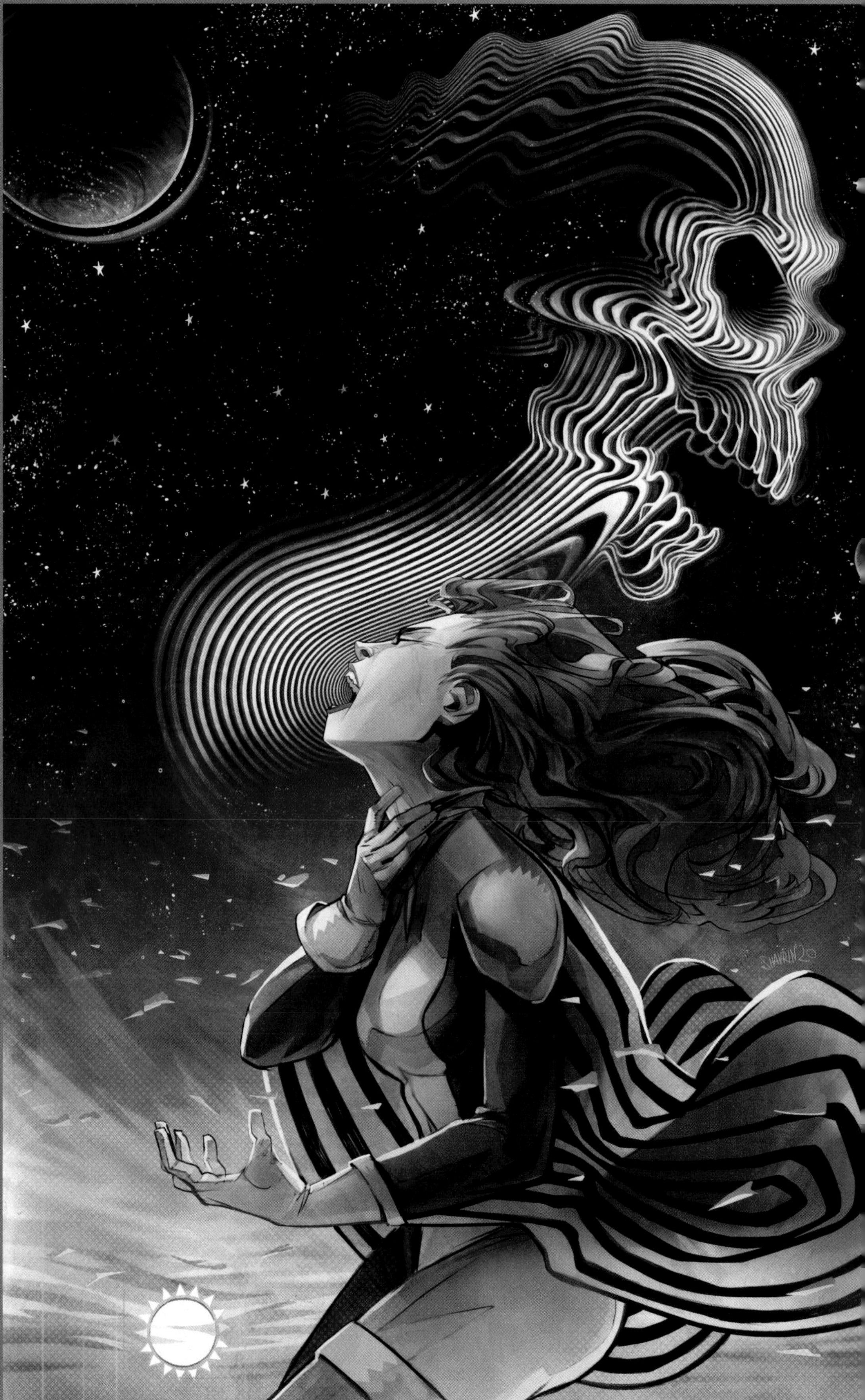

Suite N°6:
Scio Me Nihil Scire
"Second Movement"

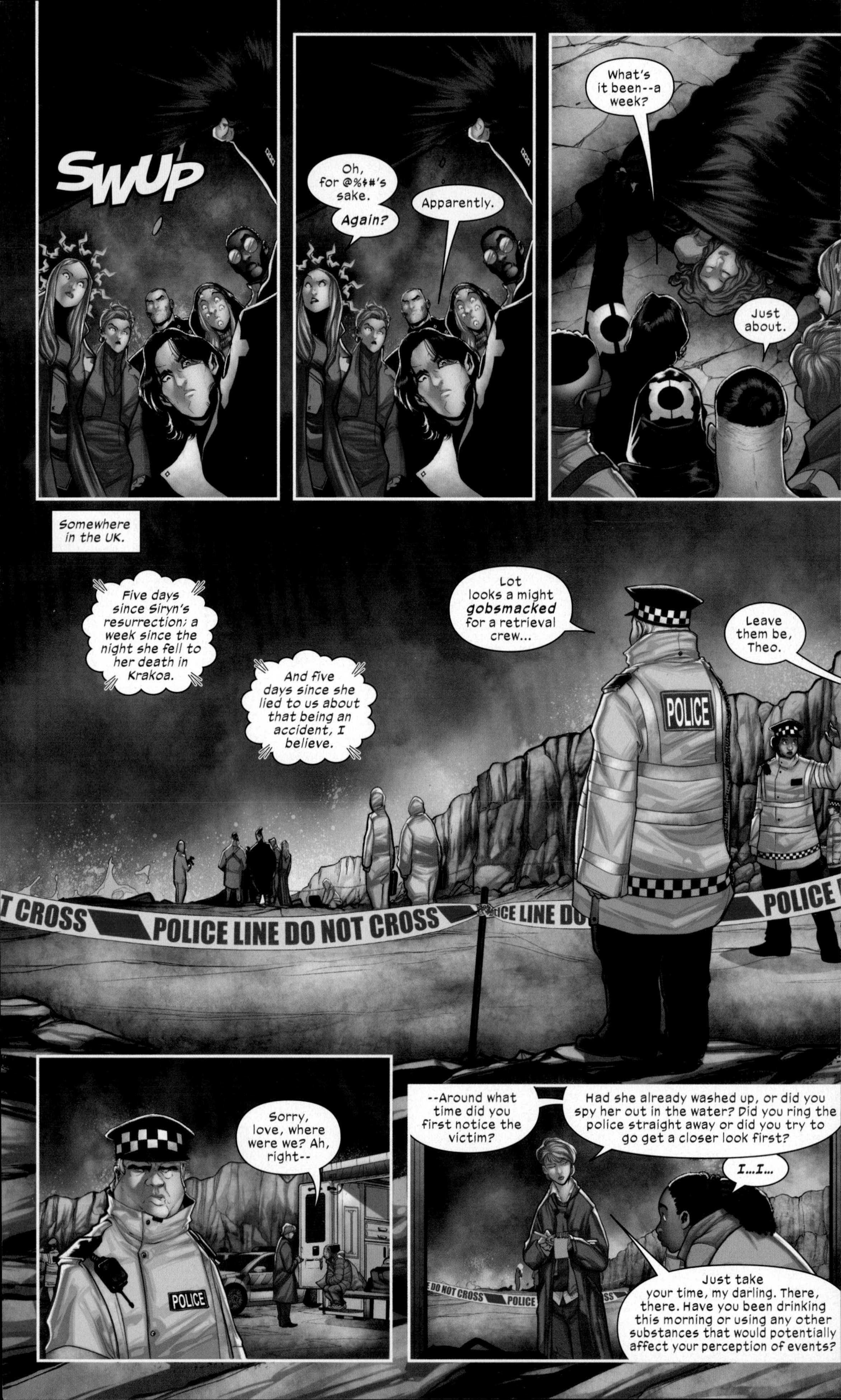
SWUP
Oh, for @%$#'s sake.
Again?
Apparently.
What's it been--a week?
Just about.
Somewhere in the UK.
Five days since Siryn's resurrection; a week since the night she fell to her death in Krakoa.
And five days since she lied to us about that being an accident, I believe.
Lot looks a might gobsmacked for a retrieval crew...
Leave them be, Theo.
POLICE
POLICE LINE DO NOT CROSS
Sorry, love, where were we? Ah, right--
--Around what time did you first notice the victim?
Had she already washed up, or did you spy her out in the water? Did you ring the police straight away or did you try to go get a closer look first?
I...I...
Just take your time, my darling. There, there. Have you been drinking this morning or using any other substances that would potentially affect your perception of events?

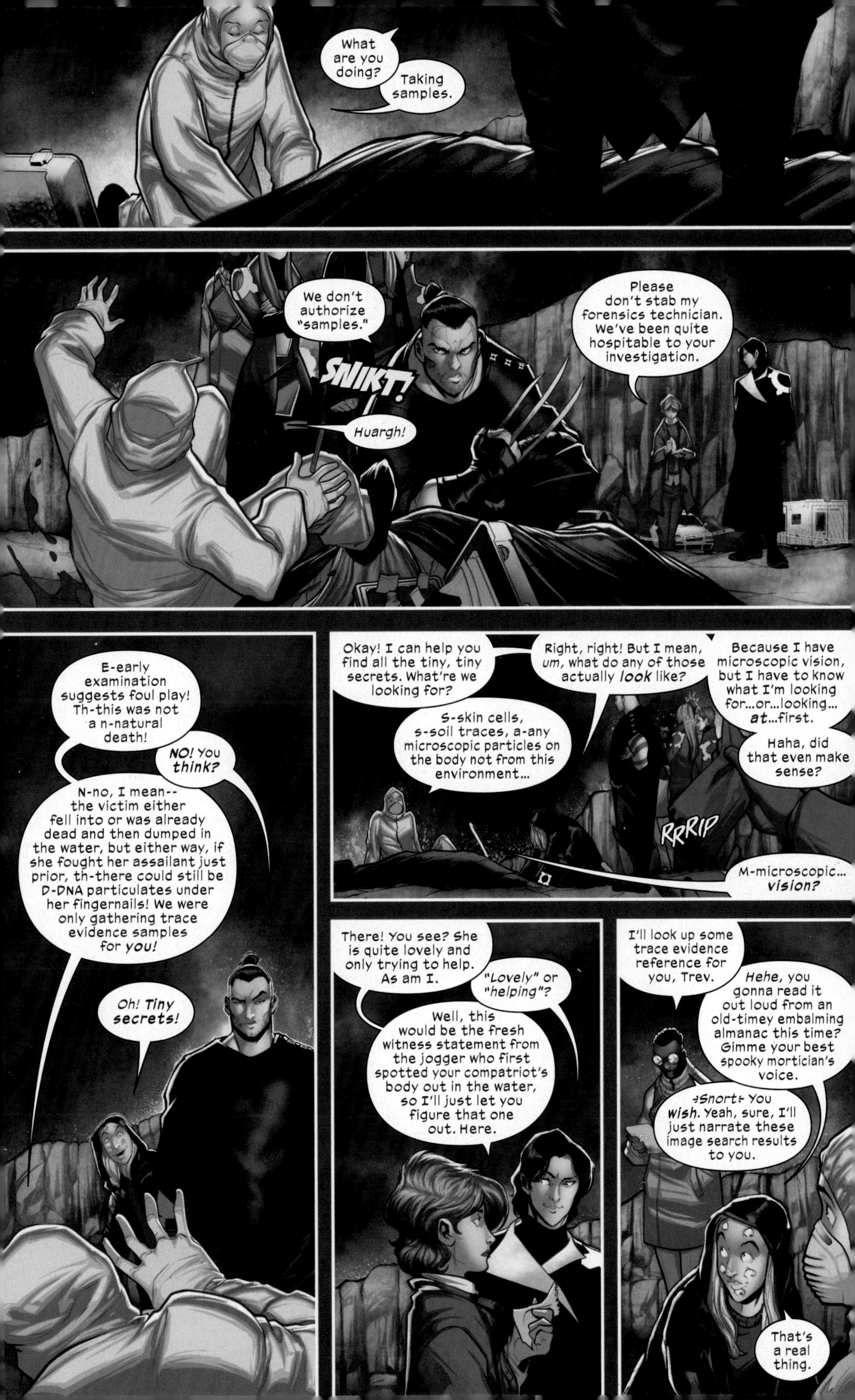
What are you doing?
Taking samples.
We don't authorize "samples."
SNIKT!
Please don't stab my forensics technician. We've been quite hospitable to your investigation.
Huargh!
E-early examination suggests foul play! Th-this was not a n-natural death!
NO! You think?
N-no, I mean-- the victim either fell into or was already dead and then dumped in the water, but either way, if she fought her assailant just prior, th-there could still be D-DNA particulates under her fingernails! We were only gathering trace evidence samples for you!
Oh! Tiny secrets!
Okay! I can help you find all the tiny, tiny secrets. What're we looking for?
S-skin cells, s-soil traces, a-any microscopic particles on the body not from this environment...
Right, right! But I mean, um, what do any of those actually look like?
Because I have microscopic vision, but I have to know what I'm looking for...or...looking... at...first.
Haha, did that even make sense?
RRRIP
M-microscopic... vision?
There! You see? She is quite lovely and only trying to help. As am I.
"Lovely" or "helping"?
Well, this would be the fresh witness statement from the jogger who first spotted your compatriot's body out in the water, so I'll just let you figure that one out. Here.
I'll look up some trace evidence reference for you, Trev.
Hehe, you gonna read it out loud from an old-timey embalming almanac this time? Gimme your best spooky mortician's voice.
=Snort= You wish. Yeah, sure, I'll just narrate these image search results to you.
That's a real thing.

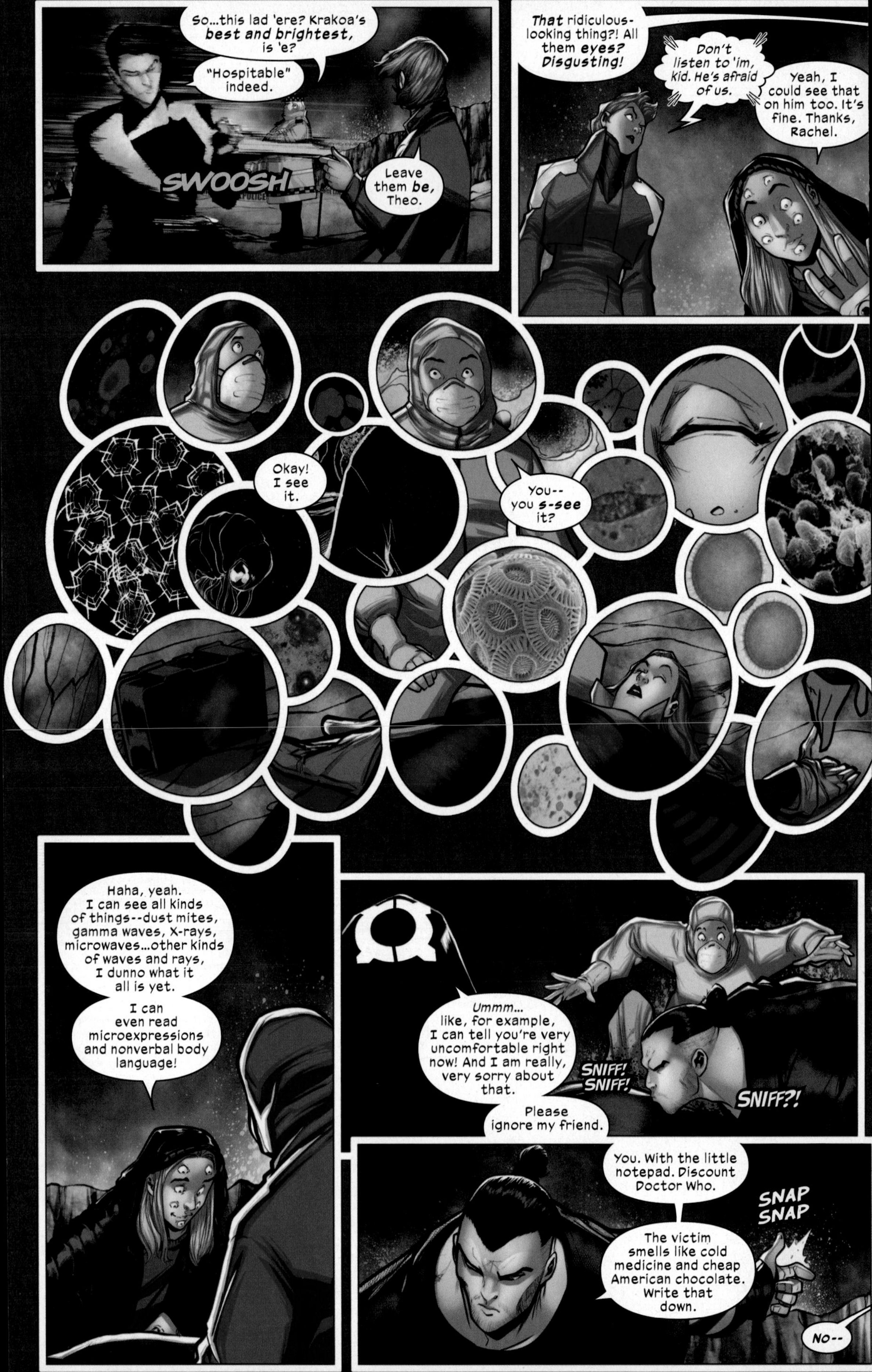
So...this lad 'ere? Krakoa's best and brightest, is 'e?
"Hospitable" indeed.
SWOOSH
POLICE
Leave them be, Theo.
That ridiculous-looking thing?! All them eyes? Disgusting!
Don't listen to 'im, kid. He's afraid of us.
Yeah, I could see that on him too. It's fine. Thanks, Rachel.
Okay! I see it.
You-- you s-see it?
Haha, yeah. I can see all kinds of things--dust mites, gamma waves, X-rays, microwaves...other kinds of waves and rays, I dunno what it all is yet.
I can even read microexpressions and nonverbal body language!
Ummm... like, for example, I can tell you're very uncomfortable right now! And I am really, very sorry about that.
Please ignore my friend.
SNIFF! SNIFF!
SNIFF?!
You. With the little notepad. Discount Doctor Who.
SNAP SNAP
The victim smells like cold medicine and cheap American chocolate. Write that down.
NO--

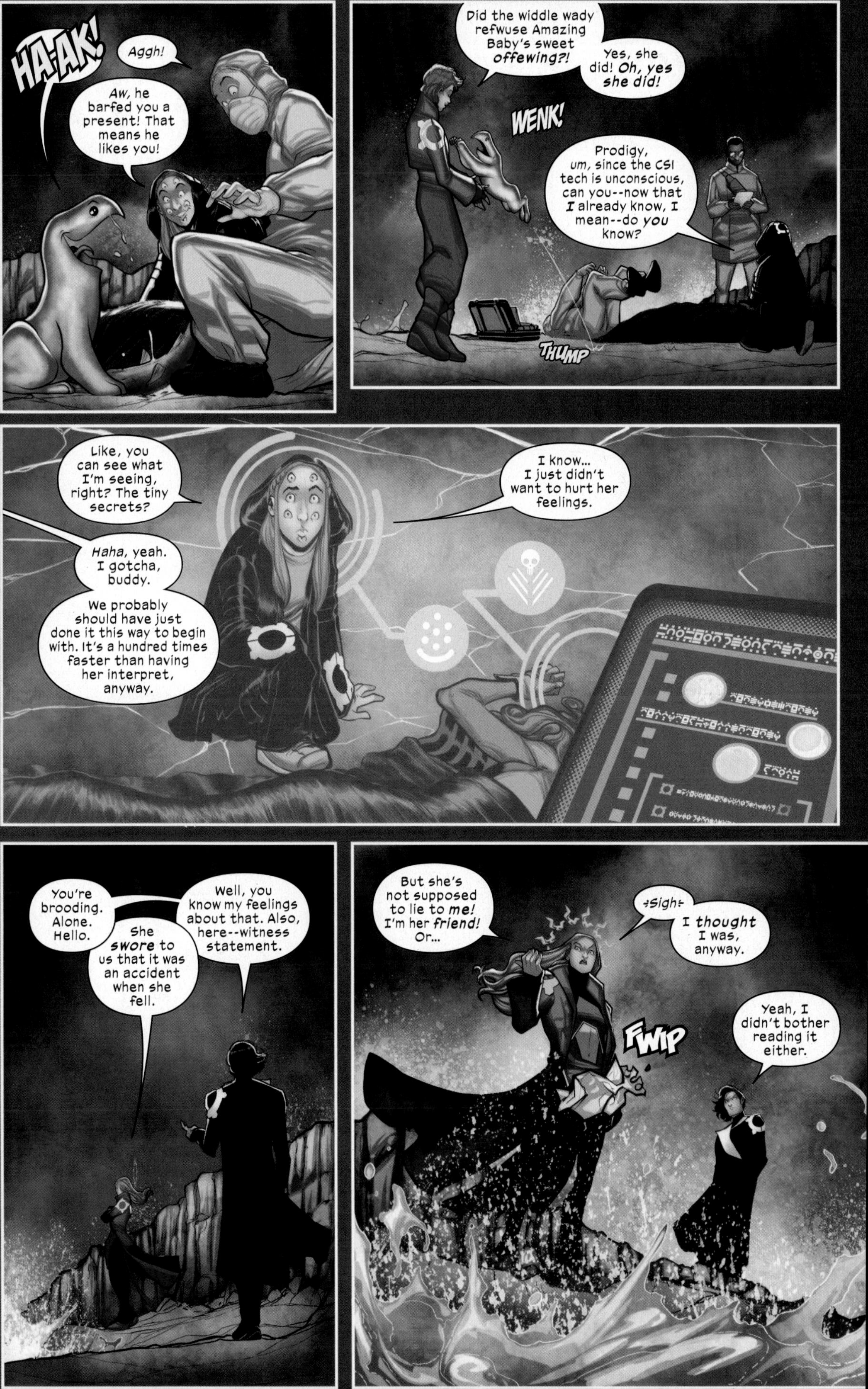

HA-AK!
Aggh!
Aw, he barfed you a present! That means he likes you!
Did the widdle wady refwuse Amazing Baby's sweet offewing?!
Yes, she did! Oh, yes she did!
WENK!
Prodigy, um, since the CSI tech is unconscious, can you--now that I already know, I mean--do you know?
THUMP
Like, you can see what I'm seeing, right? The tiny secrets?
I know... I just didn't want to hurt her feelings.
Haha, yeah. I gotcha, buddy.
We probably should have just done it this way to begin with. It's a hundred times faster than having her interpret, anyway.
You're brooding. Alone. Hello.
Well, you know my feelings about that. Also, here--witness statement.
She swore to us that it was an accident when she fell.
But she's not supposed to lie to me! I'm her friend! Or...
-Sigh-
I thought I was, anyway.
FWIP
Yeah, I didn't bother reading it either.

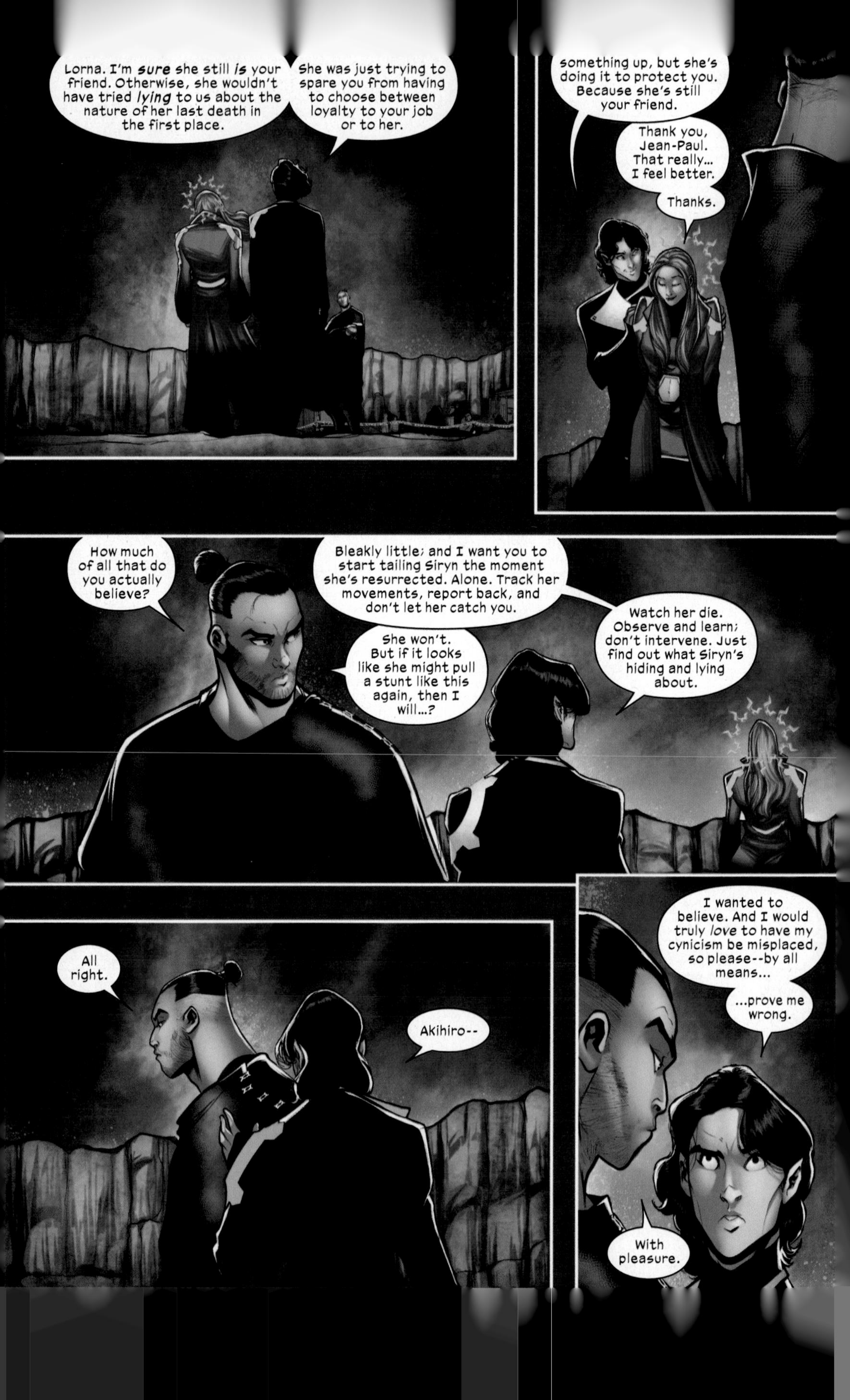
Lorna. I'm *sure* she still *is* your friend. Otherwise, she wouldn't have tried *lying* to us about the nature of her last death in the first place.
She was just trying to spare you from having to choose between loyalty to your job or to her.
something up, but she's doing it to protect you. Because she's still your friend.
Thank you, Jean-Paul. That really... I feel better.
Thanks.
How much of all that do you actually believe?
Bleakly little; and I want you to start tailing Siryn the moment she's resurrected. Alone. Track her movements, report back, and don't let her catch you.
She won't. But if it looks like she might pull a stunt like this again, then I will...?
Watch her die. Observe and learn; don't intervene. Just find out what Siryn's hiding and lying about.
All right.
Akihiro--
I wanted to believe. And I would truly *love* to have my cynicism be misplaced, so please--by all means...
...prove me wrong.
With pleasure.

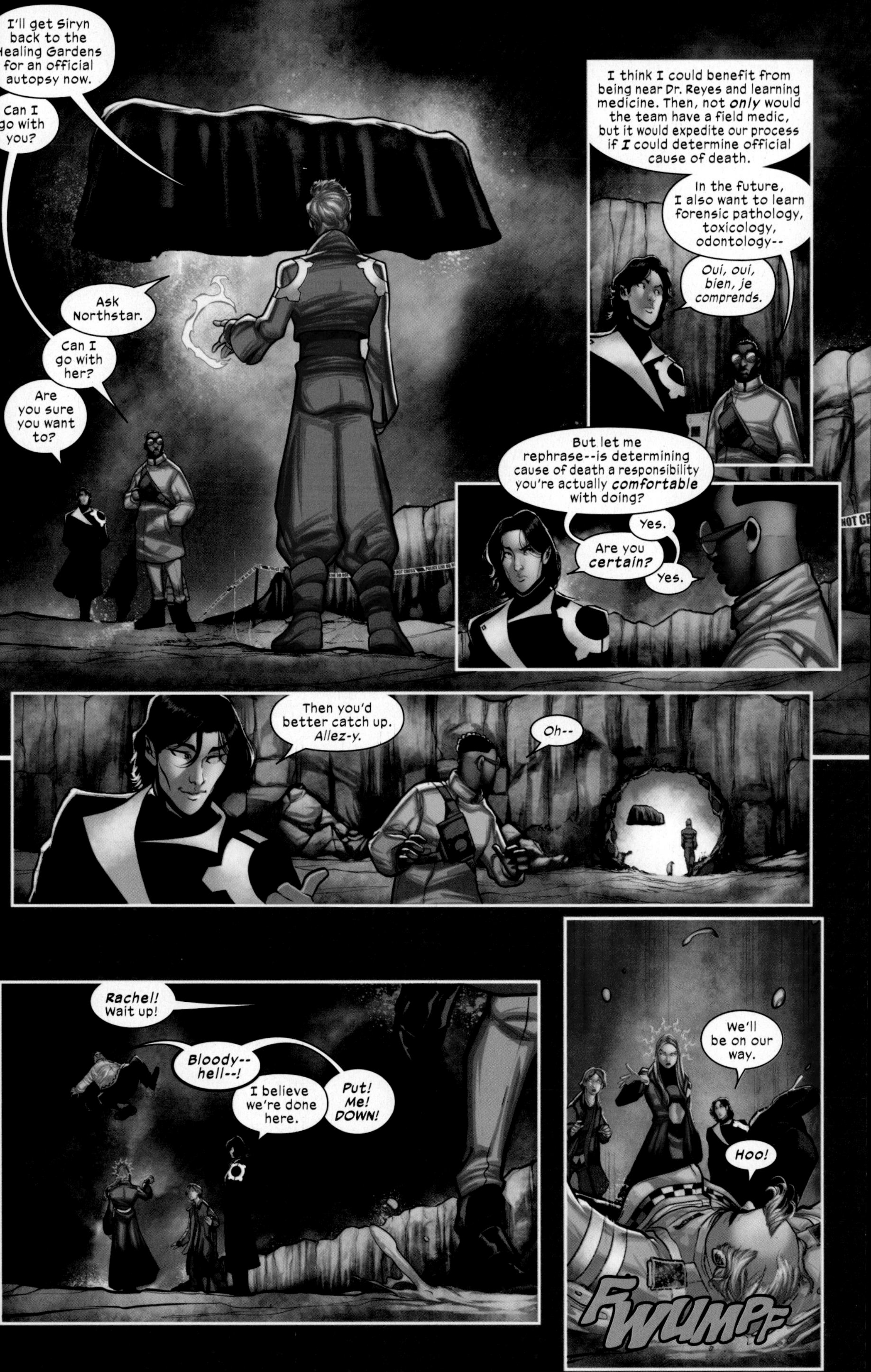
I'll get Siryn back to the Healing Gardens for an official autopsy now.
Can I go with you?
Ask Northstar.
Can I go with her?
Are you sure you want to?
I think I could benefit from being near Dr. Reyes and learning medicine. Then, not only would the team have a field medic, but it would expedite our process if I could determine official cause of death.
In the future, I also want to learn forensic pathology, toxicology, odontology--
Oui, oui, bien, je comprends.
But let me rephrase--is determining cause of death a responsibility you're actually comfortable with doing?
Yes.
Are you certain?
Yes.
Then you'd better catch up. Allez-y.
Oh--
Rachel! Wait up!
Bloody-- hell--!
I believe we're done here.
Put! Me! DOWN!
We'll be on our way.
Hoo!
FWUMPF

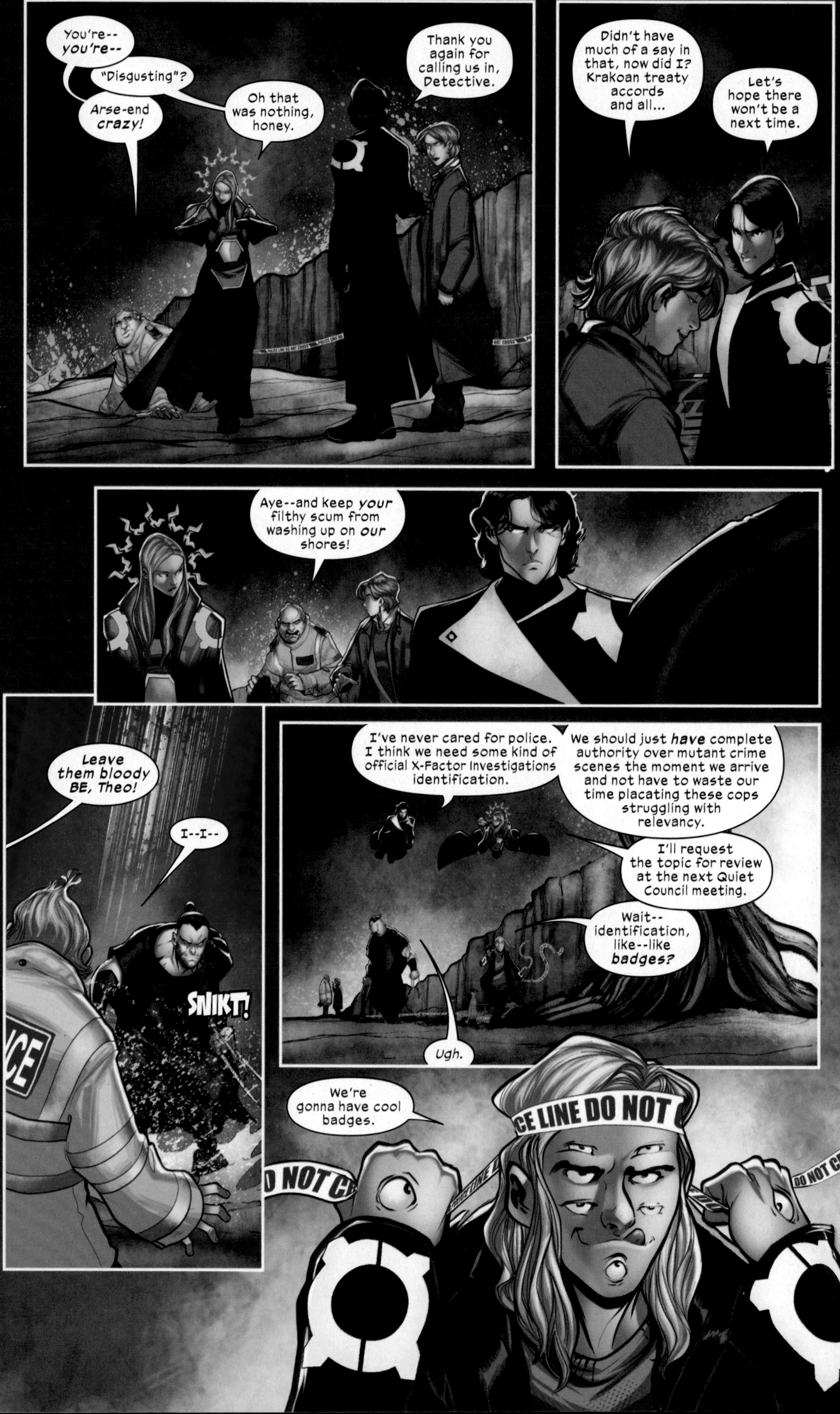

You're--
you're--
"Disgusting"?
Arse-end crazy!
Oh that was nothing, honey.
Thank you again for calling us in, Detective.
Didn't have much of a say in that, now did I? Krakoan treaty accords and all...
Let's hope there won't be a next time.
Aye--and keep your filthy scum from washing up on our shores!
Leave them bloody BE, Theo!
I--I--
SNIKT!
I've never cared for police. I think we need some kind of official X-Factor Investigations identification.
We should just have complete authority over mutant crime scenes the moment we arrive and not have to waste our time placating these cops struggling with relevancy.
I'll request the topic for review at the next Quiet Council meeting.
Wait-- identification, like--like badges?
Ugh.
We're gonna have cool badges.

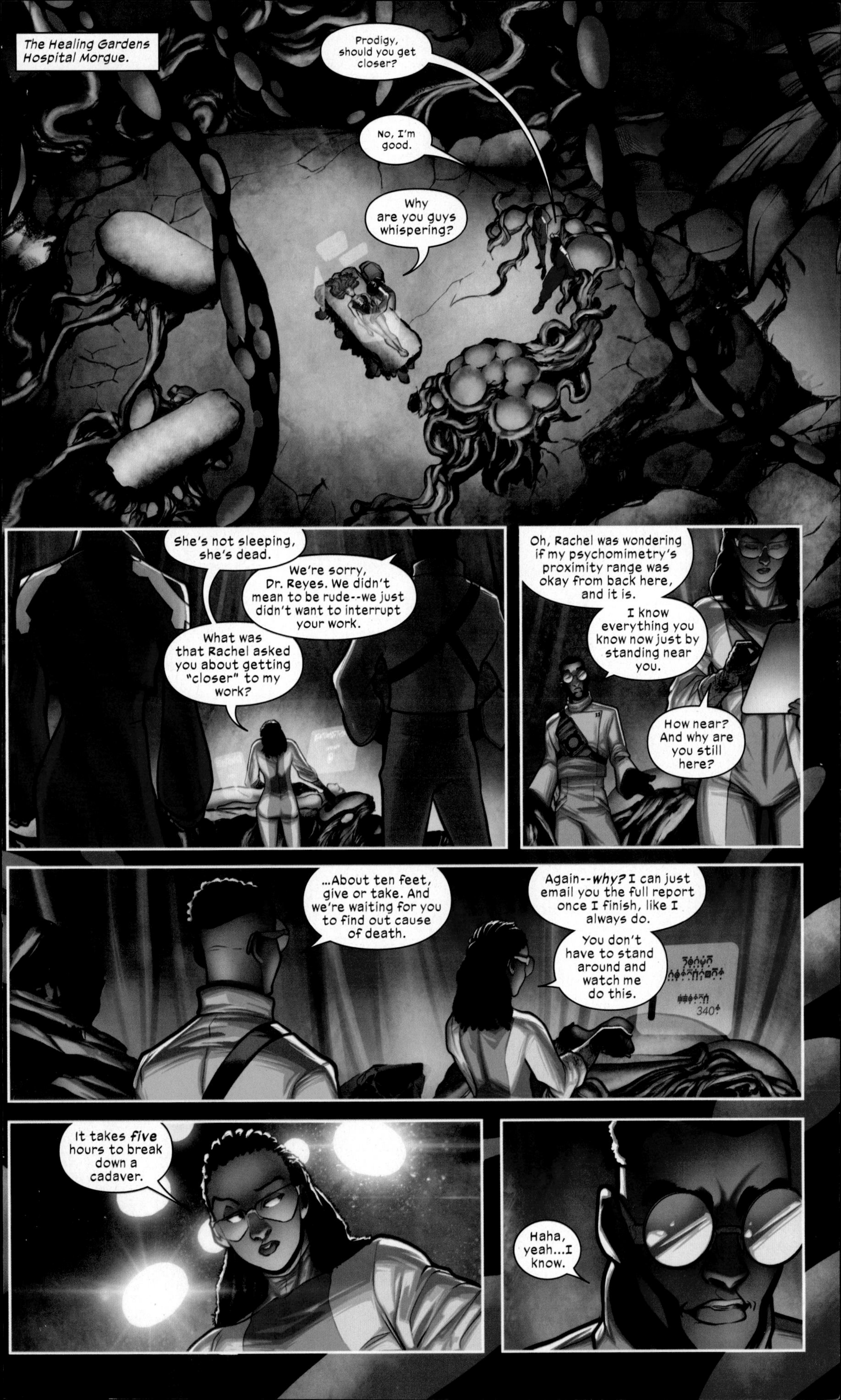

The Healing Gardens Hospital Morgue.
Prodigy, should you get closer?
No, I'm good.
Why are you guys whispering?
She's not sleeping, she's dead.
We're sorry, Dr. Reyes. We didn't mean to be rude--we just didn't want to interrupt your work.
What was that Rachel asked you about getting "closer" to my work?
Oh, Rachel was wondering if my psychomimetry's proximity range was okay from back here, and it is.
I know everything you know now just by standing near you.
How near? And why are you still here?
...About ten feet, give or take. And we're waiting for you to find out cause of death.
Again--*why?* I can just email you the full report once I finish, like I always do.
You don't have to stand around and watch me do this.
It takes *five* hours to break down a cadaver.
Haha, yeah...I know.

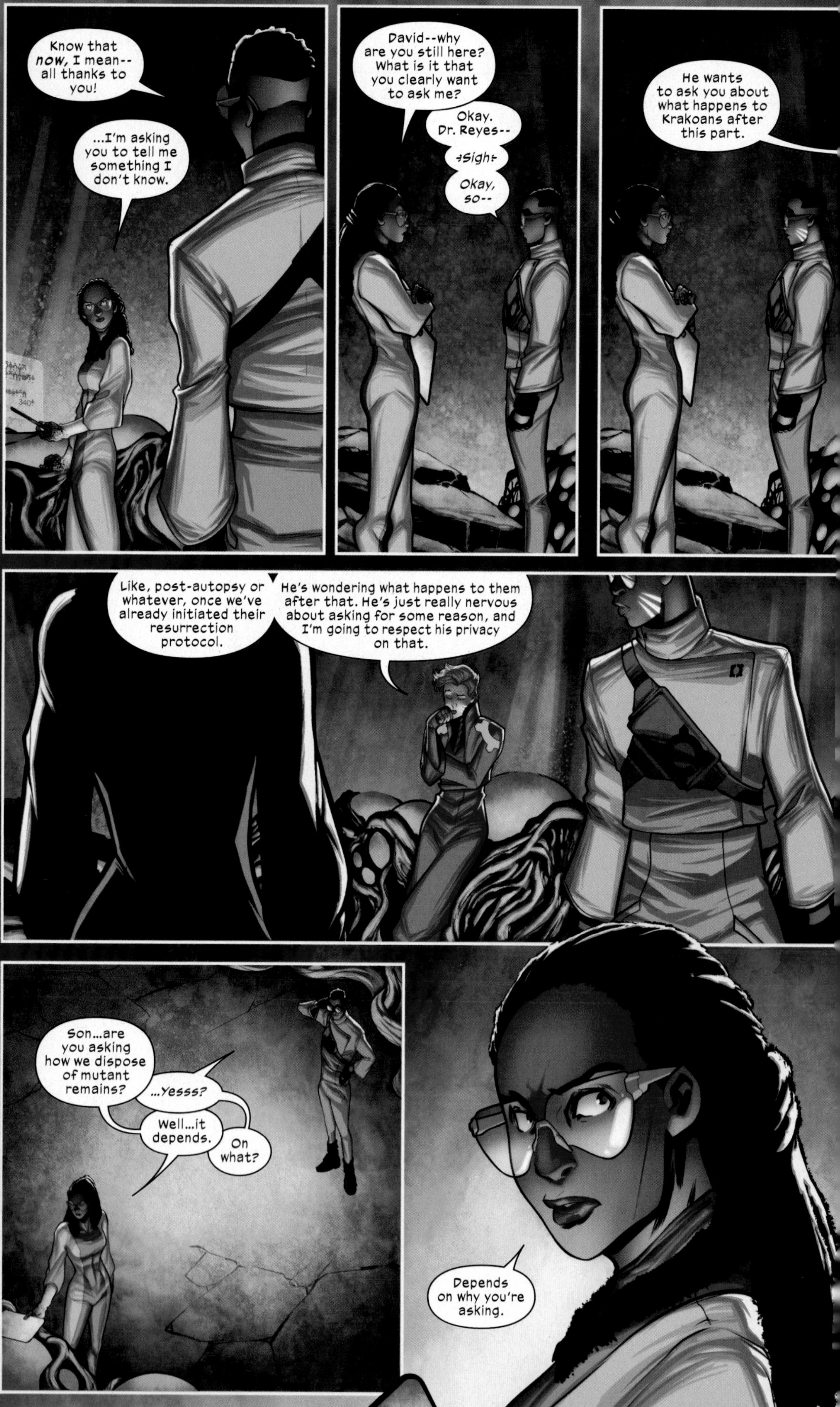
Know that *now,* I mean--all thanks to you!
...I'm asking you to tell me something I don't know.
David--why are you still here? What is it that you clearly want to ask me?
Okay. Dr. Reyes--
-Sigh-
Okay, so--
He wants to ask you about what happens to Krakoans after this part.
Like, post-autopsy or whatever, once we've already initiated their resurrection protocol.
He's wondering what happens to them after that. He's just really nervous about asking for some reason, and I'm going to respect his privacy on that.
Son...are you asking how we dispose of mutant remains?
...Yessss?
Well...it depends.
On what?
Depends on why you're asking.

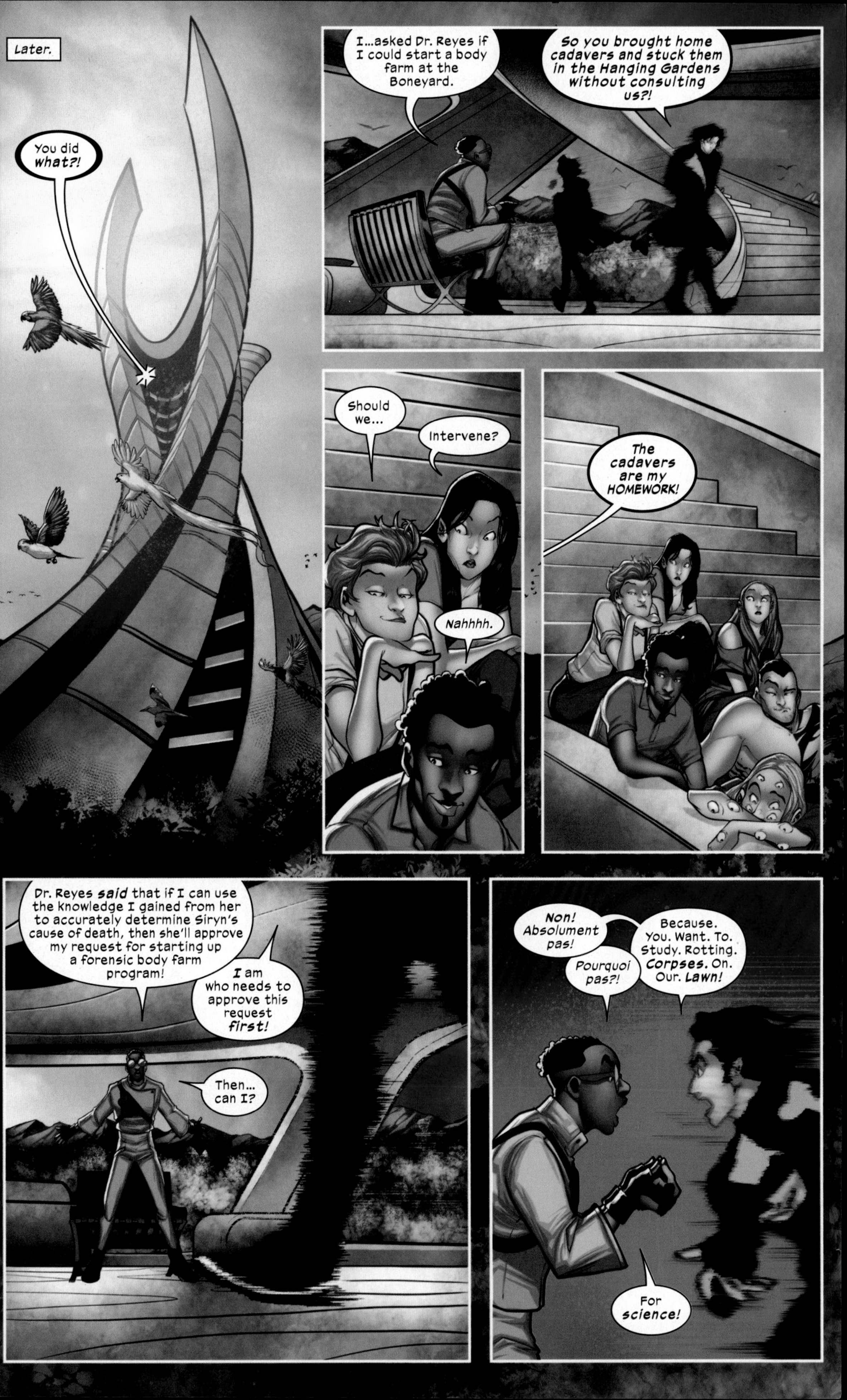
Later.
You did what?!
I...asked Dr. Reyes if I could start a body farm at the Boneyard.
So you brought home cadavers and stuck them in the Hanging Gardens without consulting us?!
Should we...
Intervene?
Nahhhh.
The cadavers are my HOMEWORK!
Dr. Reyes said that if I can use the knowledge I gained from her to accurately determine Siryn's cause of death, then she'll approve my request for starting up a forensic body farm program!
I am who needs to approve this request first!
Then... can I?
Non! Absolument pas!
Pourquoi pas?!
Because. You. Want. To. Study. Rotting. Corpses. On. Our. Lawn!
For science!

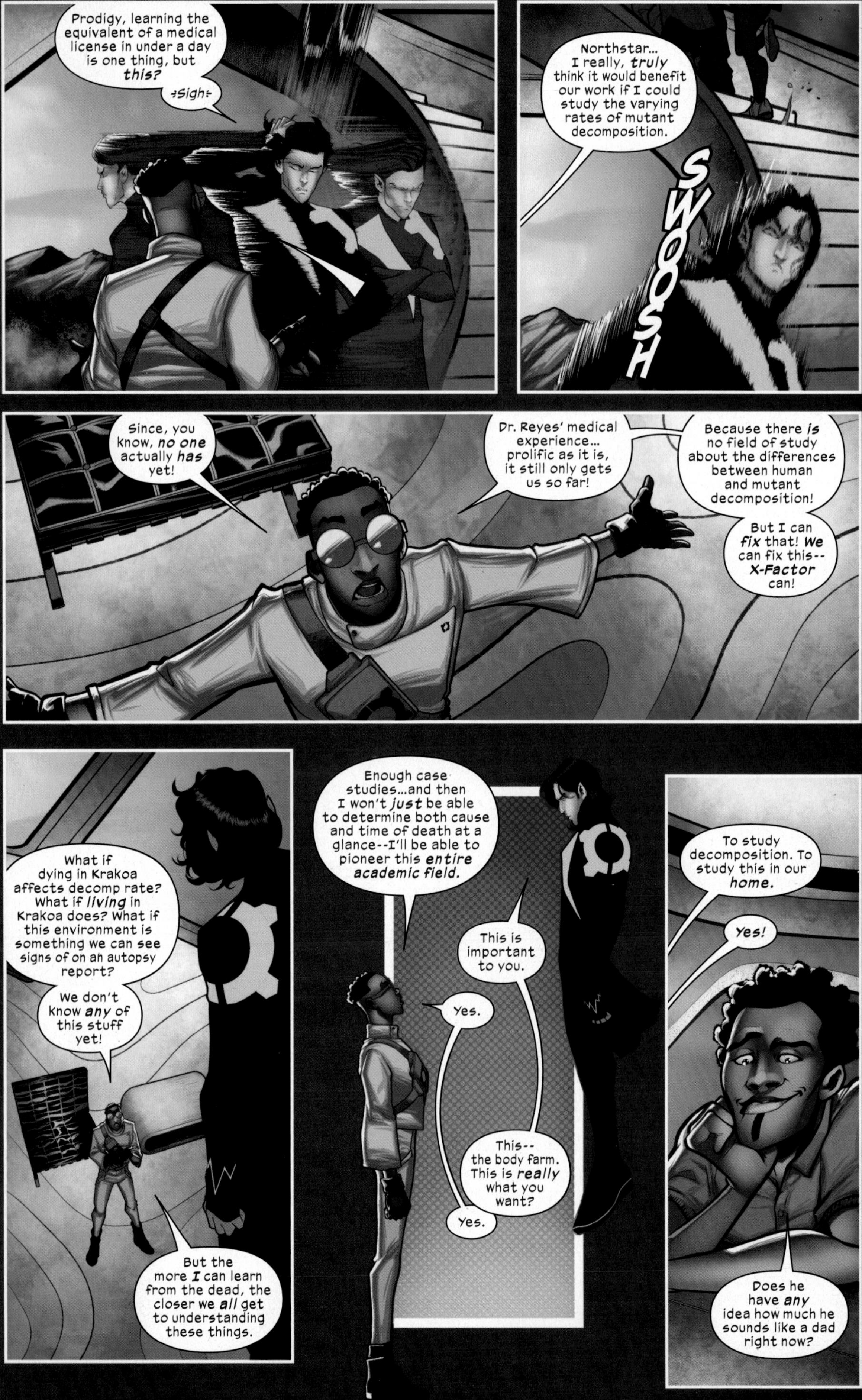
Prodigy, learning the equivalent of a medical license in under a day is one thing, but *this?*
-Sigh-
Northstar... I really, *truly* think it would benefit our work if I could study the varying rates of mutant decomposition.
SWOOSH
Since, you know, *no one* actually *has* yet!
Dr. Reyes' medical experience... prolific as it is, it still only gets us so far!
Because there *is* no field of study about the differences between human and mutant decomposition!
But I can *fix* that! *We* can fix this-- *X-Factor* can!
What if dying in Krakoa affects decomp rate? What if *living* in Krakoa does? What if this environment is something we can see signs of on an autopsy report?
We don't know *any* of this stuff yet!
But the more *I* can learn from the dead, the closer we *all* get to understanding these things.
Enough case studies...and then I won't *just* be able to determine both cause and time of death at a glance--I'll be able to pioneer this *entire academic field.*
This is important to you.
Yes.
This-- the body farm. This is *really* what you want?
Yes.
To study decomposition. To study this in our *home.*
Yes!
Does he have *any* idea how much he sounds like a dad right now?

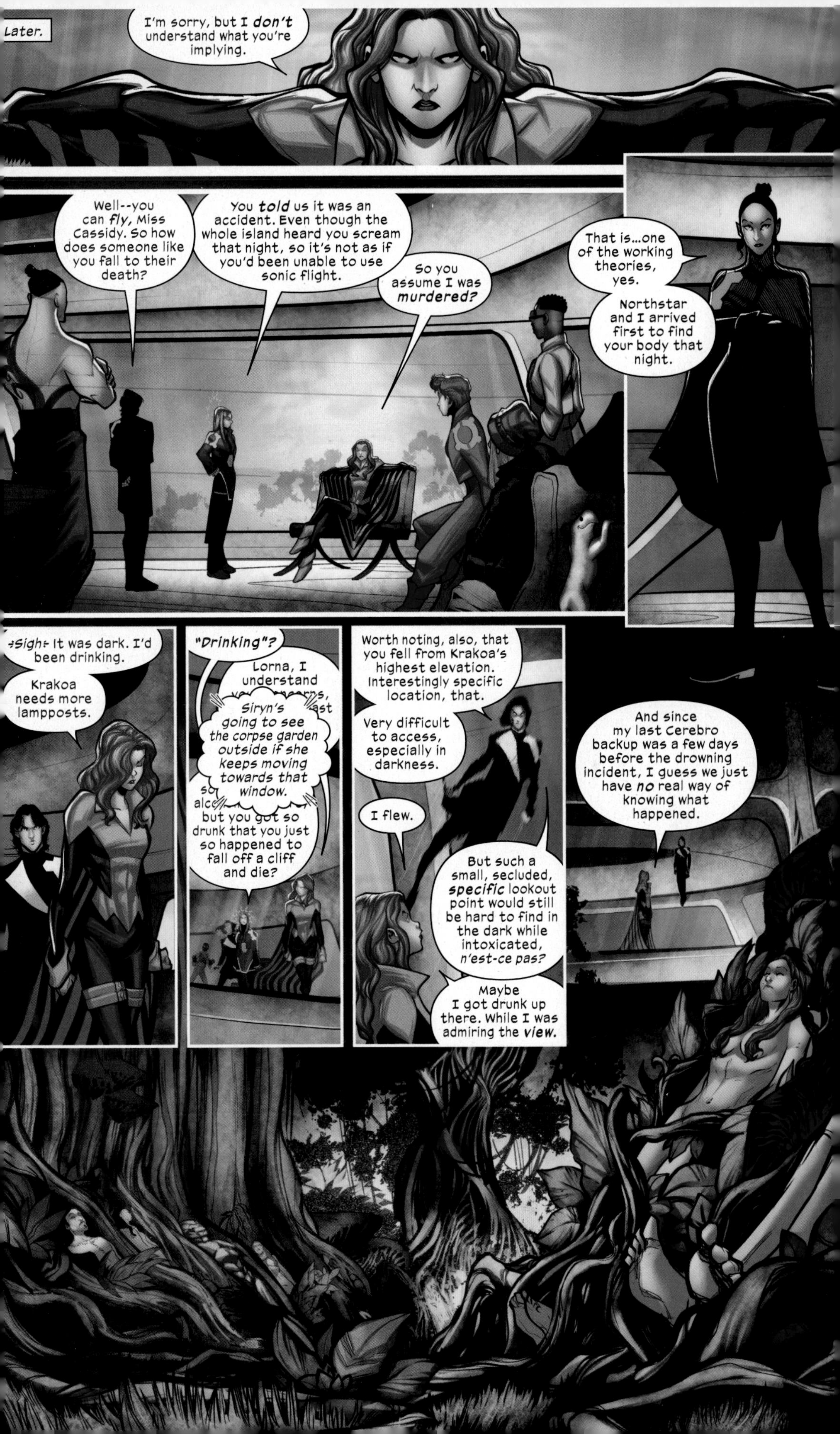
Later.
I'm sorry, but I don't understand what you're implying.
Well--you can fly, Miss Cassidy. So how does someone like you fall to their death?
You told us it was an accident. Even though the whole island heard you scream that night, so it's not as if you'd been unable to use sonic flight.
So you assume I was murdered?
That is...one of the working theories, yes.
Northstar and I arrived first to find your body that night.
Sigh It was dark. I'd been drinking.
Krakoa needs more lampposts.
"Drinking"?
Lorna, I understand
Siryn's going to see the corpse garden outside if she keeps moving towards that window.
but you got so drunk that you just so happened to fall off a cliff and die?
Worth noting, also, that you fell from Krakoa's highest elevation. Interestingly specific location, that.
Very difficult to access, especially in darkness.
I flew.
But such a small, secluded, specific lookout point would still be hard to find in the dark while intoxicated, n'est-ce pas?
Maybe I got drunk up there. While I was admiring the view.
And since my last Cerebro backup was a few days before the drowning incident, I guess we just have no real way of knowing what happened.

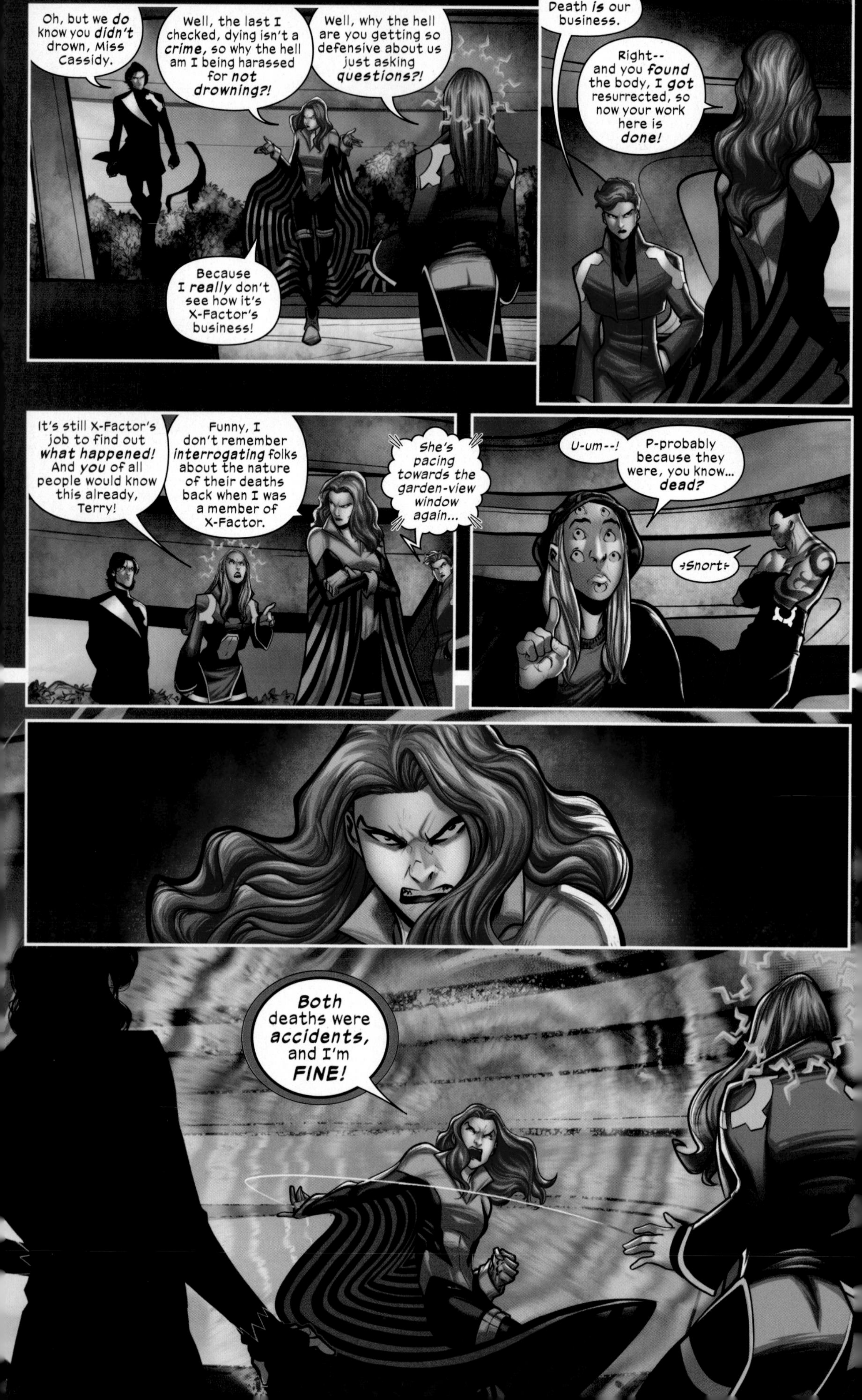
Oh, but we do know you didn't drown, Miss Cassidy.
Well, the last I checked, dying isn't a crime, so why the hell am I being harassed for not drowning?!
Well, why the hell are you getting so defensive about us just asking questions?!
Because I really don't see how it's X-Factor's business!
Death is our business.
Right-- and you found the body, I got resurrected, so now your work here is done!
It's still X-Factor's job to find out what happened! And you of all people would know this already, Terry!
Funny, I don't remember interrogating folks about the nature of their deaths back when I was a member of X-Factor.
She's pacing towards the garden-view window again...
U-um--!
P-probably because they were, you know... dead?
Snort
Both deaths were accidents, and I'm FINE!

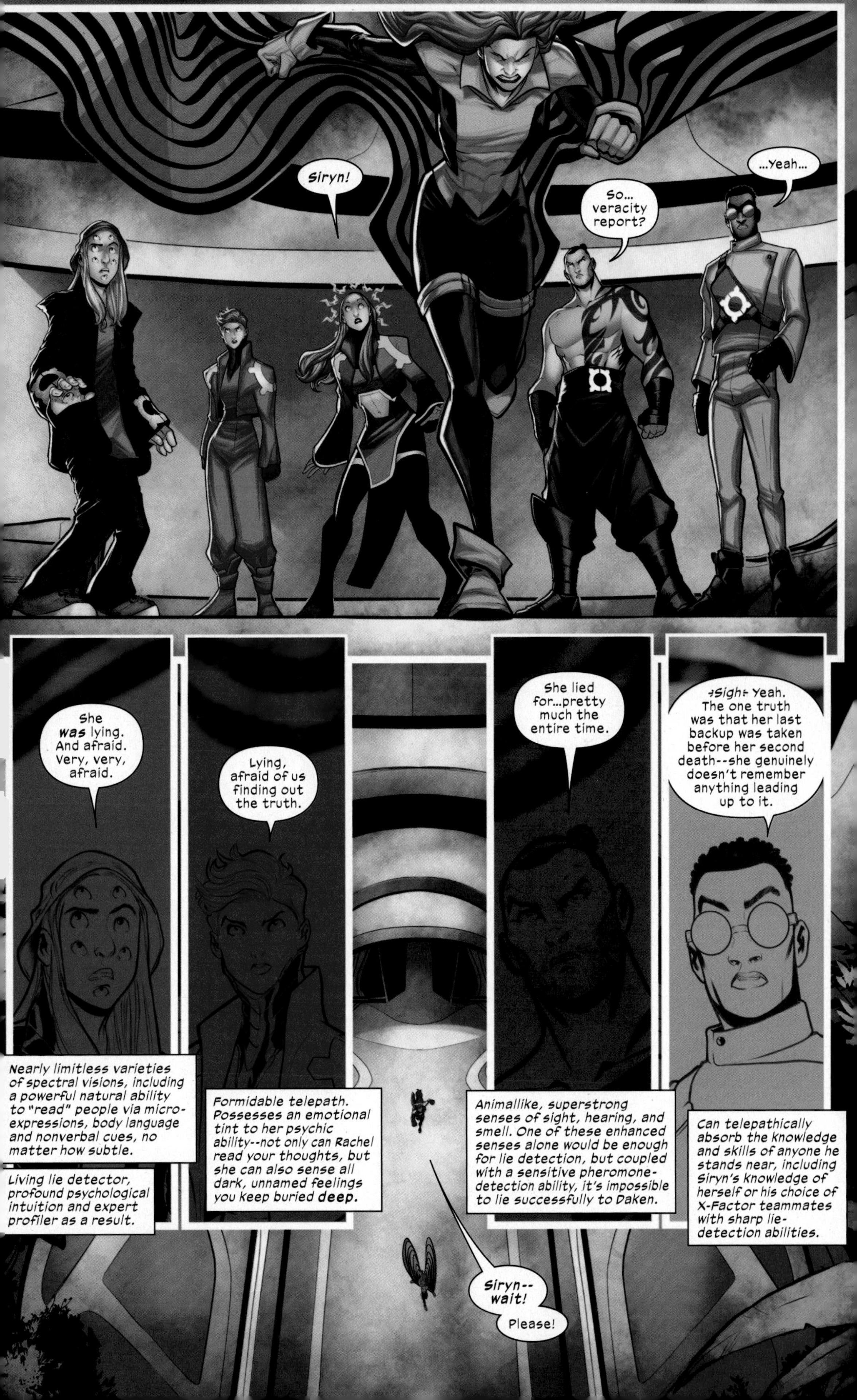
Siryn!
So... veracity report?
...Yeah...
She was lying. And afraid. Very, very, afraid.
Nearly limitless varieties of spectral visions, including a powerful natural ability to "read" people via micro-expressions, body language and nonverbal cues, no matter how subtle.
Living lie detector, profound psychological intuition and expert profiler as a result.
Lying, afraid of us finding out the truth.
Formidable telepath. Possesses an emotional tint to her psychic ability--not only can Rachel read your thoughts, but she can also sense all dark, unnamed feelings you keep buried deep.
Siryn-- wait!
Please!
She lied for...pretty much the entire time.
Animallike, superstrong senses of sight, hearing, and smell. One of these enhanced senses alone would be enough for lie detection, but coupled with a sensitive pheromone-detection ability, it's impossible to lie successfully to Daken.
Sigh Yeah. The one truth was that her last backup was taken before her second death--she genuinely doesn't remember anything leading up to it.
Can telepathically absorb the knowledge and skills of anyone he stands near, including Siryn's knowledge of herself or his choice of X-Factor teammates with sharp lie-detection abilities.

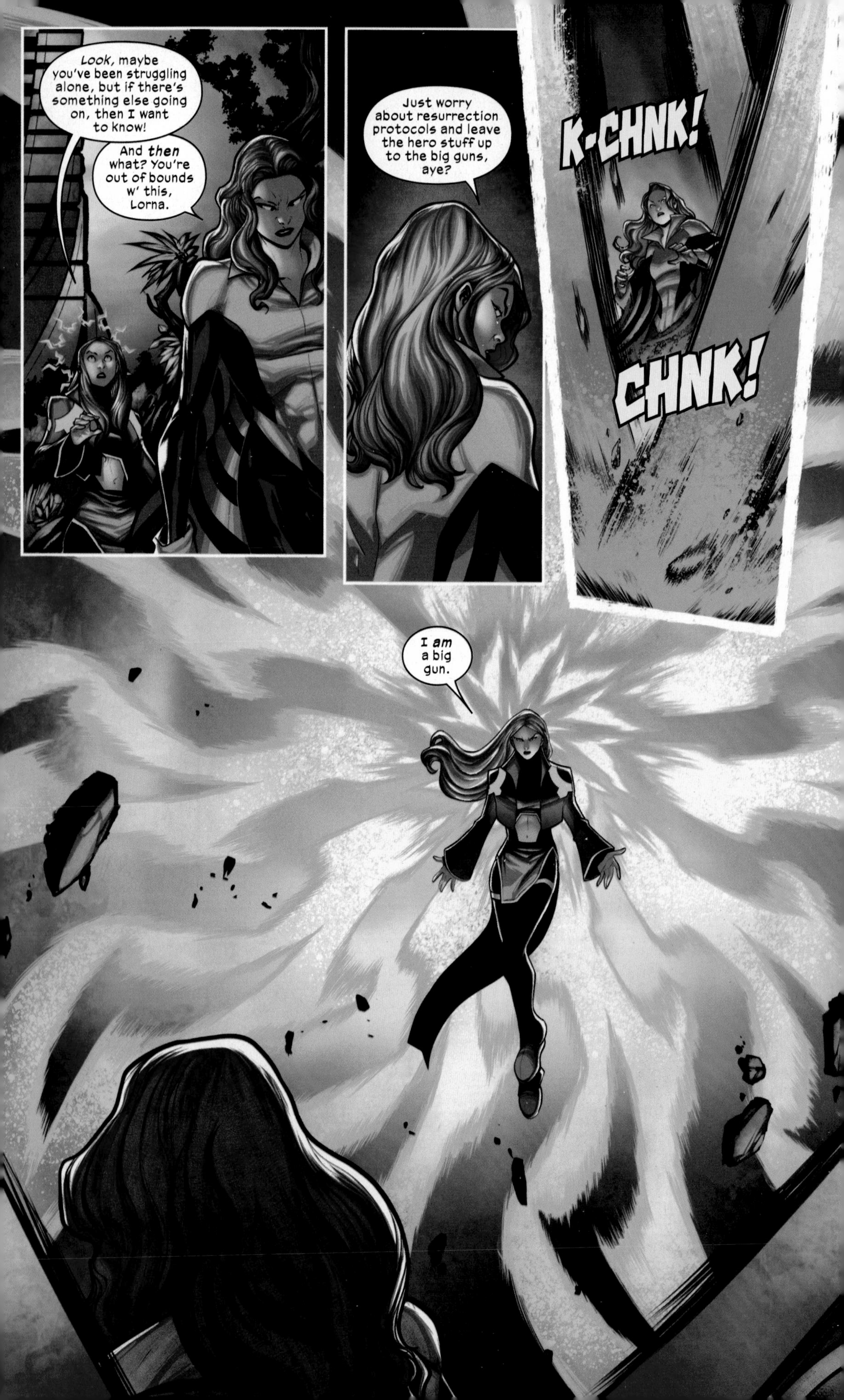
Look, maybe you've been struggling alone, but if there's something else going on, then I want to know!
And then what? You're out of bounds w' this, Lorna.
Just worry about resurrection protocols and leave the hero stuff up to the big guns, aye?
K-CHNK!
CHNK!
I am a big gun.

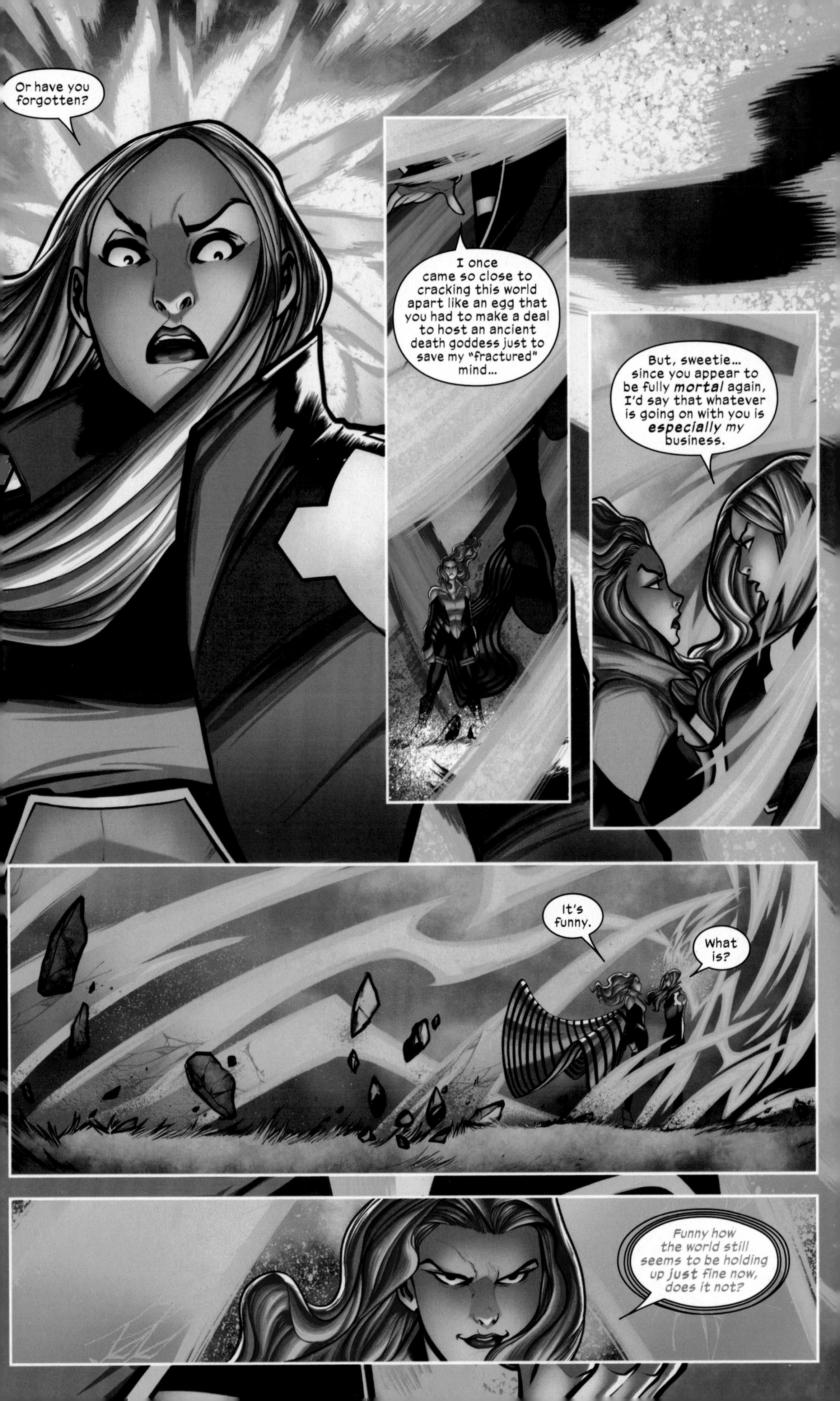
Or have you forgotten?
I once came so close to cracking this world apart like an egg that you had to make a deal to host an ancient death goddess just to save my "fractured" mind...
But, sweetie... since you appear to be fully *mortal* again, I'd say that whatever is going on with you is ***especially*** *my* business.
It's funny.
What is?
Funny how the world still seems to be holding up **just** *fine now, does it not?*

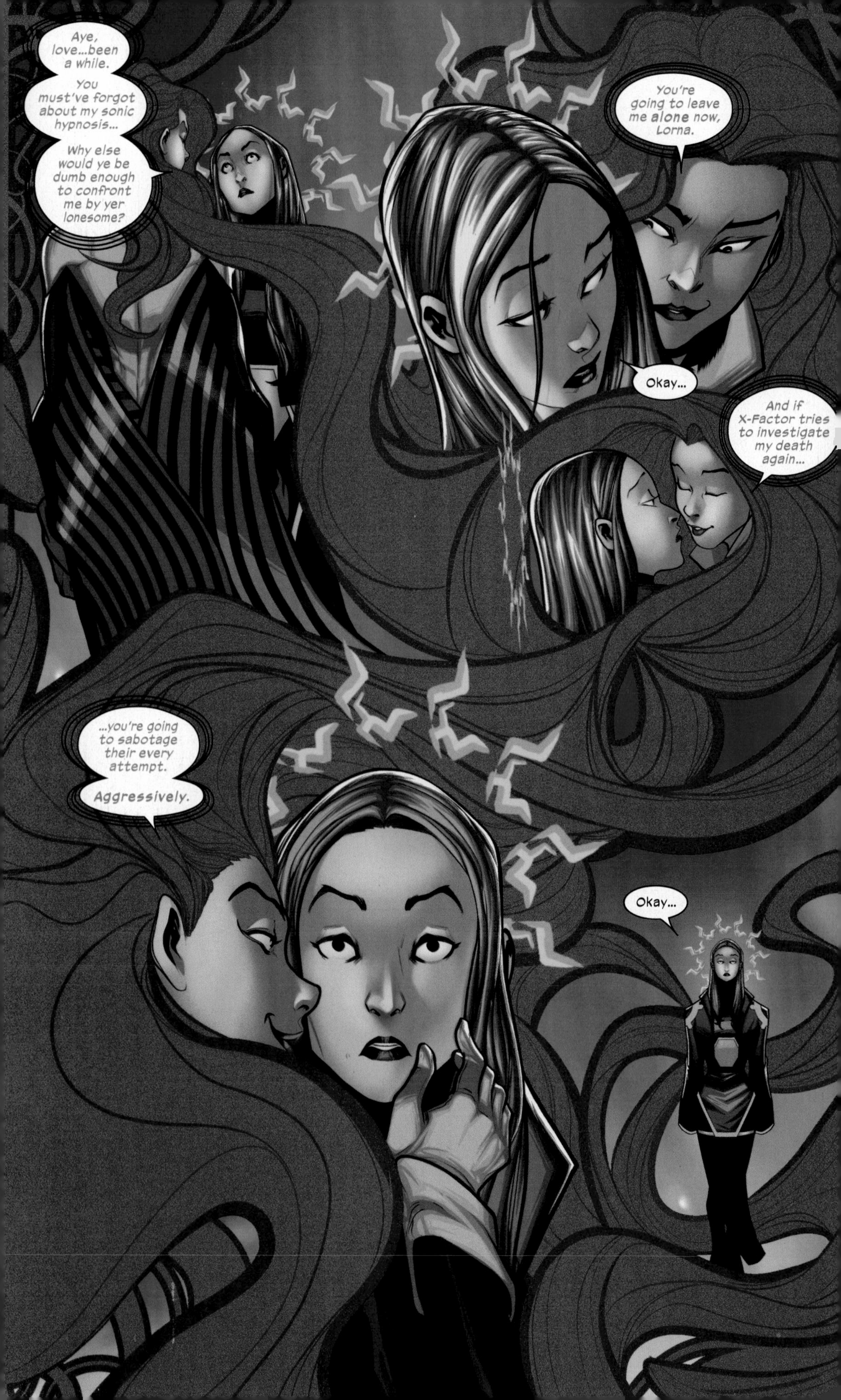

Aye, love...been a while.
You must've forgot about my sonic hypnosis...
Why else would ye be dumb enough to confront me by yer lonesome?
You're going to leave me alone now, Lorna.
Okay...
And if X-Factor tries to investigate my death again...
...you're going to sabotage their every attempt.
Aggressively.
Okay...

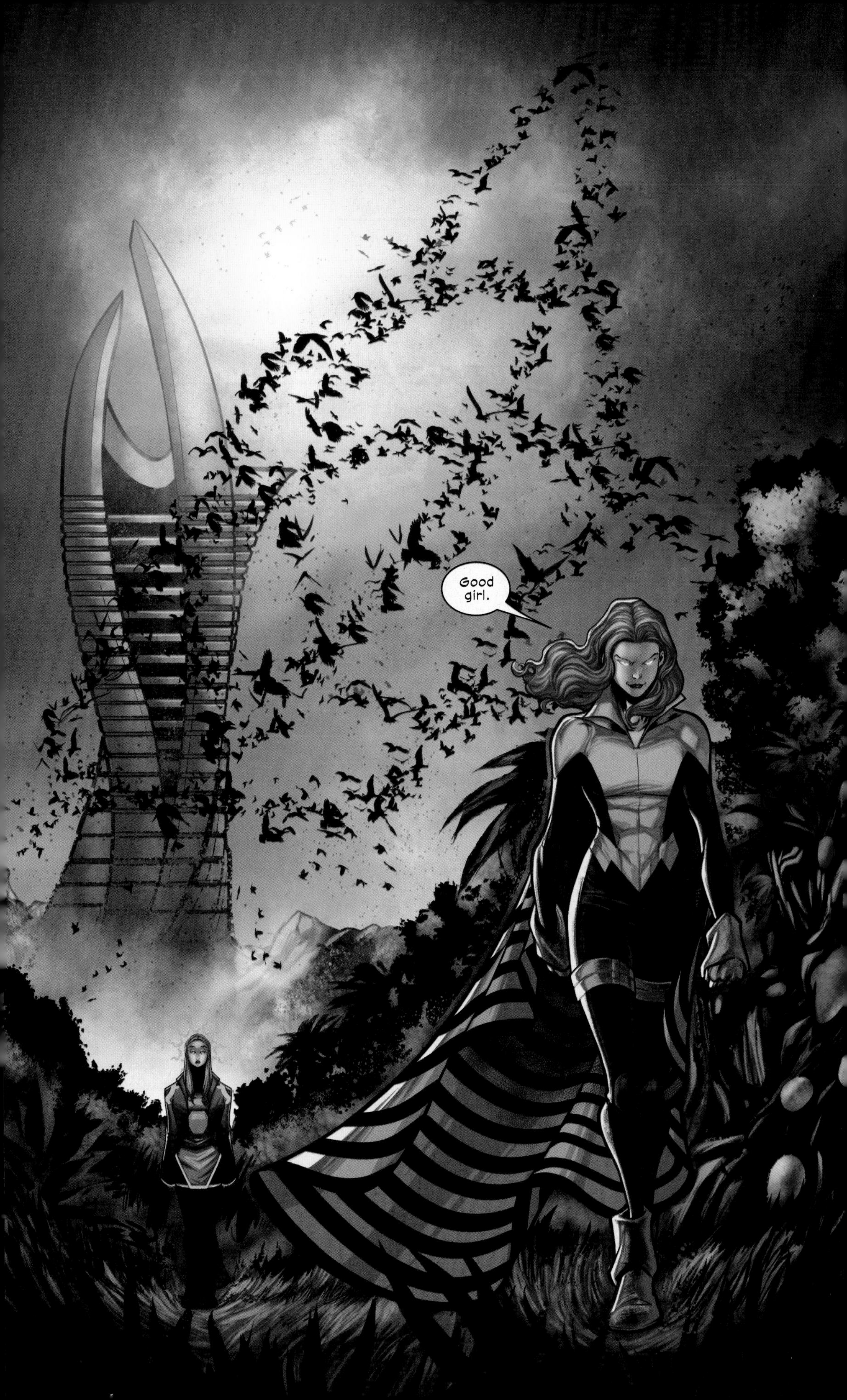
Good girl.

FROM THE PHONE OF DAVID ALLEYNE

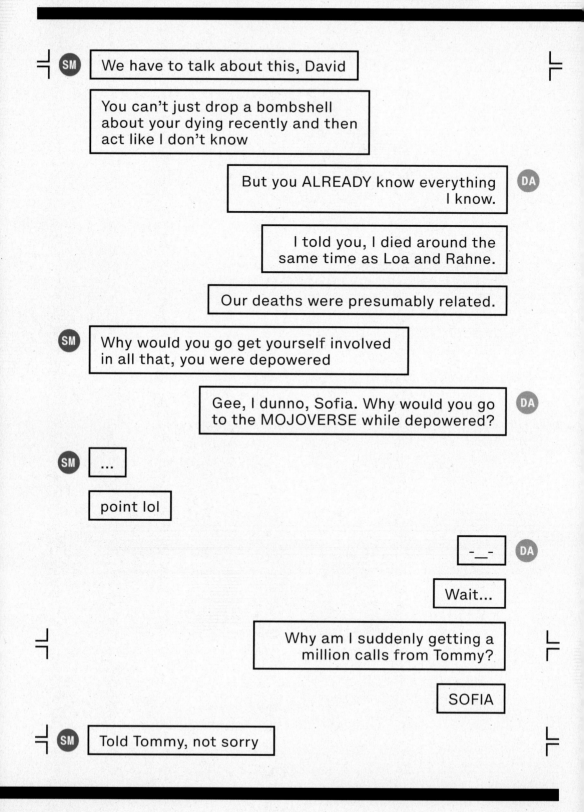

SM: We have to talk about this, David

SM: You can't just drop a bombshell about your dying recently and then act like I don't know

DA: But you ALREADY know everything I know.

DA: I told you, I died around the same time as Loa and Rahne.

DA: Our deaths were presumably related.

SM: Why would you go get yourself involved in all that, you were depowered

DA: Gee, I dunno, Sofia. Why would you go to the MOJOVERSE while depowered?

SM: ...

SM: point lol

DA: -_-

DA: Wait...

DA: Why am I suddenly getting a million calls from Tommy?

DA: SOFIA

SM: Told Tommy, not sorry

[reign_of_x]

[proof_X]
[death_X]

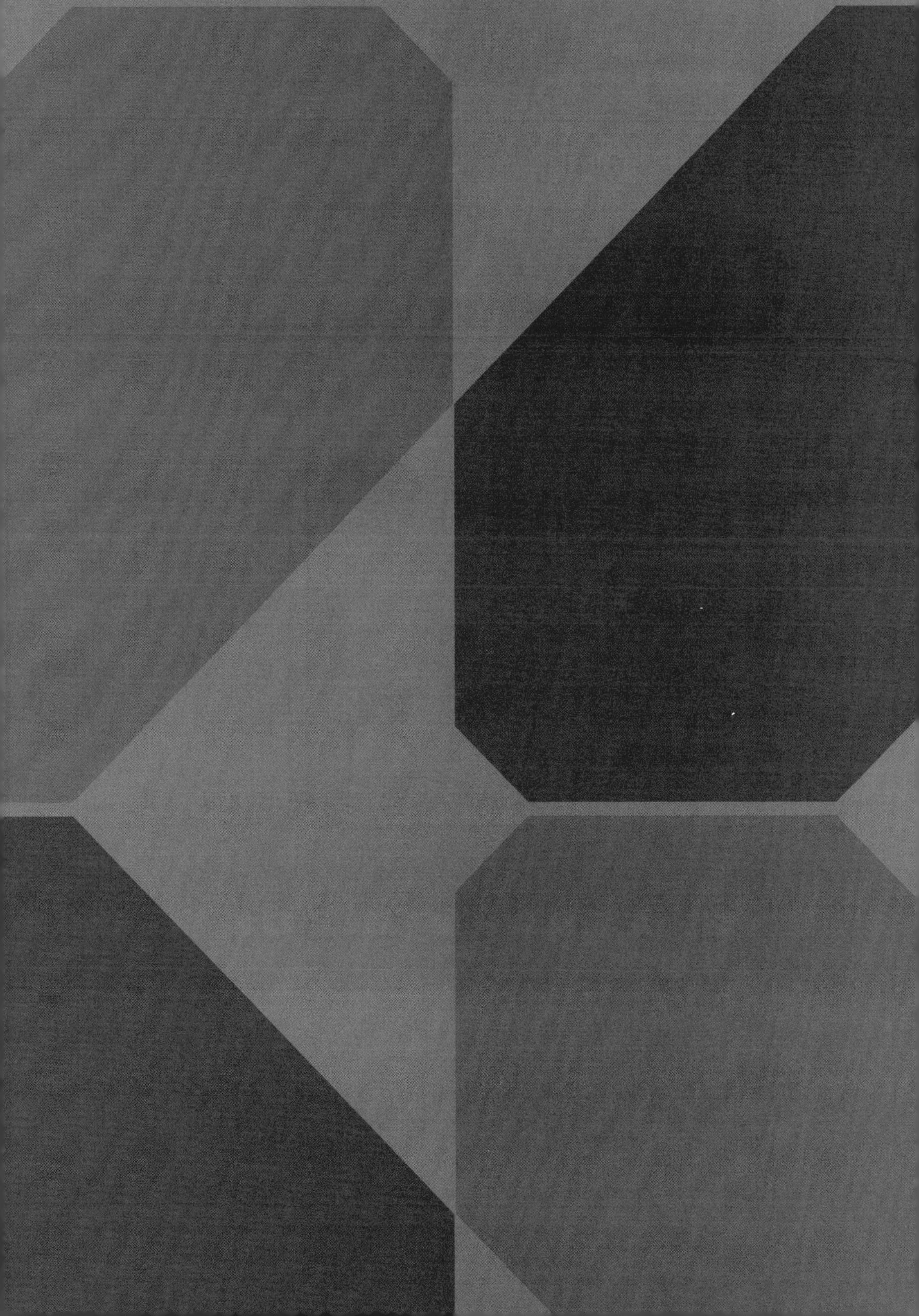

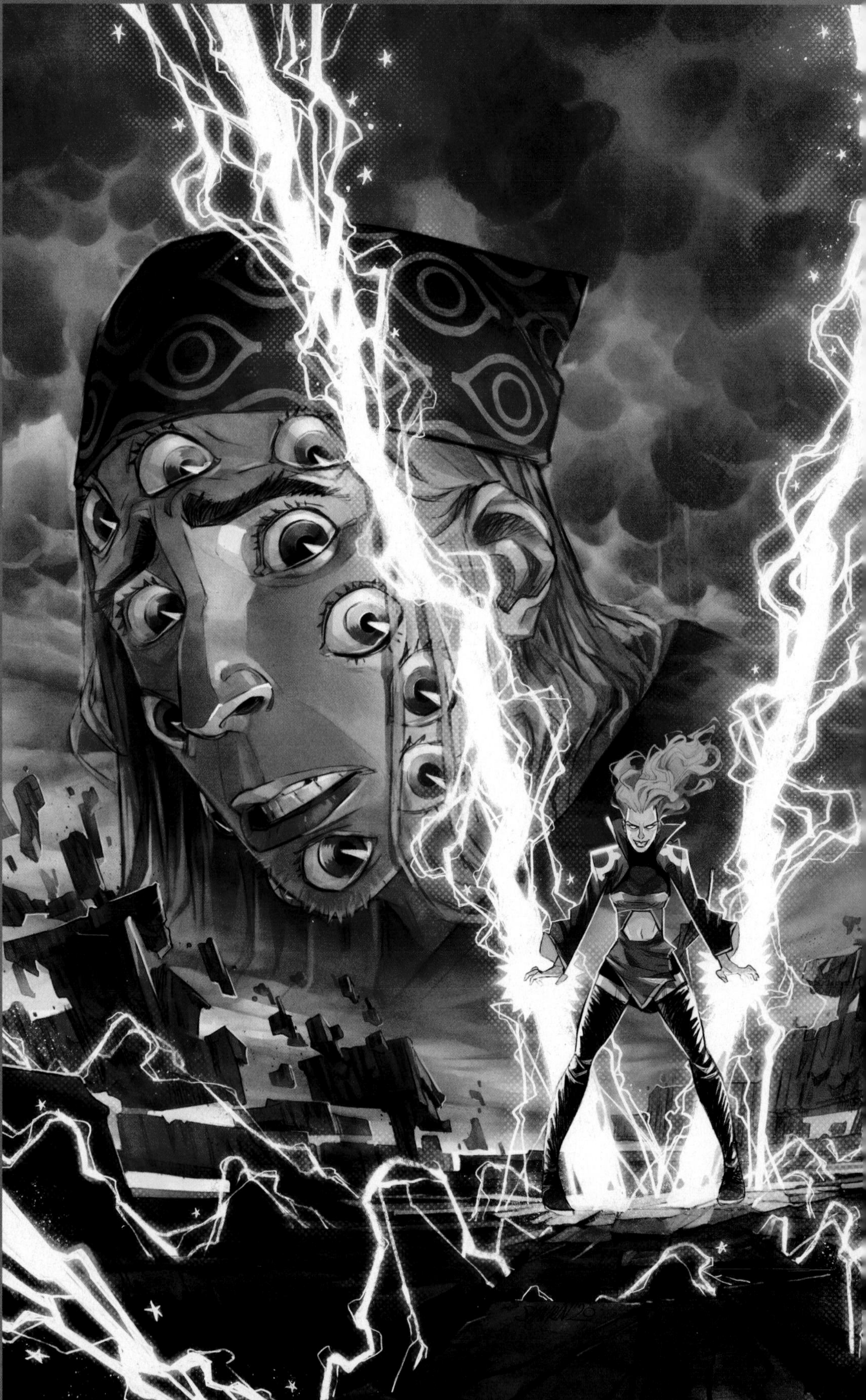

Suite Nº7:
Scientia Vincere Tenebras

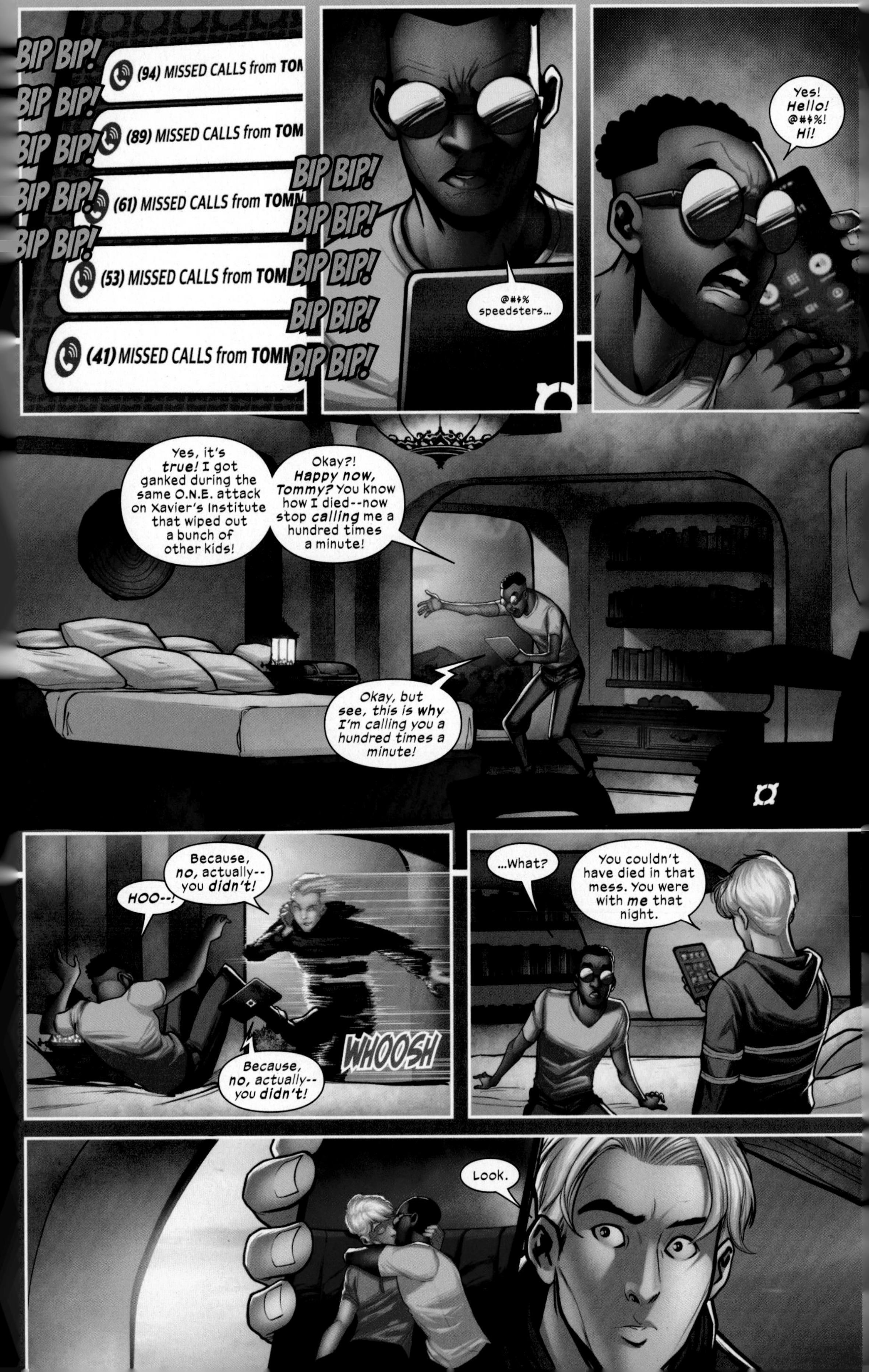
BIP BIP!
BIP BIP!
BIP BIP!
BIP BIP!
BIP BIP!
(94) MISSED CALLS from TOM
(89) MISSED CALLS from TOM
(61) MISSED CALLS from TOMM
(53) MISSED CALLS from TOM
(41) MISSED CALLS from TOMM
BIP BIP!
BIP BIP!
BIP BIP!
BIP BIP!
BIP BIP!
@#$% speedsters...
Yes! Hello! @#$%! Hi!
Yes, it's true! I got ganked during the same O.N.E. attack on Xavier's Institute that wiped out a bunch of other kids!
Okay?! Happy now, Tommy? You know how I died--now stop calling me a hundred times a minute!
Okay, but see, this is why I'm calling you a hundred times a minute!
HOO--!
Because, no, actually--you didn't!
Because, no, actually--you didn't!
WHOOSH
...What?
You couldn't have died in that mess. You were with me that night.
Look.

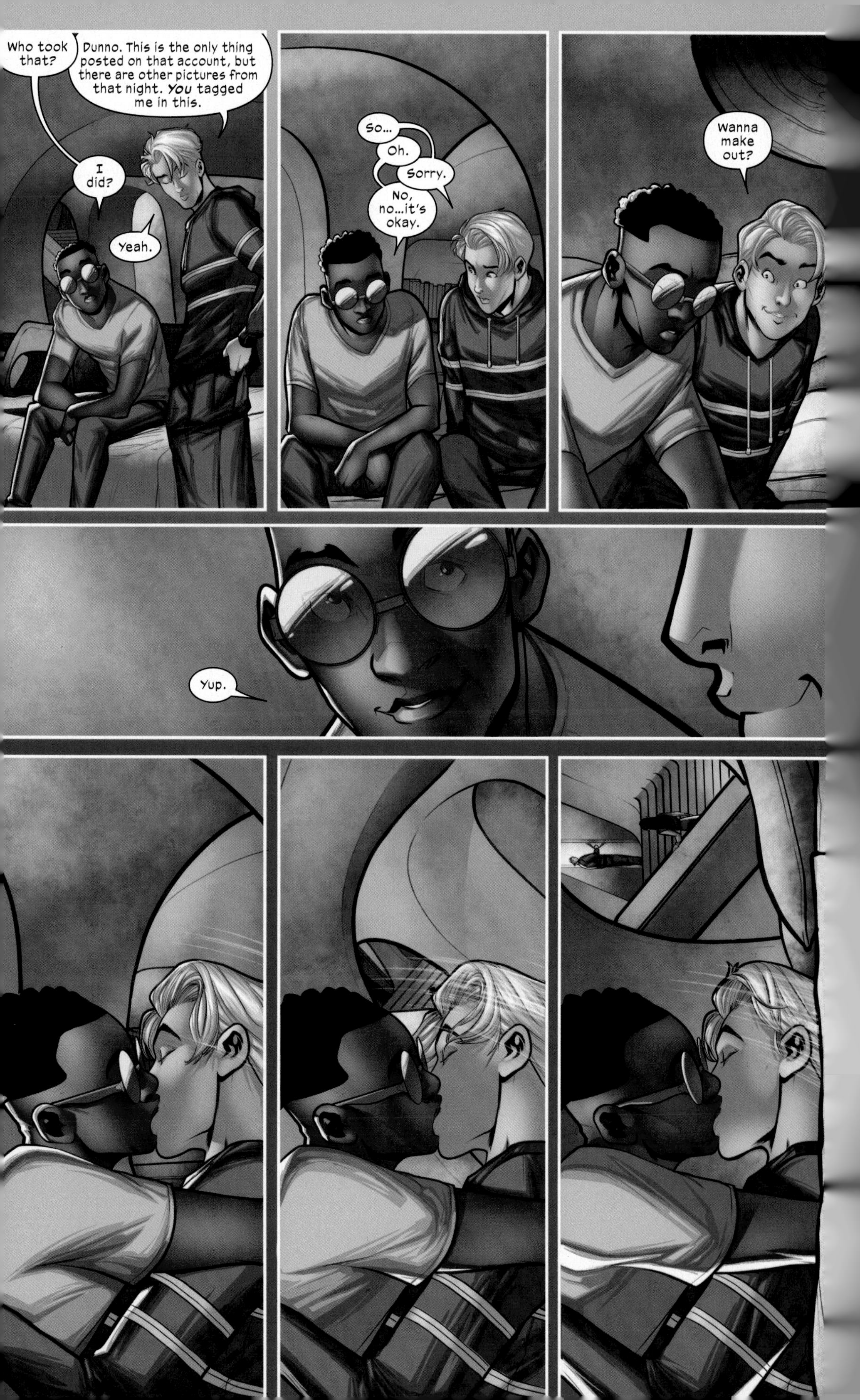
Who took that?
Dunno. This is the only thing posted on that account, but there are other pictures from that night. *You* tagged me in this.
I did?
Yeah.
So...
Oh.
Sorry.
No, no...it's okay.
Wanna make out?
Yup.

Hey, Prodigy. Here's the info you asked for. We knew to resurrect you without a body because the official incident report of your death was mailed to us along with Loa's, Rahne's, and everyone else who bit it around that same time. This was before X-Factor was established, so there was no formalized proof of death protocol back then, but since Wolverine and Cyclops were able to confirm so many of these deaths, we didn't question yours either. I hope this helps, and let me know if there's anything else I can do! What's this for, anyway?

Hugs 'n' kisses,
Elixir

Club Pepper
West Hollywood, CA

THE FIVE
Arbor Magna Hatchery, Krakoa

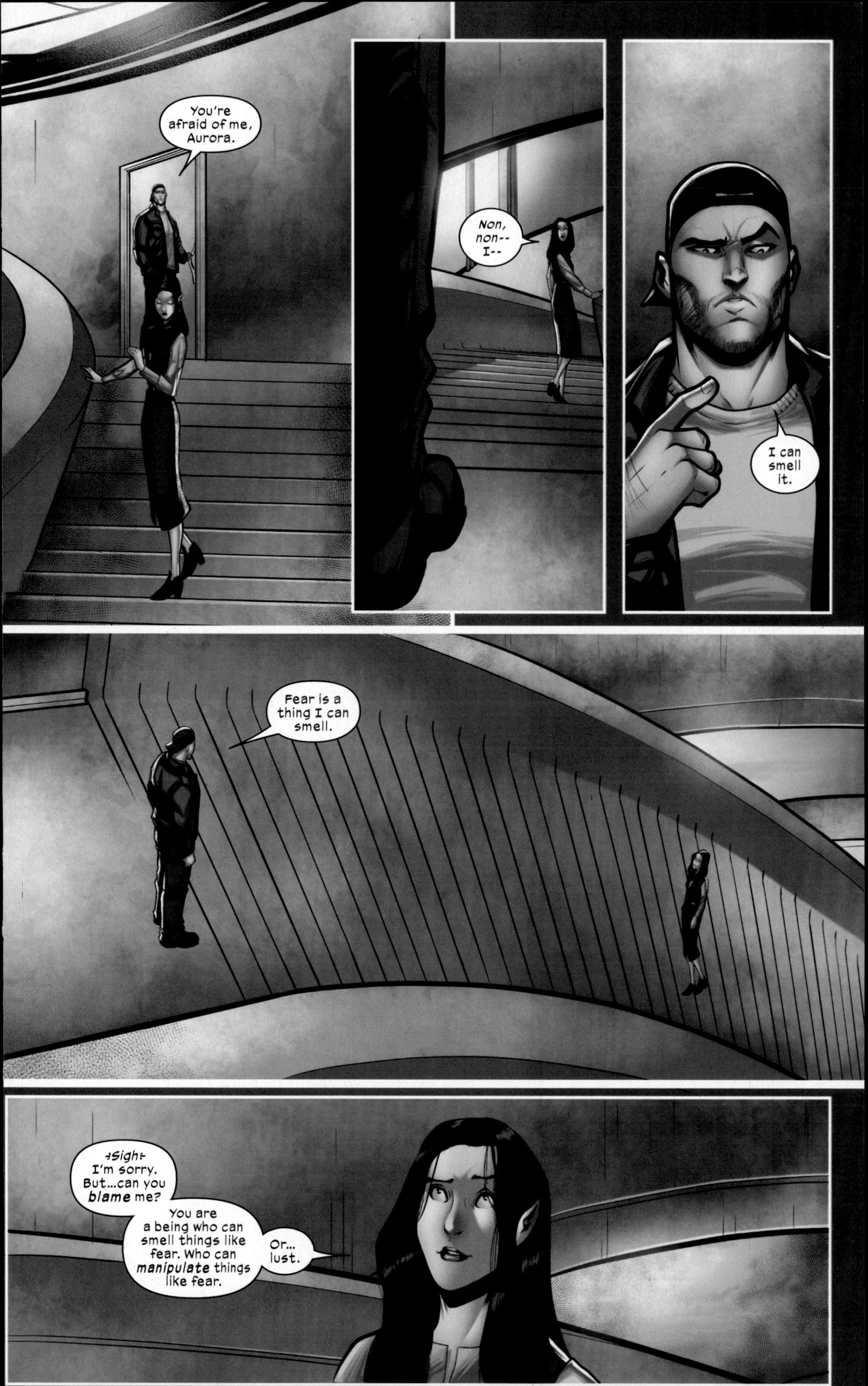
You're afraid of me, Aurora.
Non, non-- I--
I can smell it.
Fear is a thing I can smell.
-Sigh- I'm sorry. But...can you *blame* me?
You are a being who can smell things like fear. Who can *manipulate* things like fear.
Or... lust.

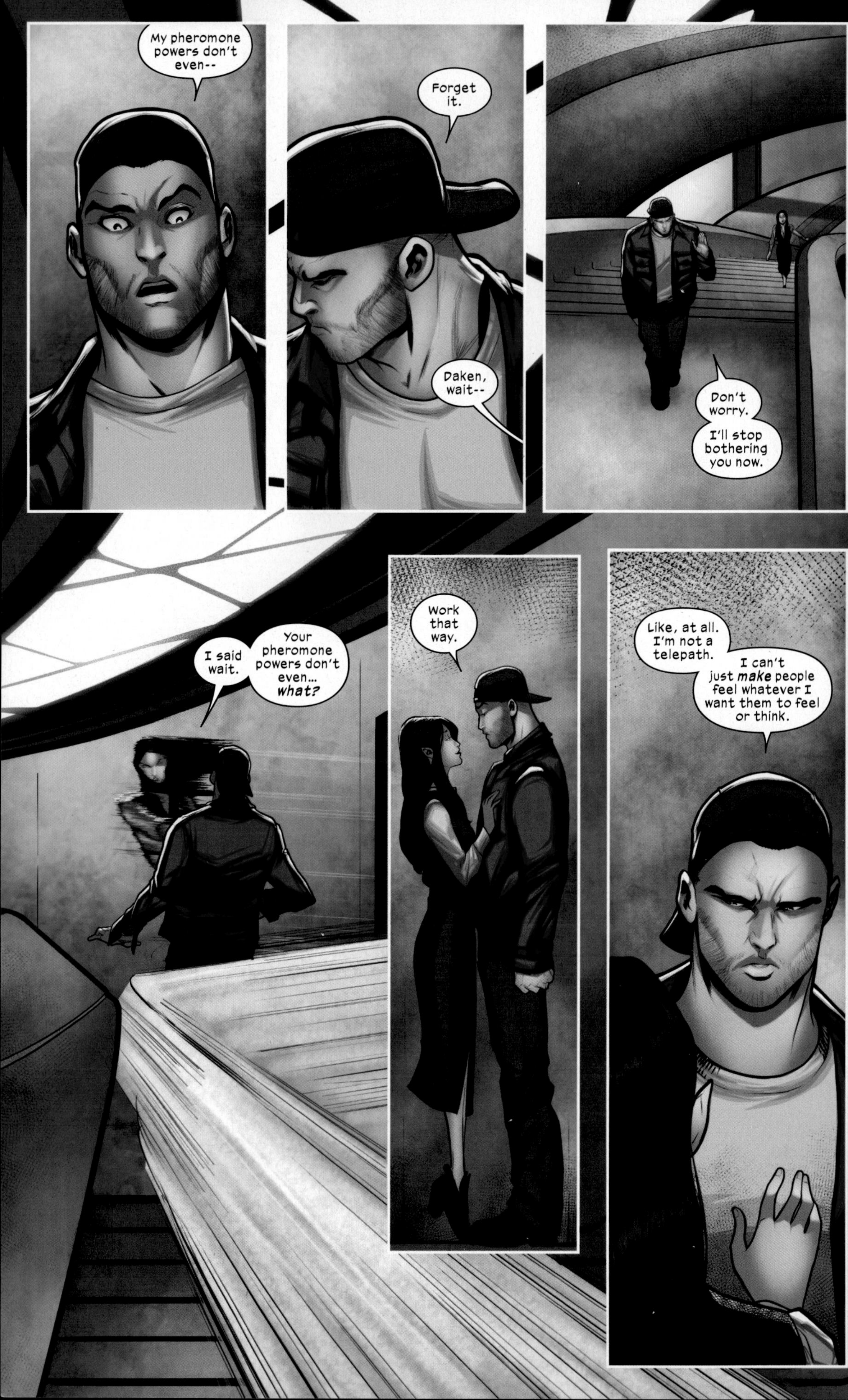
My pheromone powers don't even--
Forget it.
Daken, wait--
Don't worry.
I'll stop bothering you now.
I said wait.
Your pheromone powers don't even... *what?*
Work that way.
Like, at all. I'm not a telepath.
I can't just *make* people feel whatever I want them to feel or think.

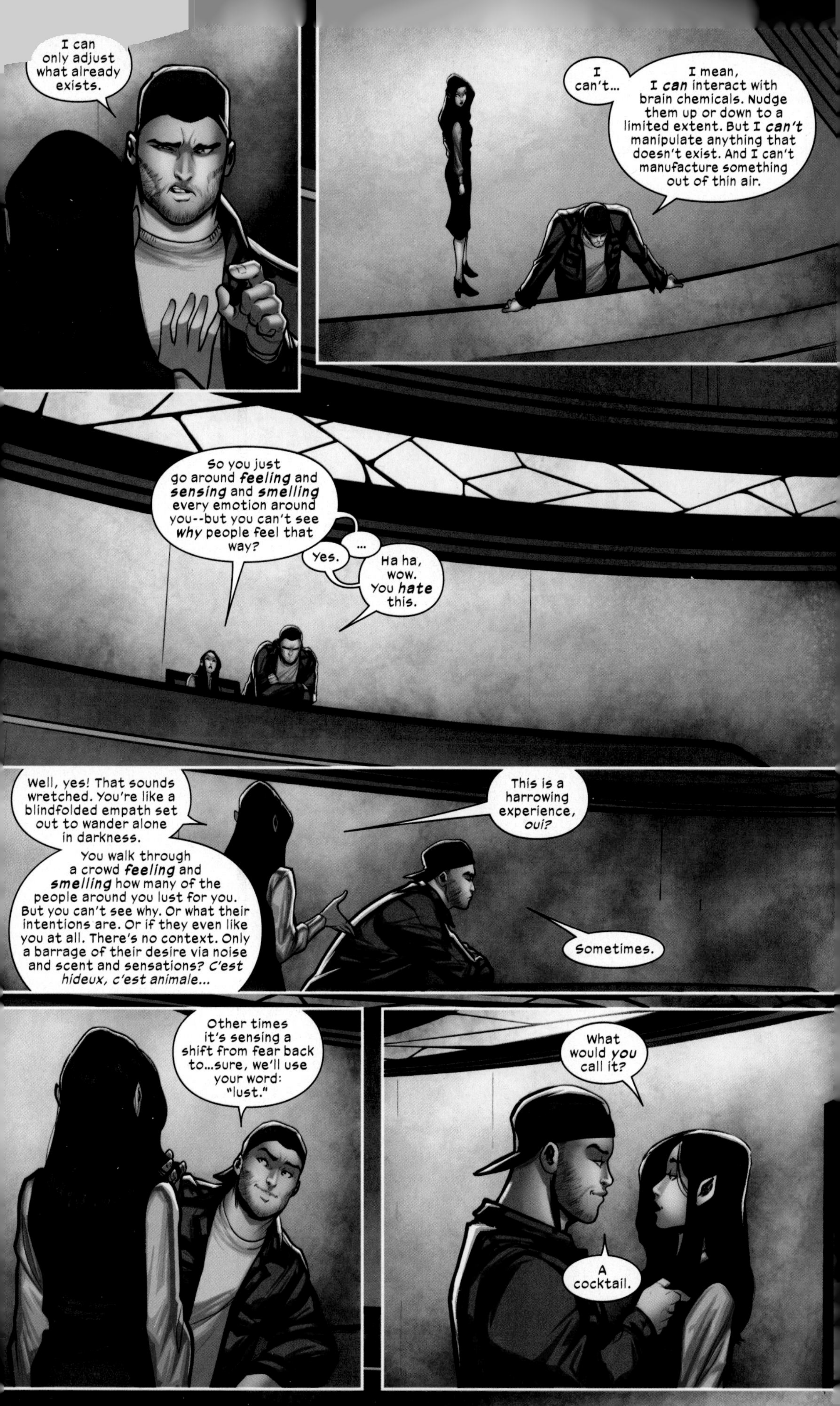
I can only adjust what already exists.
I can't...
I mean, I *can* interact with brain chemicals. Nudge them up or down to a limited extent. But I *can't* manipulate anything that doesn't exist. And I can't manufacture something out of thin air.
So you just go around *feeling* and *sensing* and *smelling* every emotion around you--but you can't see *why* people feel that way?
...
Yes.
Ha ha, wow. You *hate* this.
Well, yes! That sounds wretched. You're like a blindfolded empath set out to wander alone in darkness.
You walk through a crowd *feeling* and *smelling* how many of the people around you lust for you. But you can't see why. Or what their intentions are. Or if they even like you at all. There's no context. Only a barrage of their desire via noise and scent and sensations? *C'est hideux, c'est animale...*
This is a harrowing experience, *oui?*
Sometimes.
Other times it's sensing a shift from fear back to...sure, we'll use your word: "lust."
What would *you* call it?
A cocktail.

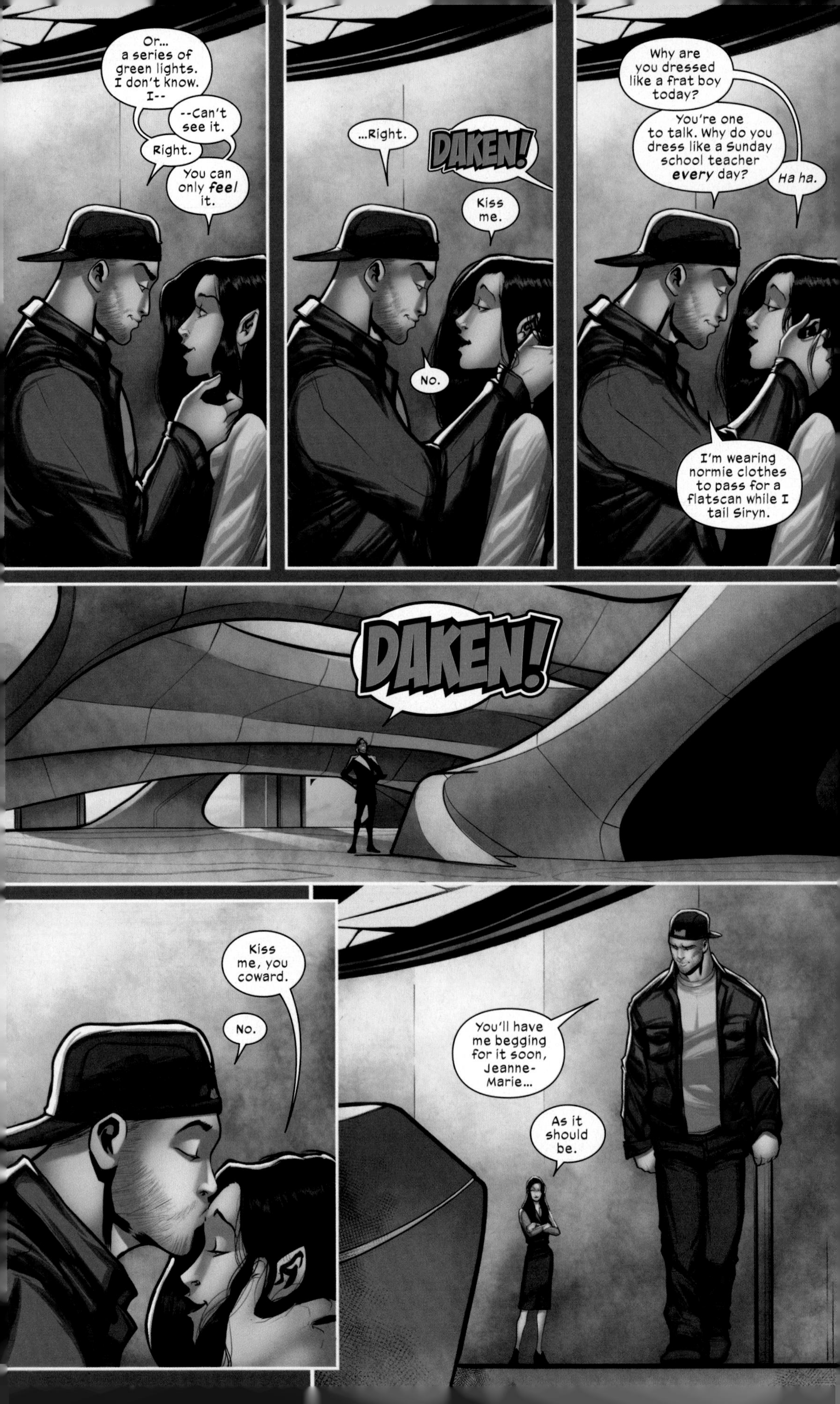
Or... a series of green lights. I don't know. I--
--Can't see it.
Right.
You can only *feel* it.
...Right.
DAKEN!
Kiss me.
No.
Why are you dressed like a frat boy today?
You're one to talk. Why do you dress like a Sunday school teacher **every** day?
Ha ha.
I'm wearing normie clothes to pass for a flatscan while I tail Siryn.
DAKEN!
Kiss me, you coward.
No.
You'll have me begging for it soon, Jeanne-Marie...
As it should be.

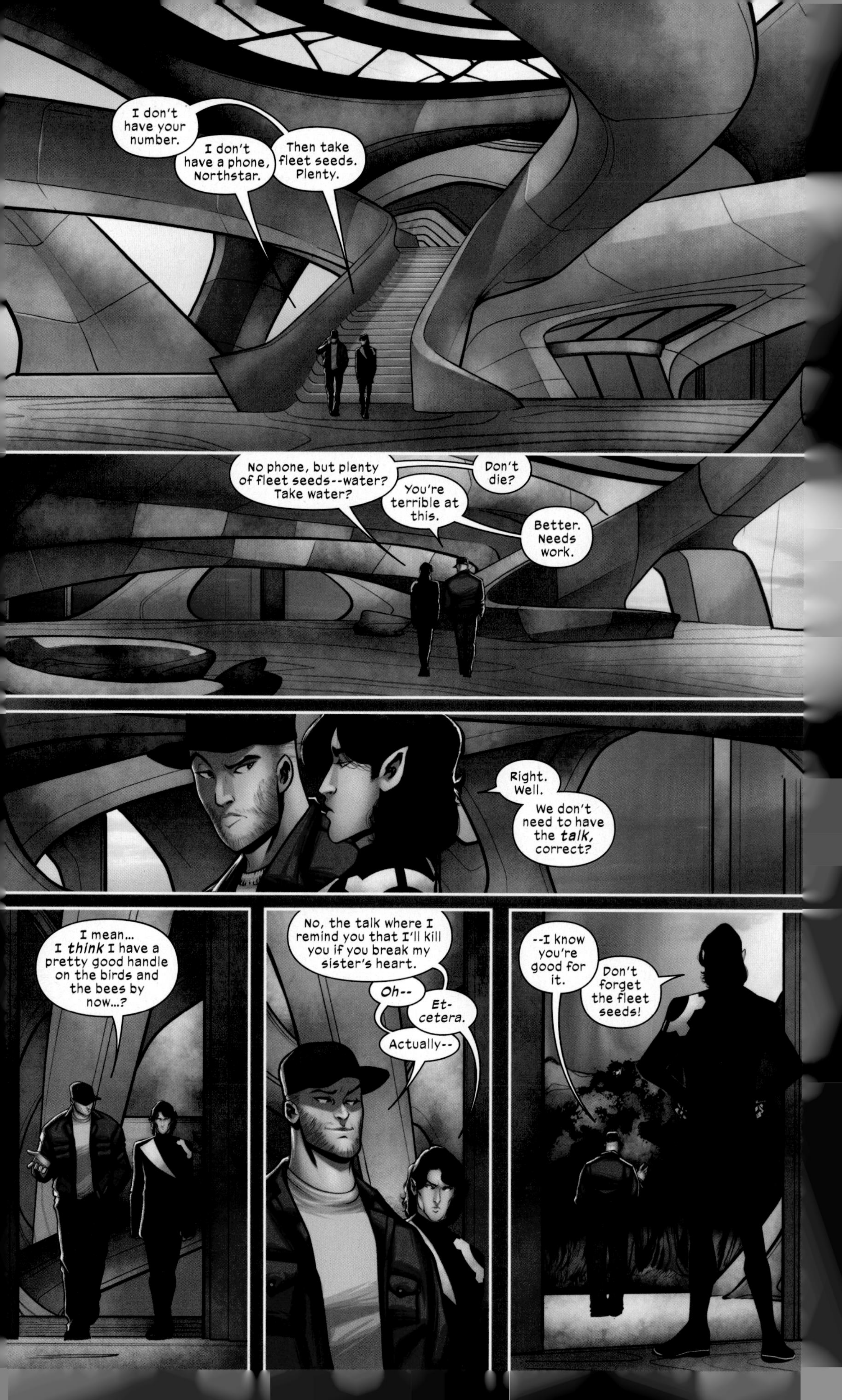

I don't have your number.
I don't have a phone, Northstar.
Then take fleet seeds. Plenty.
No phone, but plenty of fleet seeds--water? Take water?
Don't die?
You're terrible at this.
Better. Needs work.
Right. Well.
We don't need to have the *talk,* correct?
I mean... I *think* I have a pretty good handle on the birds and the bees by now...?
No, the talk where I remind you that I'll kill you if you break my sister's heart.
Oh--
Et-cetera.
Actually--
--I know you're good for it.
Don't forget the fleet seeds!

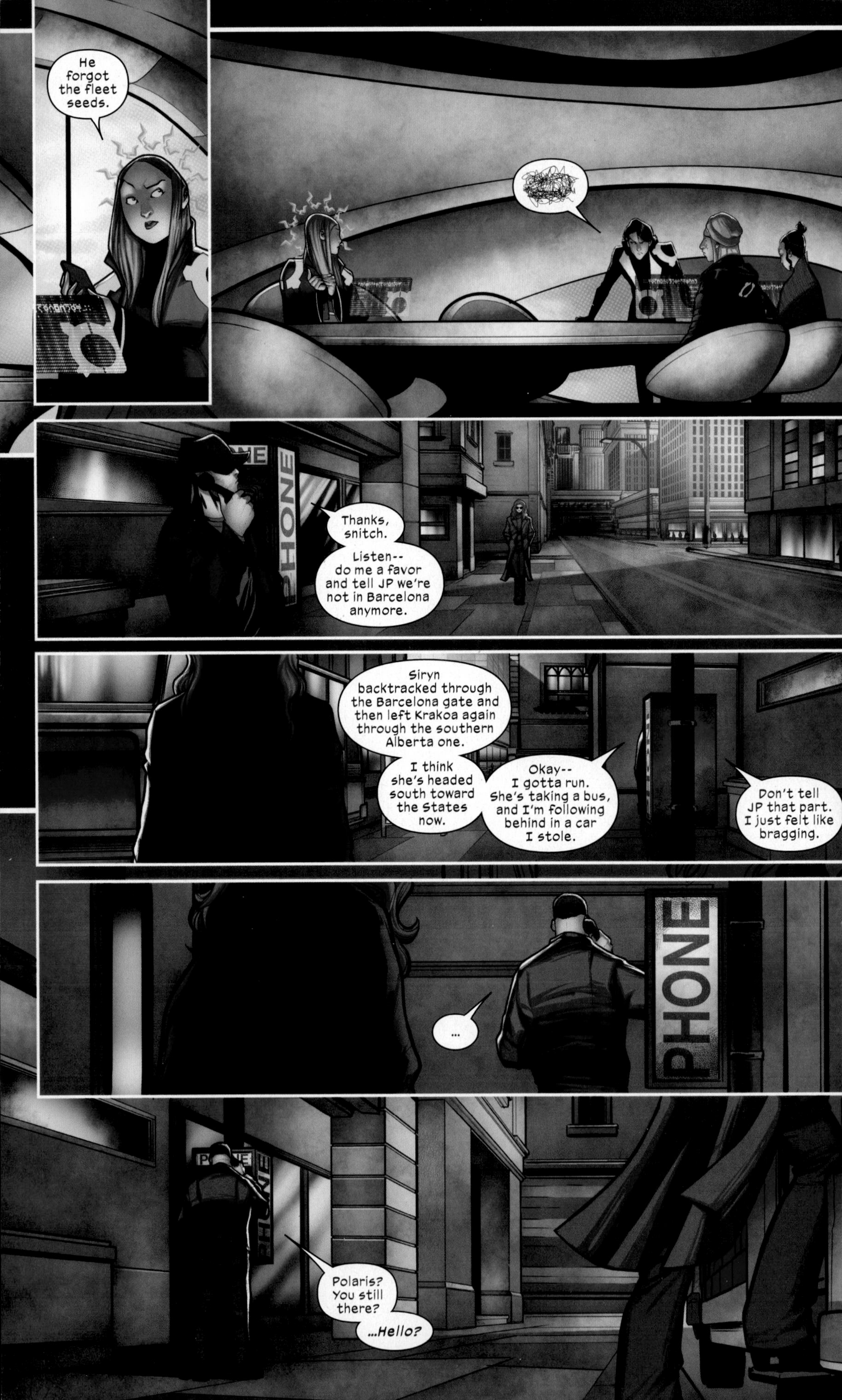
He forgot the fleet seeds.
Thanks, snitch.
Listen-- do me a favor and tell JP we're not in Barcelona anymore.
PHONE
Siryn backtracked through the Barcelona gate and then left Krakoa again through the southern Alberta one.
I think she's headed south toward the States now.
Okay-- I gotta run. She's taking a bus, and I'm following behind in a car I stole.
Don't tell JP that part. I just felt like bragging.
...
PHONE
Polaris? You still there?
...Hello?

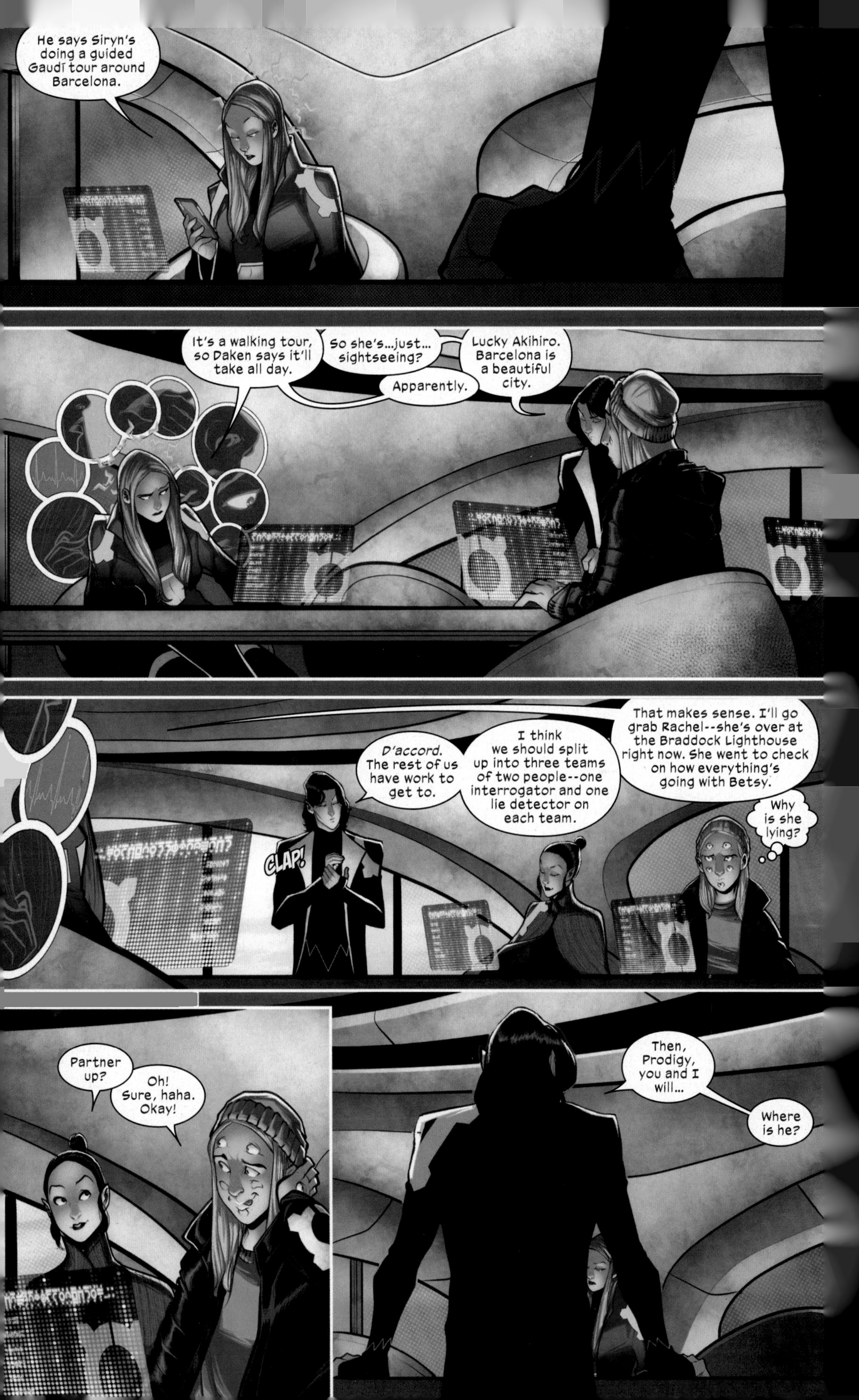

He says Siryn's doing a guided Gaudí tour around Barcelona.
It's a walking tour, so Daken says it'll take all day.
So she's...just... sightseeing?
Apparently.
Lucky Akihiro. Barcelona is a beautiful city.
D'accord. The rest of us have work to get to.
CLAP!
I think we should split up into three teams of two people--one interrogator and one lie detector on each team.
That makes sense. I'll go grab Rachel--she's over at the Braddock Lighthouse right now. She went to check on how everything's going with Betsy.
Why is she lying?
Partner up?
Oh! Sure, haha. Okay!
Then, Prodigy, you and I will...
Where is he?

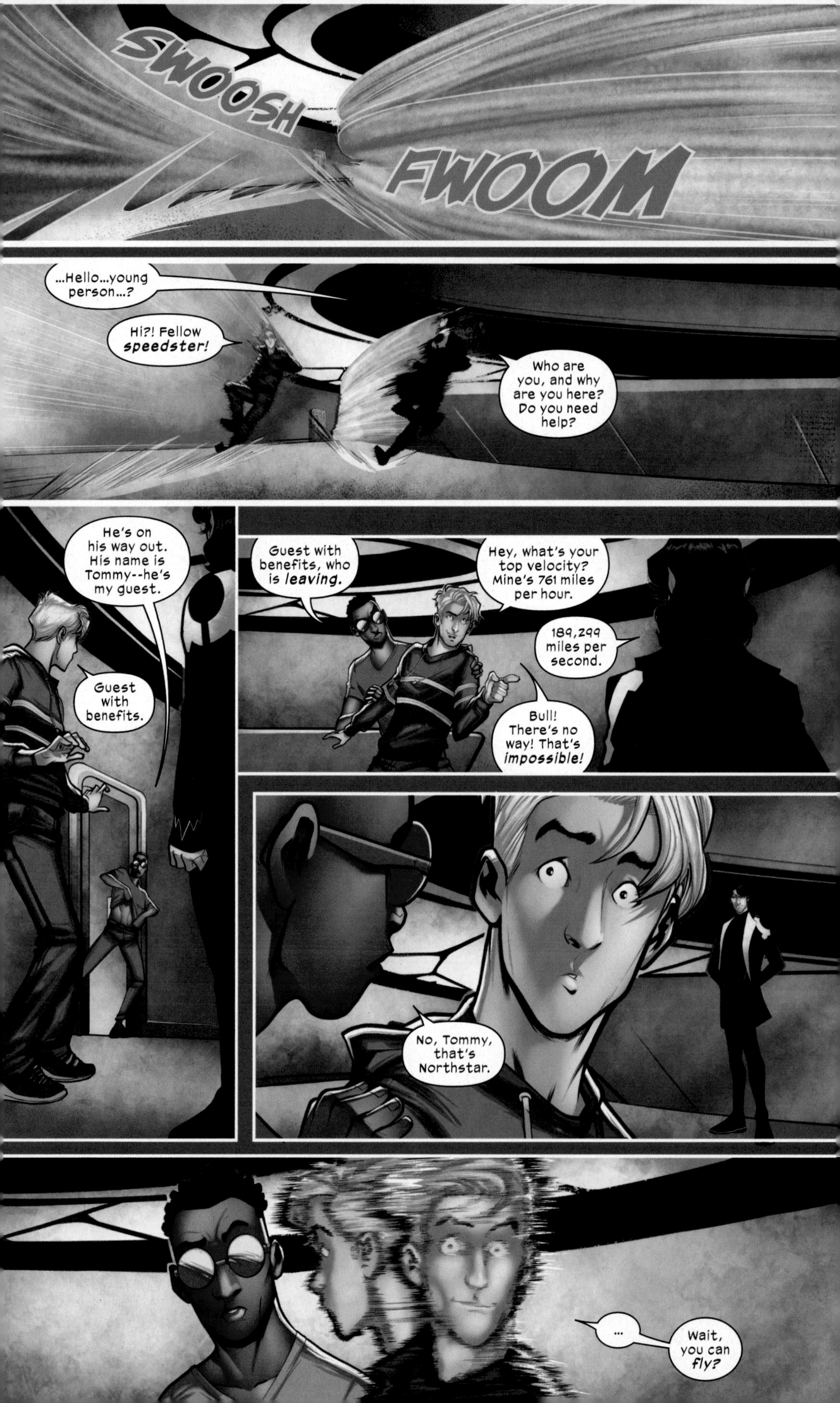
SWOOSH
FWOOM
...Hello...young person...?
Hi?! Fellow *speedster!*
Who are you, and why are you here? Do you need help?
He's on his way out. His name is Tommy--he's my guest.
Guest with benefits.
Guest with benefits, who is *leaving.*
Hey, what's your top velocity? Mine's 761 miles per hour.
189,299 miles per second.
Bull! There's no way! That's *impossible!*
No, Tommy, that's Northstar.
...
Wait, you can *fly?*

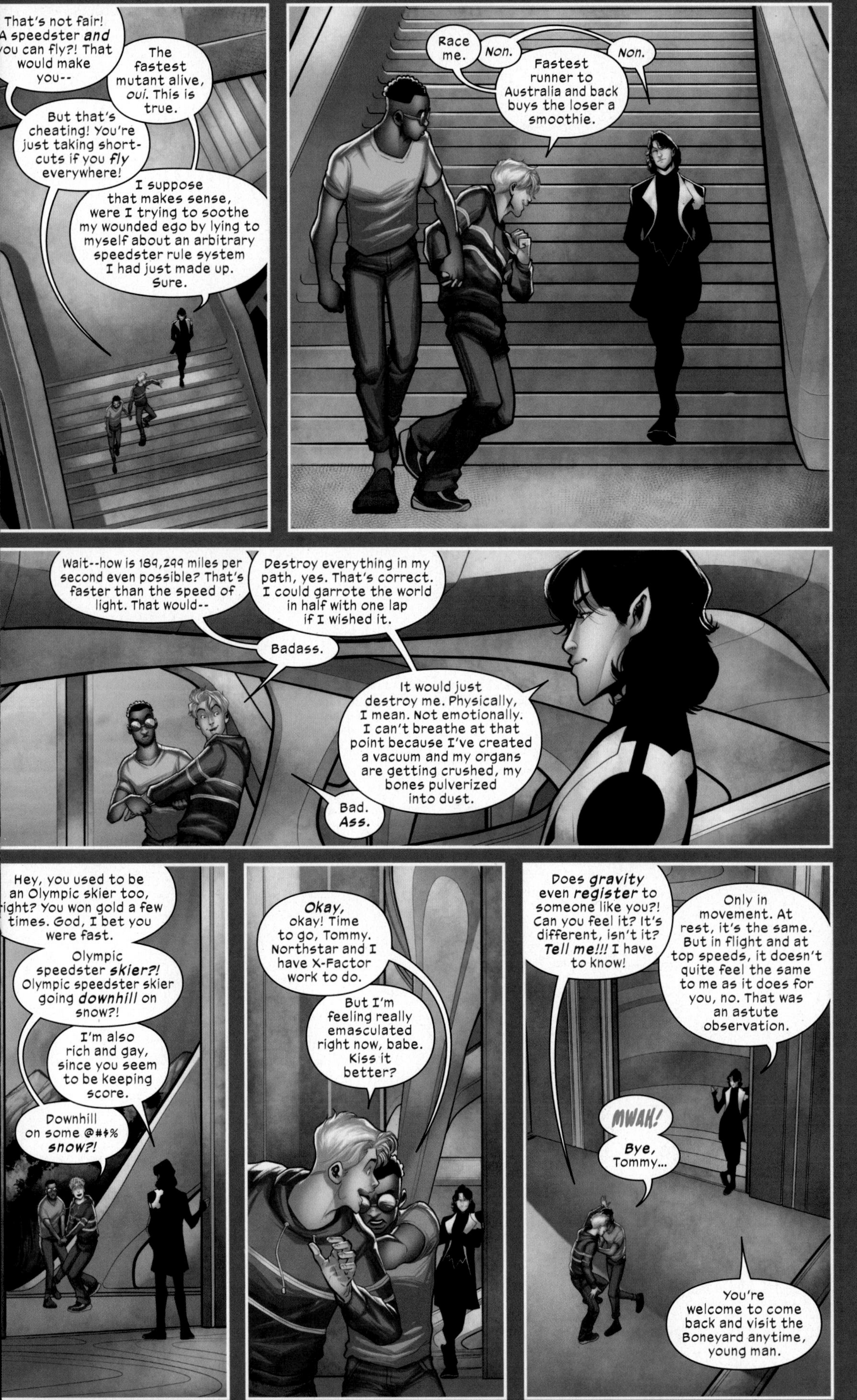

That's not fair! A speedster *and* you can fly?! That would make you--
The fastest mutant alive, *oui*. This is true.
But that's cheating! You're just taking short-cuts if you *fly* everywhere!
I suppose that makes sense, were I trying to soothe my wounded ego by lying to myself about an arbitrary speedster rule system I had just made up. Sure.
Race me.
Non.
Fastest runner to Australia and back buys the loser a smoothie.
Non.
Wait--how is 189,299 miles per second even possible? That's faster than the speed of light. That would--
Destroy everything in my path, yes. That's correct. I could garrote the world in half with one lap if I wished it.
Badass.
It would just destroy me. Physically, I mean. Not emotionally. I can't breathe at that point because I've created a vacuum and my organs are getting crushed, my bones pulverized into dust.
Bad. *Ass.*
Hey, you used to be an Olympic skier too, right? You won gold a few times. God, I bet you were fast.
Olympic speedster *skier?!* Olympic speedster skier going *downhill* on snow?!
I'm also rich and gay, since you seem to be keeping score.
Downhill on some @#$% *snow?!*
Okay, okay! Time to go, Tommy. Northstar and I have X-Factor work to do.
But I'm feeling really emasculated right now, babe. Kiss it better?
Does *gravity* even *register* to someone like you?! Can you feel it? It's different, isn't it? *Tell me!!!* I have to know!
Only in movement. At rest, it's the same. But in flight and at top speeds, it doesn't quite feel the same to me as it does for you, no. That was an astute observation.
MWAH!
Bye, Tommy...
You're welcome to come back and visit the Boneyard anytime, young man.

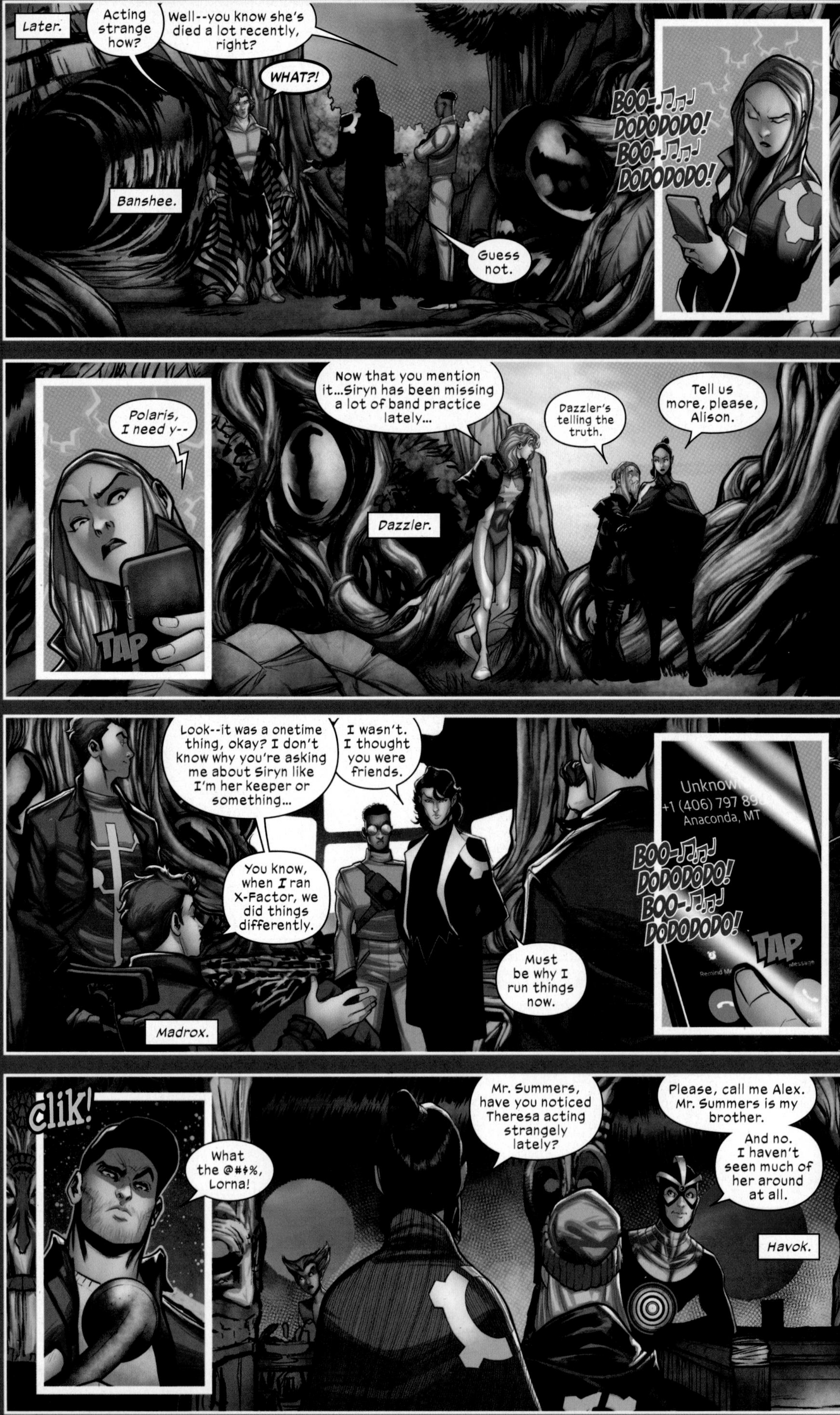

Later.
Acting strange how?
Well--you know she's died a lot recently, right?
WHAT?!
Banshee.
Guess not.
BOO-♫♫♩ DODODODO! BOO-♫♫♩ DODODODO!
Polaris, I need y--
TAP
Now that you mention it...Siryn has been missing a lot of band practice lately...
Dazzler's telling the truth.
Tell us more, please, Alison.
Dazzler.
Look--it was a onetime thing, okay? I don't know why you're asking me about Siryn like I'm her keeper or something...
I wasn't. I thought you were friends.
You know, when I ran X-Factor, we did things differently.
Must be why I run things now.
Madrox.
Anaconda, MT
BOO-♫♫♩ DODODODO! BOO-♫♫♩ DODODODO!
TAP
clik!
What the @#$%, Lorna!
Mr. Summers, have you noticed Theresa acting strangely lately?
Please, call me Alex. Mr. Summers is my brother.
And no. I haven't seen much of her around at all.
Havok.

The Morrigan, Goddess of Death and Battle.

Some claim she has existed since death itself began and has taken many different forms and different names as ages pass. It is said she is a shape-shifter who can affect areas of death and battle in all ways, including both bestowing and removing abilities in others. She can weaken victims to the brink of death or heal the sick back from the very same edge if she wills it.

Our history of her begins in the year 250 B.C.E., in which the Morrigan battles for her new host body. Her original form has long since been lost to time, and thusly the Morrigan may only pass into a new host upon death of the former host, though her window of time to do so is limited. It is death itself that permits the transfer, whether or not the intended host, who is always female, consents.

The source of the Morrigan's powers is by her own account ageless, drawn from the font of death and battles themselves. Celts and druids made ritual sacrifices in praise of her name, and some texts tell of death rite rituals found across many a different ancient heathen society of eras gone.

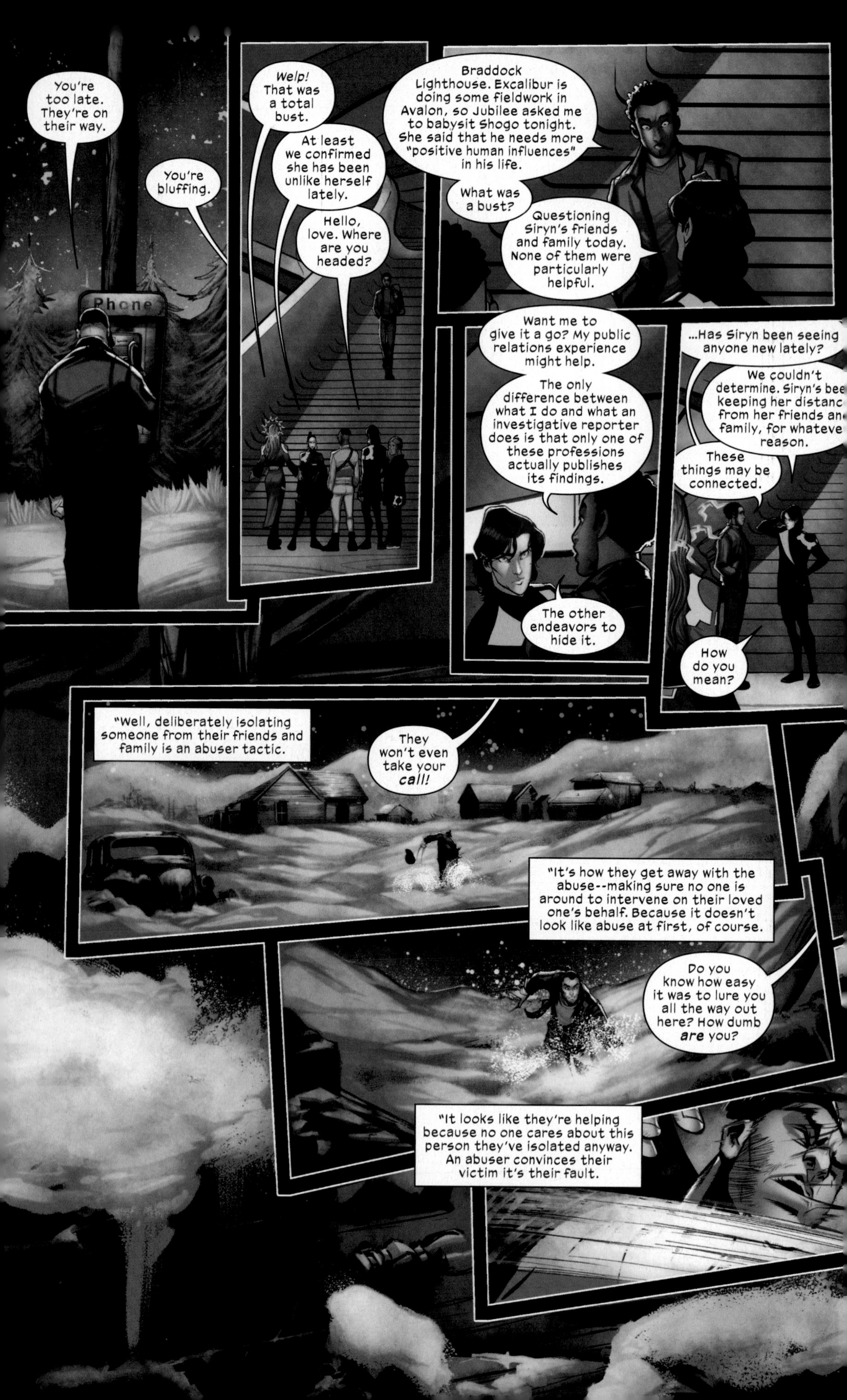
You're too late. They're on their way.
You're bluffing.
Welp! That was a total bust.
At least we confirmed she has been unlike herself lately.
Hello, love. Where are you headed?
Braddock Lighthouse. Excalibur is doing some fieldwork in Avalon, so Jubilee asked me to babysit Shogo tonight. She said that he needs more "positive human influences" in his life.
What was a bust?
Questioning Siryn's friends and family today. None of them were particularly helpful.
Want me to give it a go? My public relations experience might help.
The only difference between what I do and what an investigative reporter does is that only one of these professions actually publishes its findings.
The other endeavors to hide it.
...Has Siryn been seeing anyone new lately?
We couldn't determine. Siryn's bee keeping her distanc from her friends an family, for whateve reason.
These things may be connected.
How do you mean?
"Well, deliberately isolating someone from their friends and family is an abuser tactic.
They won't even take your call!
"It's how they get away with the abuse--making sure no one is around to intervene on their loved one's behalf. Because it doesn't look like abuse at first, of course.
Do you know how easy it was to lure you all the way out here? How dumb are you?
"It looks like they're helping because no one cares about this person they've isolated anyway. An abuser convinces their victim it's their fault.
Phone

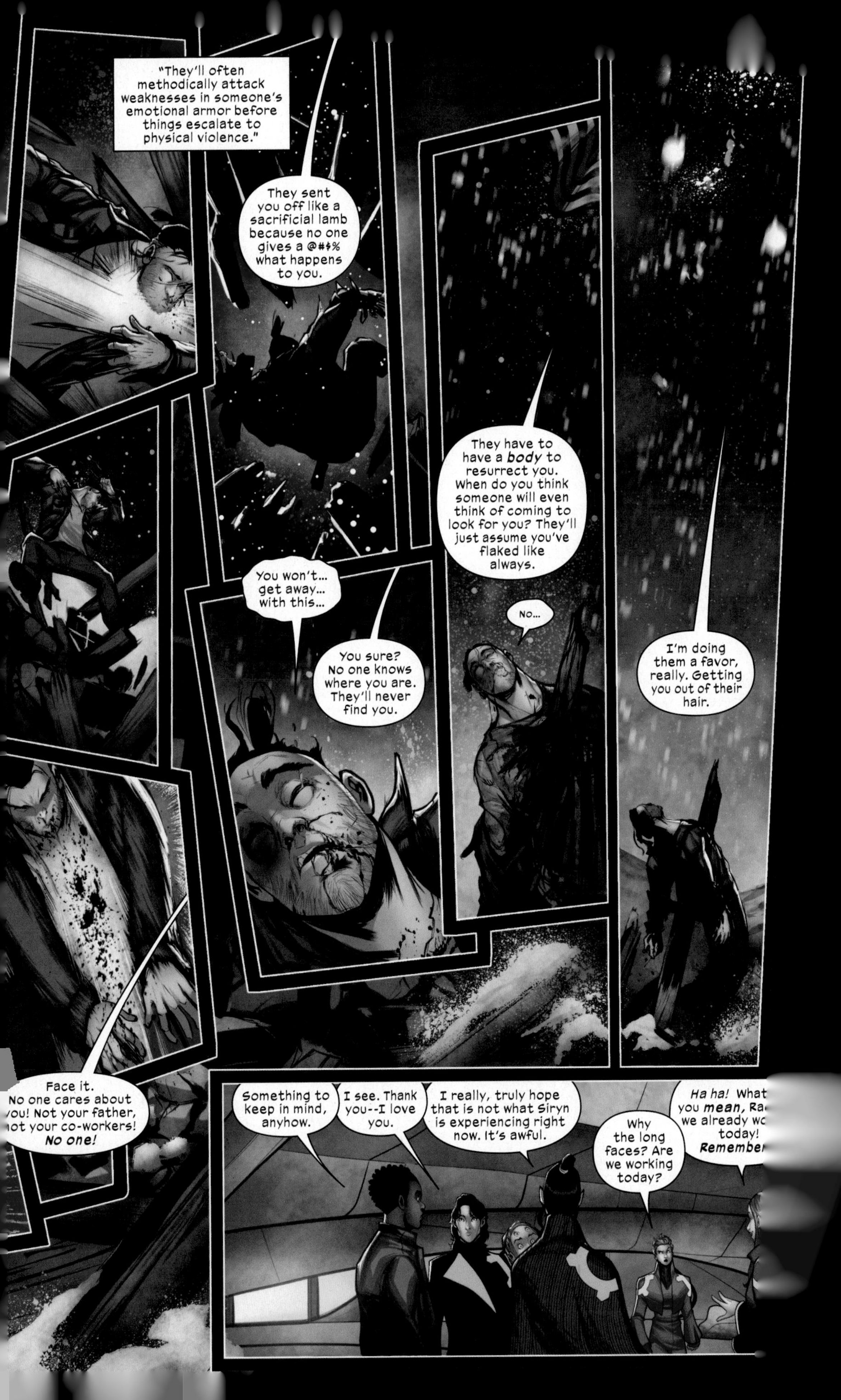
"They'll often methodically attack weaknesses in someone's emotional armor before things escalate to physical violence."
They sent you off like a sacrificial lamb because no one gives a @#$% what happens to you.
They have to have a *body* to resurrect you. When do you think someone will even think of coming to look for you? They'll just assume you've flaked like always.
You won't... get away... with this...
You sure? No one knows where you are. They'll never find you.
No...
I'm doing them a favor, really. Getting you out of their hair.
Face it. No one cares about you! Not your father, not your co-workers! *No one!*
Something to keep in mind, anyhow.
I see. Thank you--I love you.
I really, truly hope that is not what Siryn is experiencing right now. It's awful.
Why the long faces? Are we working today?
Ha ha! What you *mean,* Ra we already wo today! *Remember*

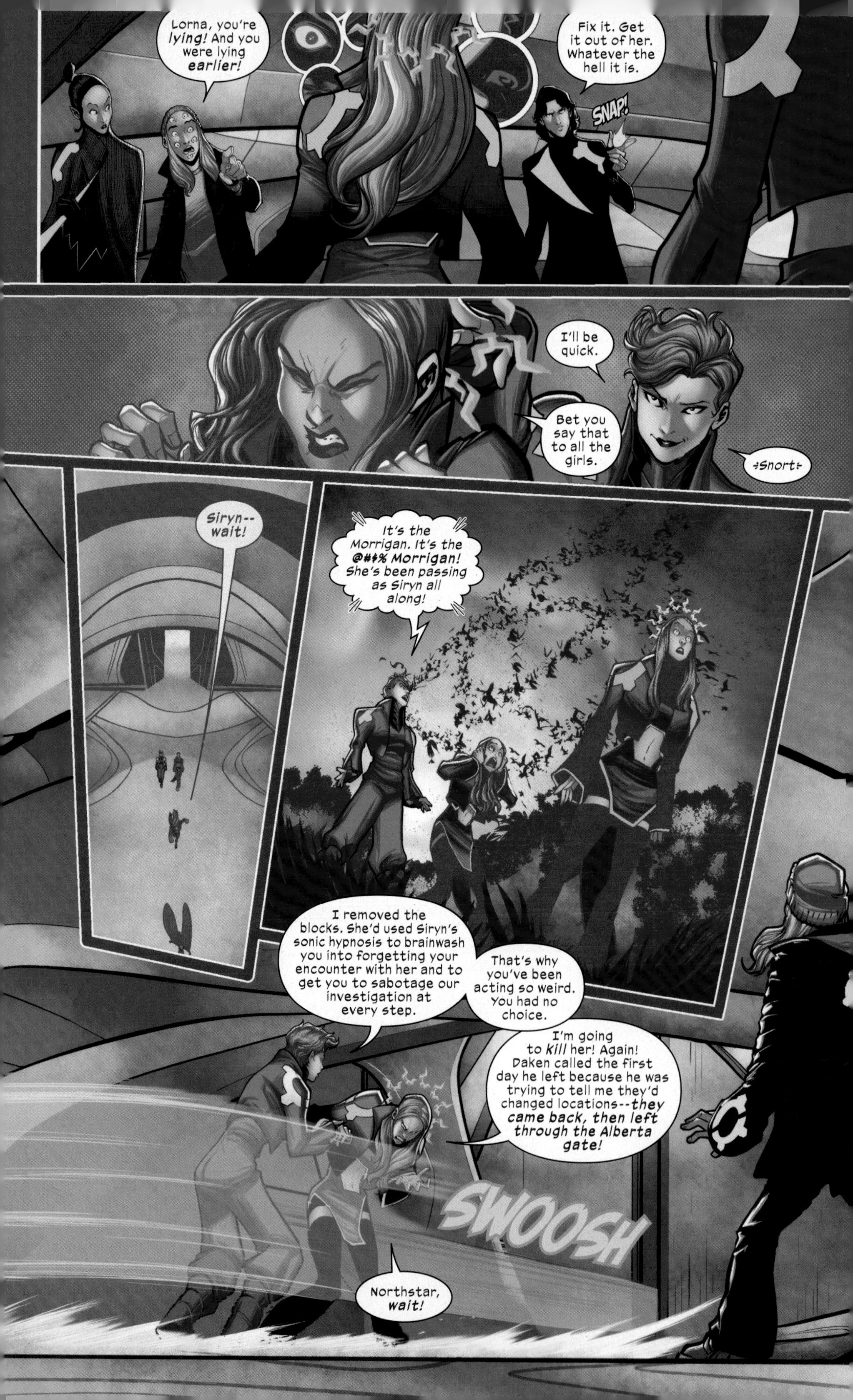

Lorna, you're *lying!* And you were lying *earlier!*
Fix it. Get it out of her. Whatever the hell it is.
SNAP!
I'll be quick.
Bet you say that to all the girls.
-Snort-
Siryn--wait!
It's the Morrigan. It's the @#$% Morrigan! She's been passing as Siryn all along!
I removed the blocks. She'd used Siryn's sonic hypnosis to brainwash you into forgetting your encounter with her and to get you to sabotage our investigation at every step.
That's why you've been acting so weird. You had no choice.
I'm going to *kill* her! Again! Daken called the first day he left because he was trying to tell me they'd changed locations--*they came back, then left through the Alberta gate!*
SWOOSH
Northstar, *wait!*

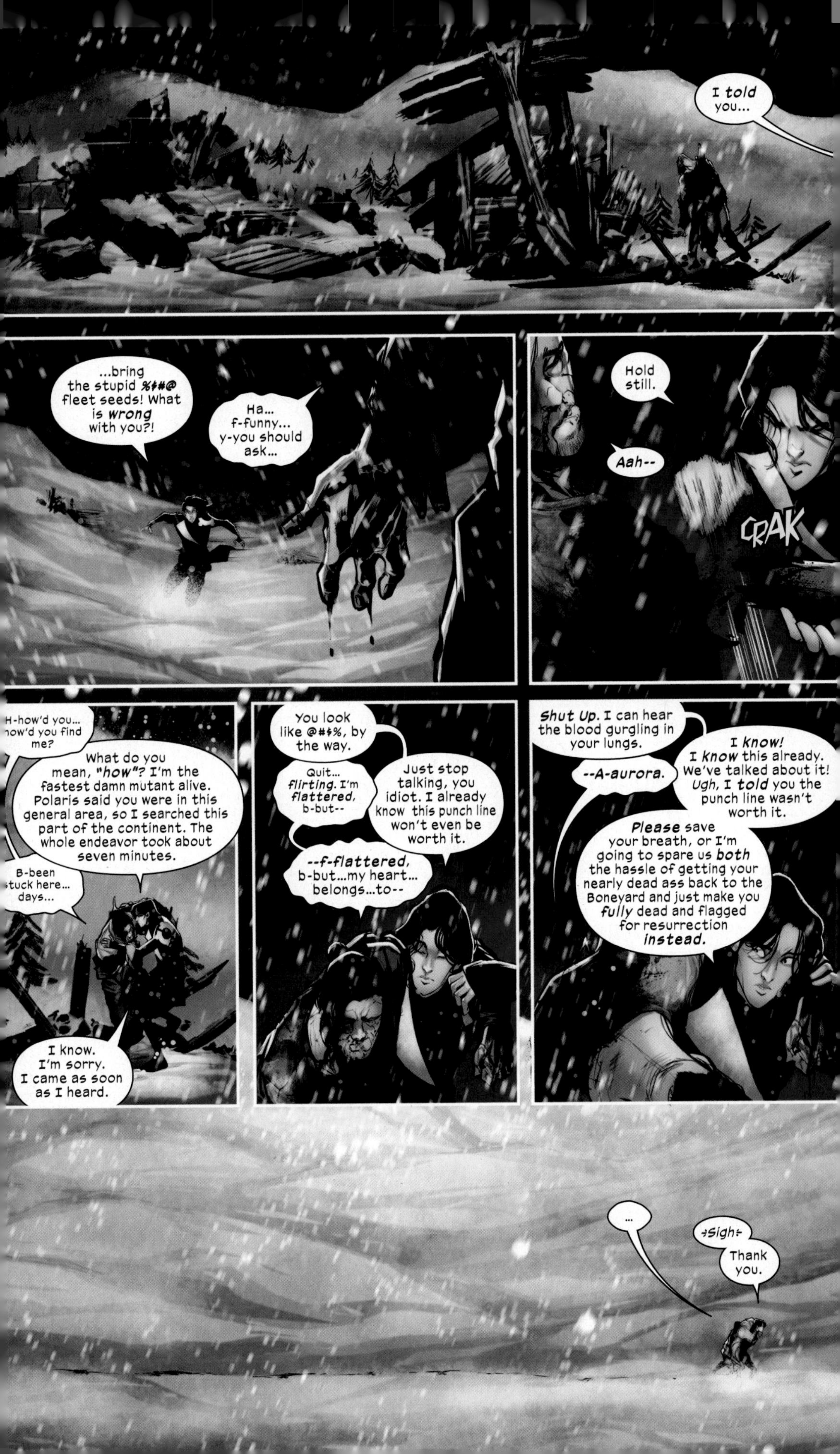

I told you...
...bring the stupid %$#@ fleet seeds! What is wrong with you?!
Ha... f-funny... y-you should ask...
Hold still.
Aah--
CRAK
H-how'd you... how'd you find me?
What do you mean, "how"? I'm the fastest damn mutant alive. Polaris said you were in this general area, so I searched this part of the continent. The whole endeavor took about seven minutes.
B-been stuck here... days...
I know. I'm sorry. I came as soon as I heard.
You look like @#$%, by the way.
Quit... flirting. I'm flattered, b-but--
Just stop talking, you idiot. I already know this punch line won't even be worth it.
--f-flattered, b-but...my heart... belongs...to--
Shut Up. I can hear the blood gurgling in your lungs.
--A-aurora.
I know! I know this already. We've talked about it! Ugh, I told you the punch line wasn't worth it.
Please save your breath, or I'm going to spare us both the hassle of getting your nearly dead ass back to the Boneyard and just make you fully dead and flagged for resurrection instead.
...
=Sigh=
Thank you.

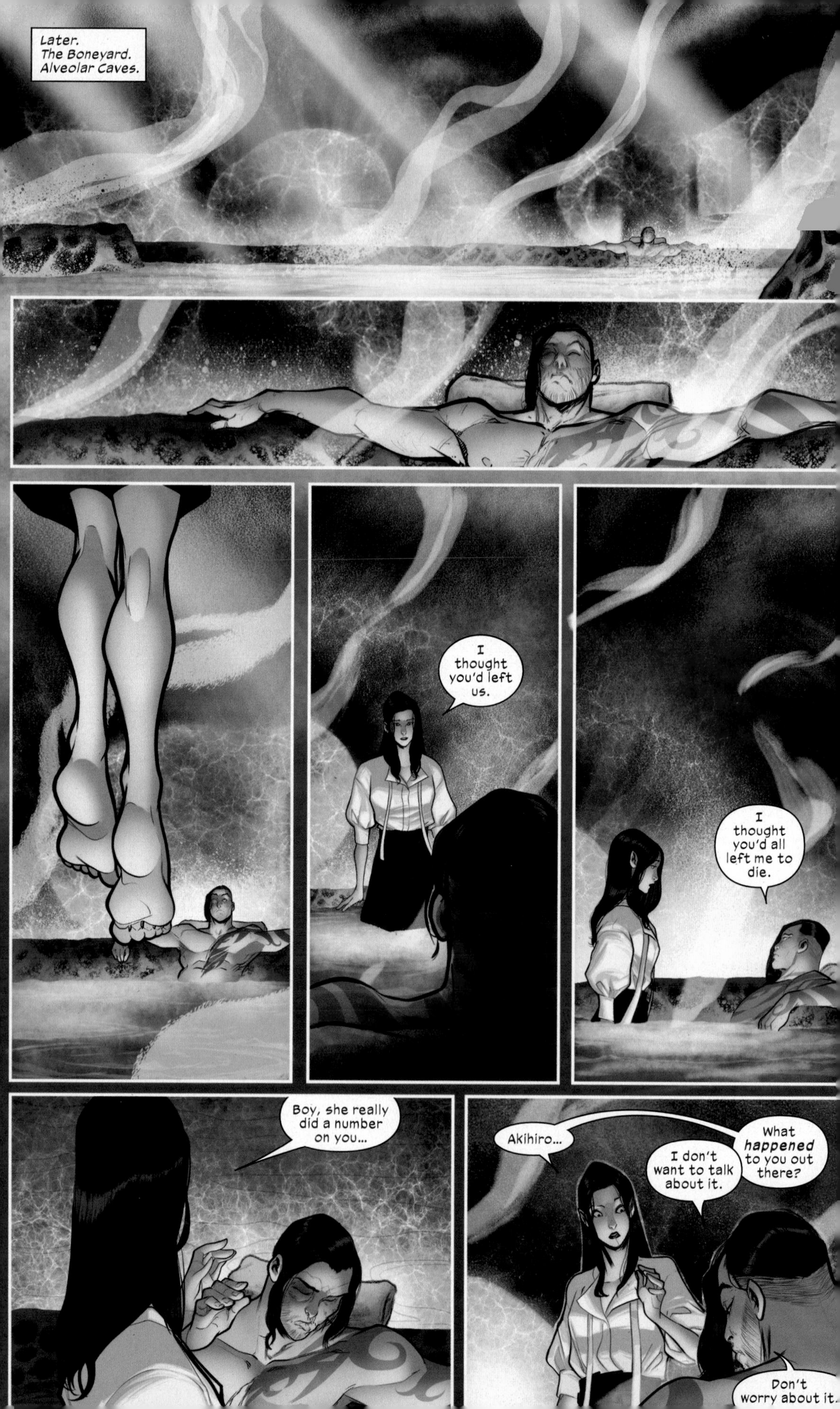
Later.
The Boneyard.
Alveolar Caves.
I thought you'd left us.
I thought you'd all left me to die.
Boy, she really did a number on you...
Akihiro...
What *happened* to you out there?
I don't want to talk about it.
Don't worry about it.

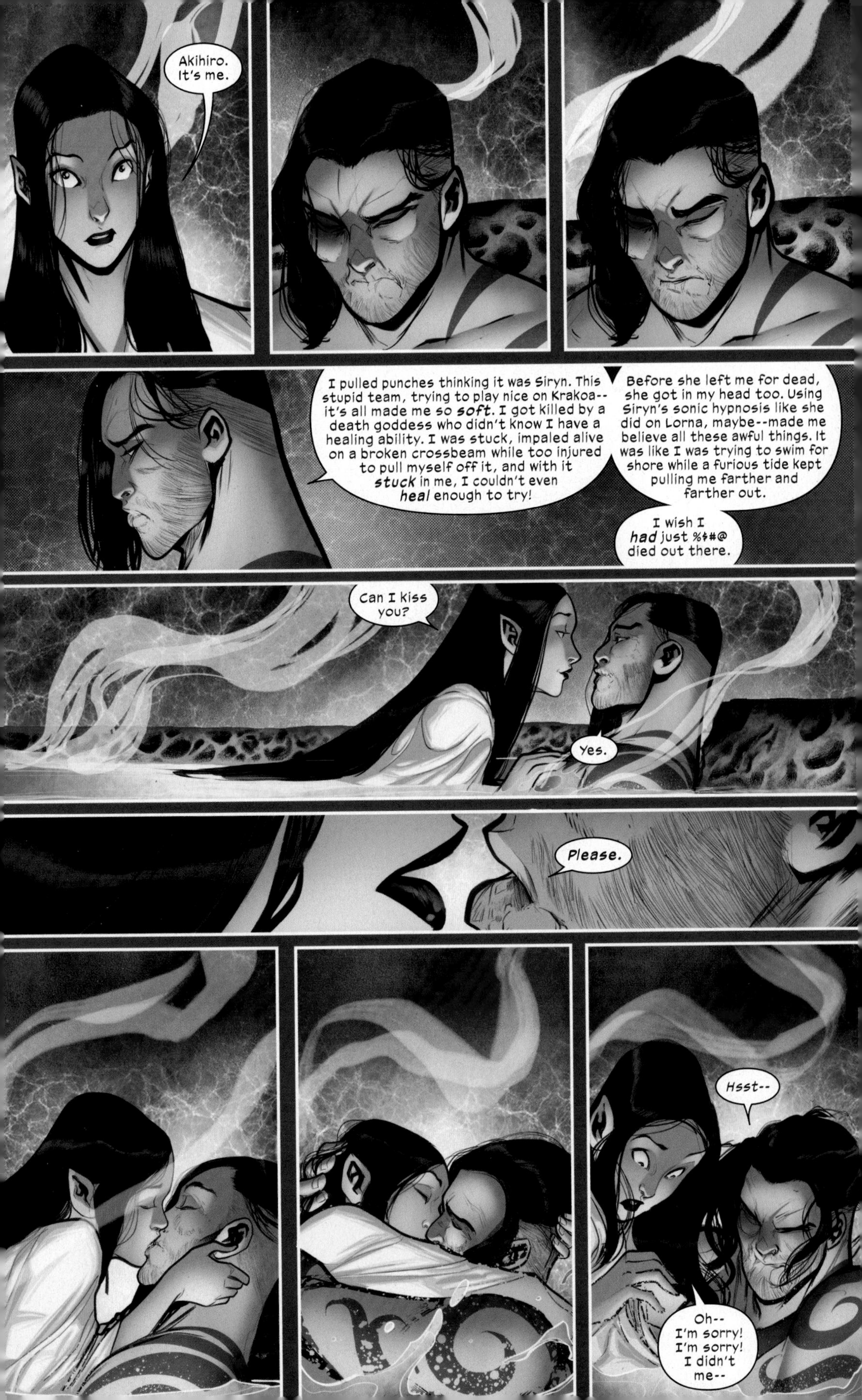
Akihiro. It's me.
I pulled punches thinking it was Siryn. This stupid team, trying to play nice on Krakoa-- it's all made me so soft. I got killed by a death goddess who didn't know I have a healing ability. I was stuck, impaled alive on a broken crossbeam while too injured to pull myself off it, and with it stuck in me, I couldn't even heal enough to try!
Before she left me for dead, she got in my head too. Using Siryn's sonic hypnosis like she did on Lorna, maybe--made me believe all these awful things. It was like I was trying to swim for shore while a furious tide kept pulling me farther and farther out.
I wish I had just %$#@ died out there.
Can I kiss you?
Yes.
Please.
Hsst--
Oh-- I'm sorry! I'm sorry! I didn't me--

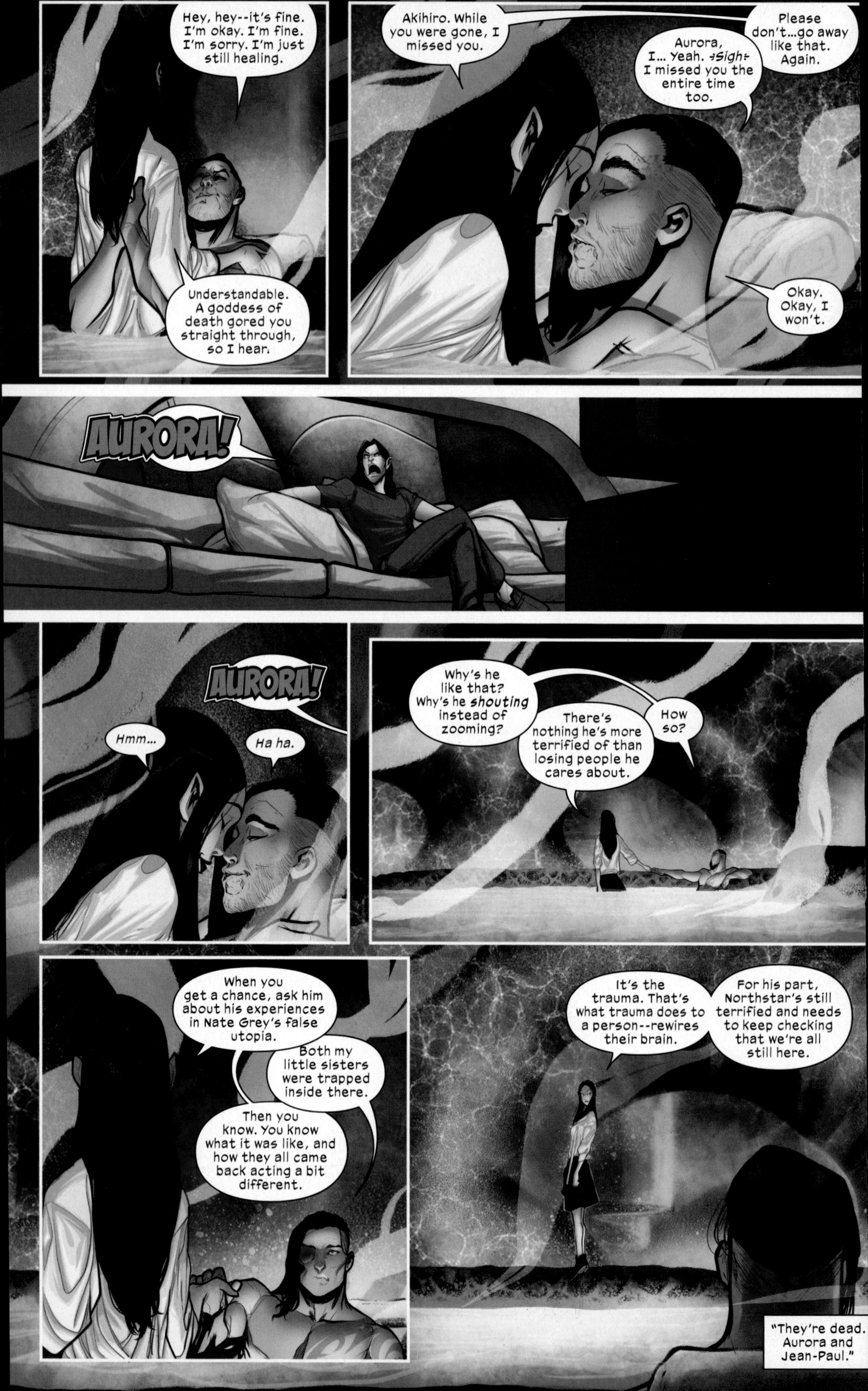
Hey, hey--it's fine. I'm okay. I'm fine. I'm sorry. I'm just still healing.
Understandable. A goddess of death gored you straight through, so I hear.
Akihiro. While you were gone, I missed you.
Aurora, I... Yeah. -Sigh- I missed you the entire time too.
Please don't...go away like that. Again.
Okay. Okay, I won't.
AURORA!
AURORA!
Hmm...
Ha ha.
Why's he like that? Why's he *shouting* instead of zooming?
How so?
There's nothing he's more terrified of than losing people he cares about.
When you get a chance, ask him about his experiences in Nate Grey's false utopia.
Both my little sisters were trapped inside there.
Then you know. You know what it was like, and how they all came back acting a bit different.
It's the trauma. That's what trauma does to a person--rewires their brain.
For his part, Northstar's still terrified and needs to keep checking that we're all still here.
"They're dead. Aurora and Jean-Paul."

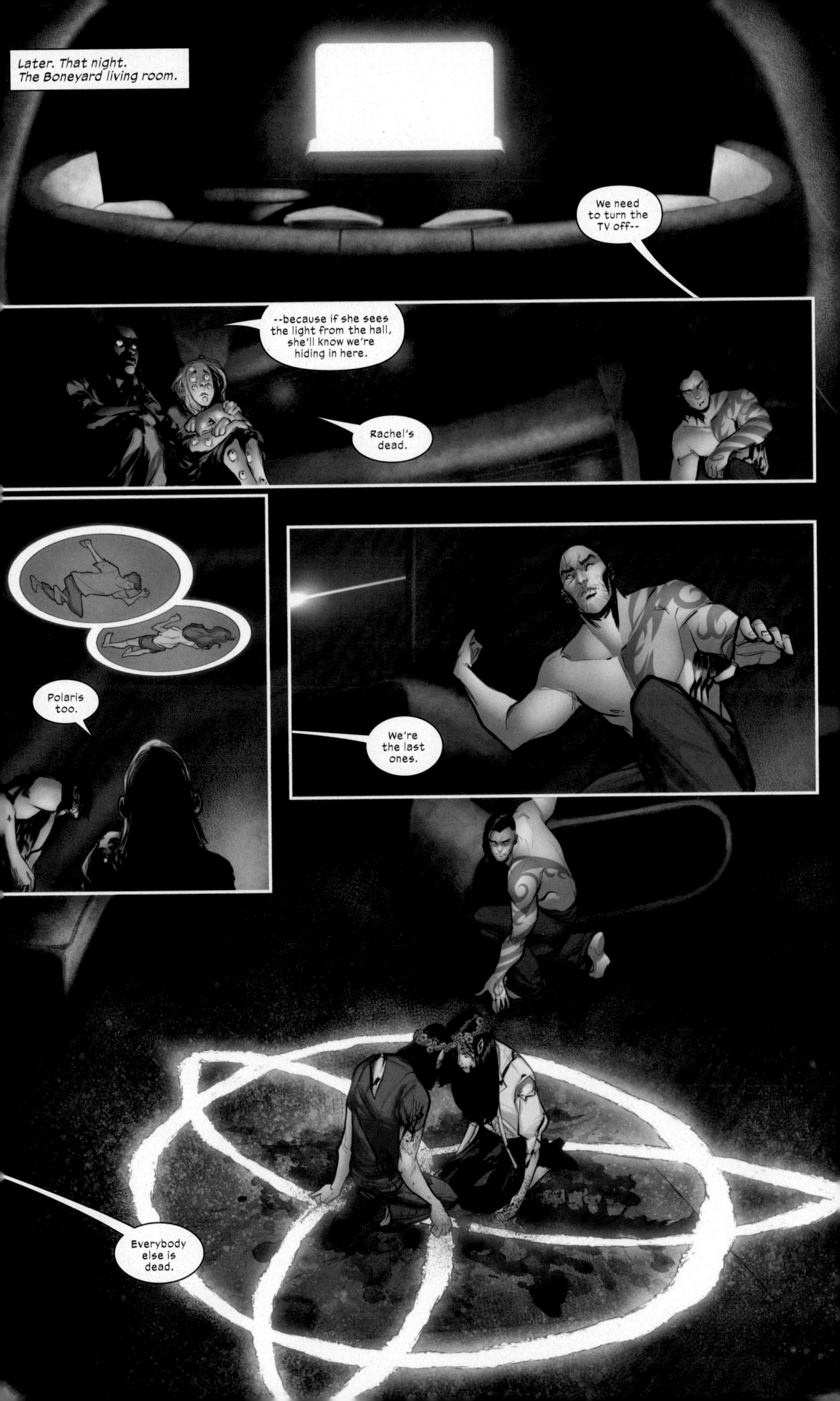
Later. That night.
The Boneyard living room.
We need to turn the TV off--
--because if she sees the light from the hall, she'll know we're hiding in here.
Rachel's dead.
Polaris too.
We're the last ones.
Everybody else is dead.

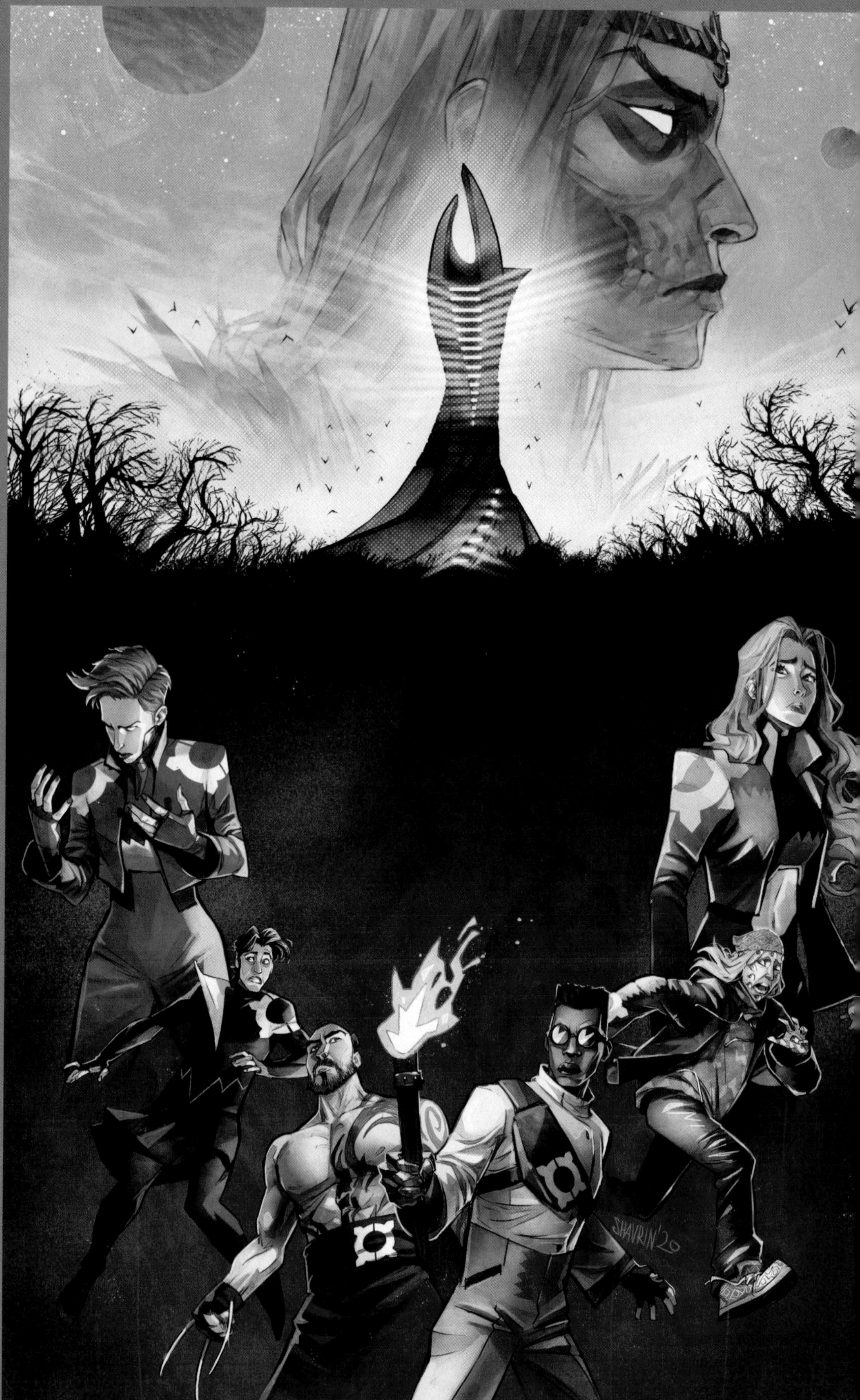
SHAVRIN'20

Suite Nº8:
Scio Me Nihil Scire
(Tritone Substitution —
Jazz Arrangement)

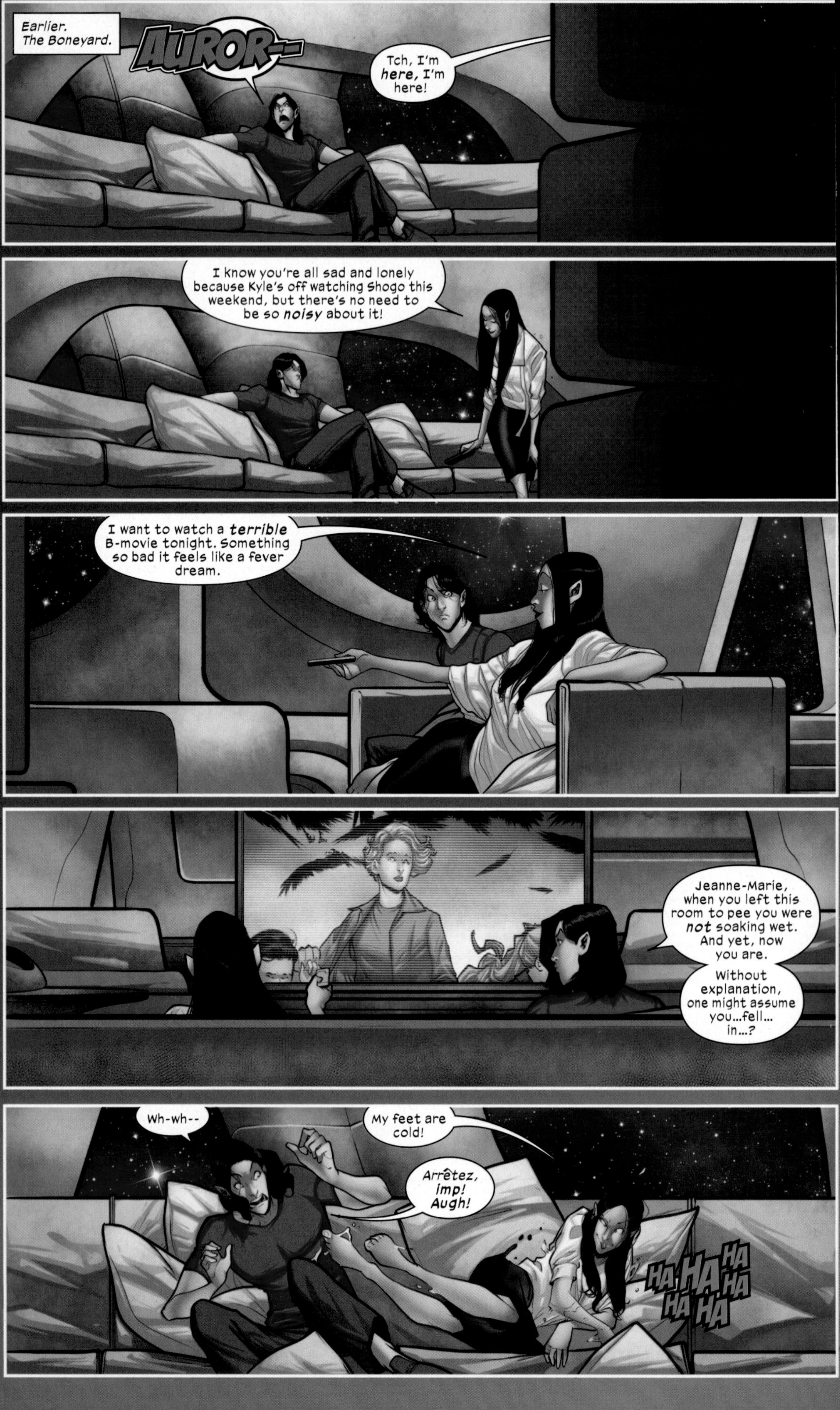
Earlier.
The Boneyard.
AUROR--
Tch, I'm here, I'm here!
I know you're all sad and lonely because Kyle's off watching Shogo this weekend, but there's no need to be so noisy about it!
I want to watch a terrible B-movie tonight. Something so bad it feels like a fever dream.
Jeanne-Marie, when you left this room to pee you were not soaking wet. And yet, now you are.
Without explanation, one might assume you...fell... in...?
Wh-wh--
My feet are cold!
Arrêtez, imp! Augh!
HA HA HA HA HA HA HA

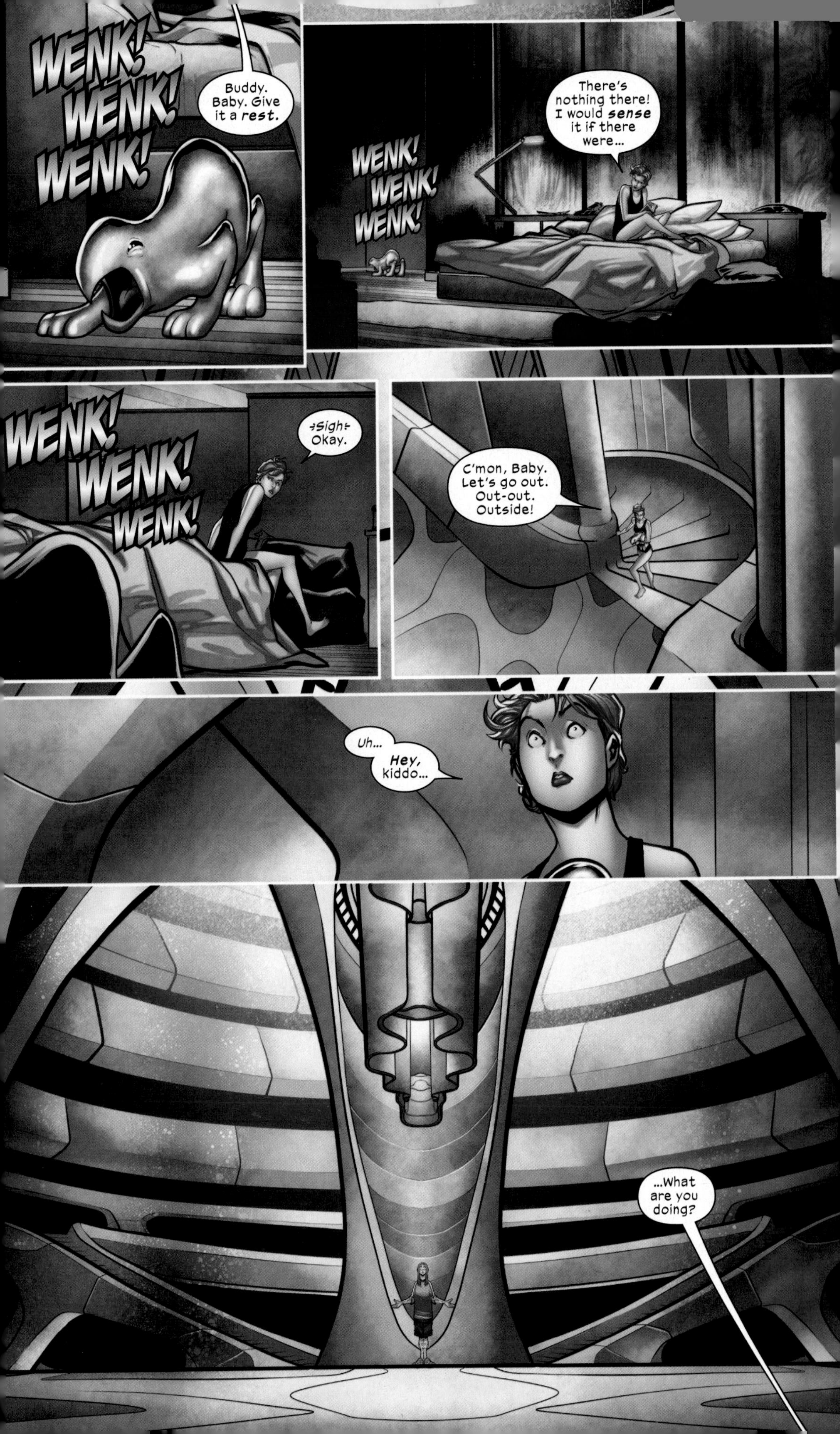
WENK! WENK! WENK!
Buddy. Baby. Give it a rest.
WENK! WENK! WENK!
There's nothing there! I would sense it if there were...
WENK! WENK! WENK!
-Sigh- Okay.
C'mon, Baby. Let's go out. Out-out. Outside!
Uh...
Hey, kiddo...
...What are you doing?

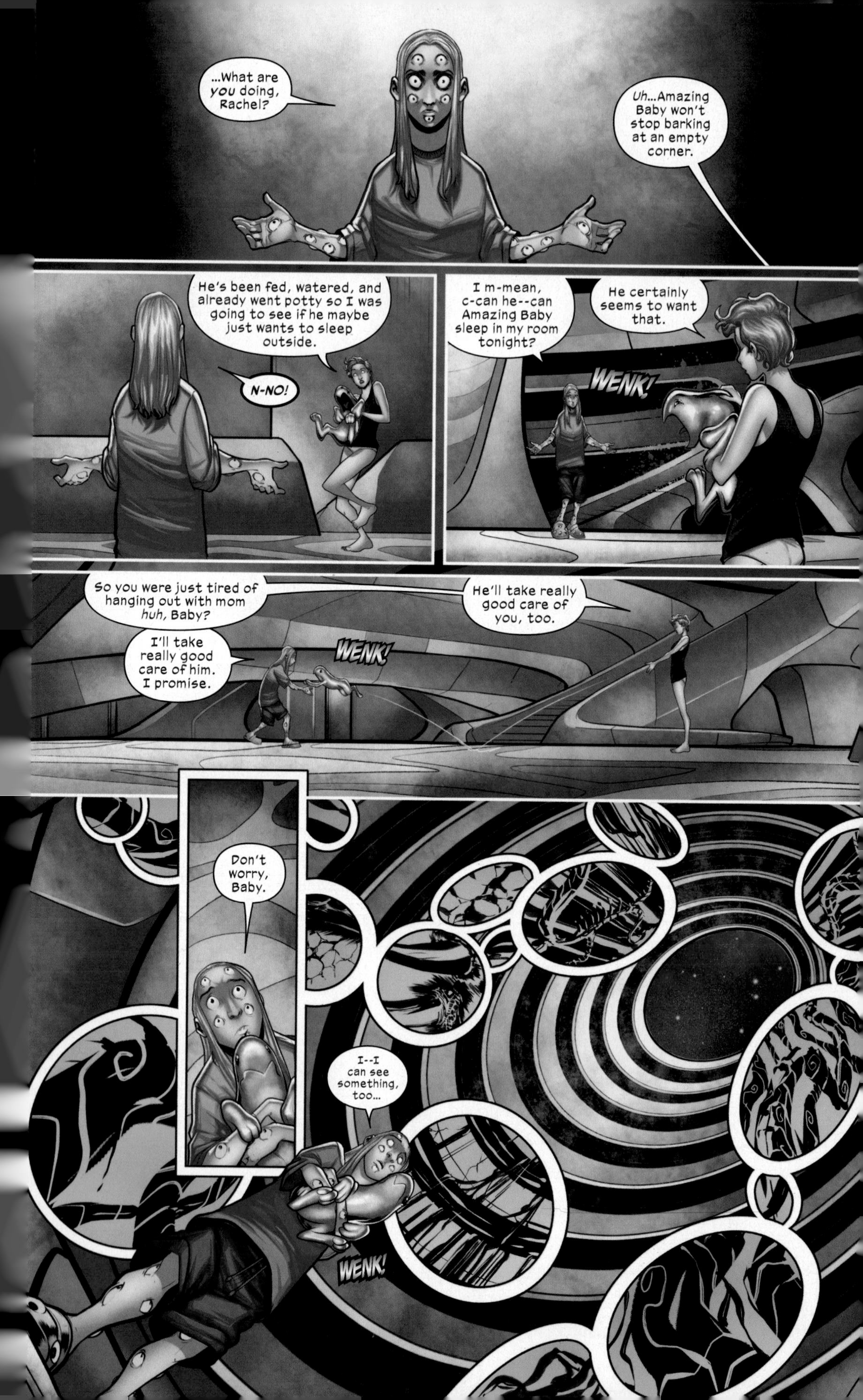
...What are you doing, Rachel?
Uh...Amazing Baby won't stop barking at an empty corner.
He's been fed, watered, and already went potty so I was going to see if he maybe just wants to sleep outside.
N-NO!
I m-mean, c-can he--can Amazing Baby sleep in my room tonight?
He certainly seems to want that.
WENK!
So you were just tired of hanging out with mom huh, Baby?
He'll take really good care of you, too.
I'll take really good care of him. I promise.
WENK!
Don't worry, Baby.
I--I can see something, too...
WENK!

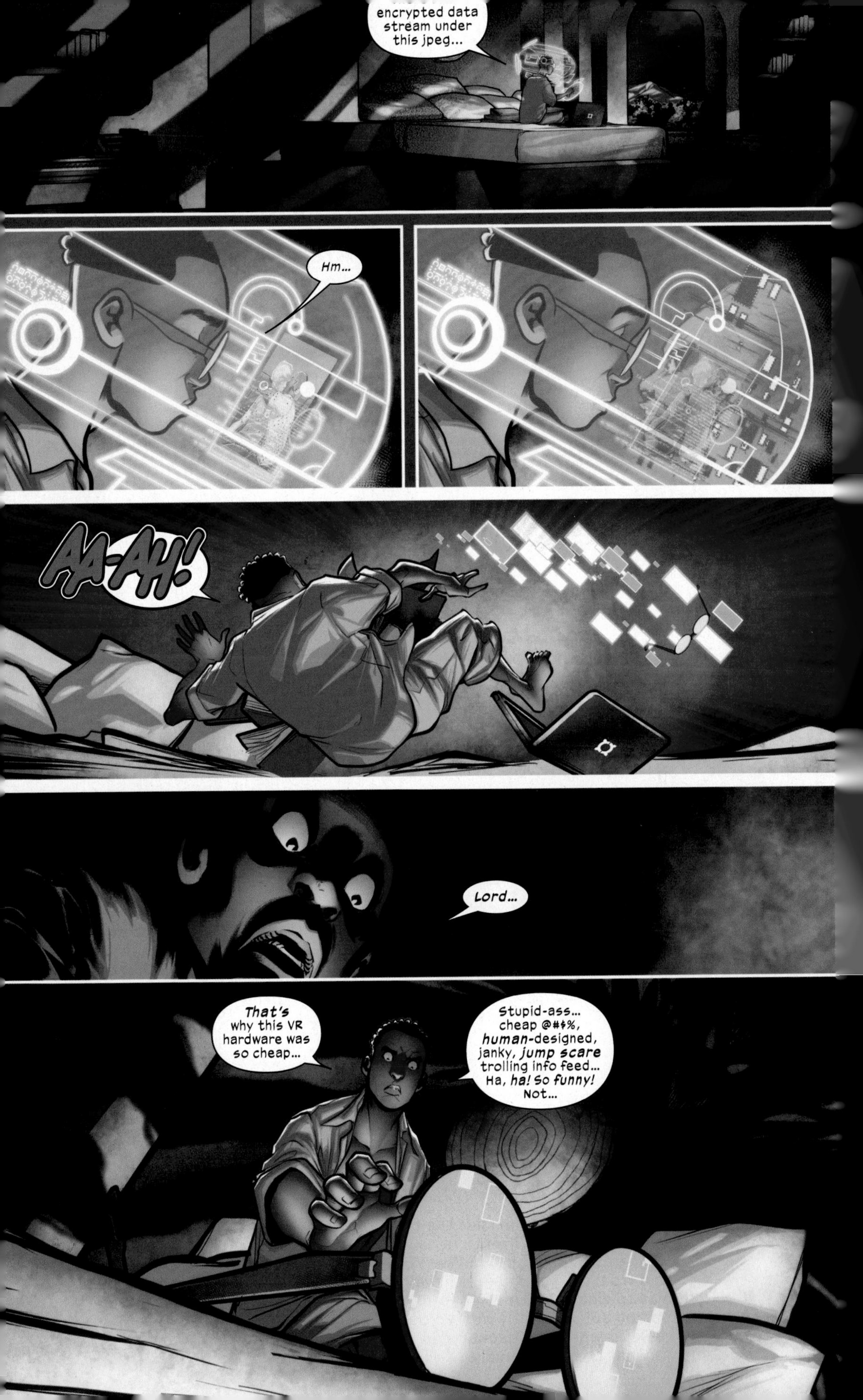
encrypted data stream under this jpeg...
Hm...
AA-AH!
Lord...
That's why this VR hardware was so cheap...
Stupid-ass... cheap @#$%, human-designed, janky, jump scare trolling info feed... Ha, ha! So funny! Not...

PERSONAL LOG: DAVID ALLEYNE

i. First hidden layer reveals photo edits.

ii. Second hidden layer reveals GPS coordinates and a date/time stamp embedded in JPEG metadata.

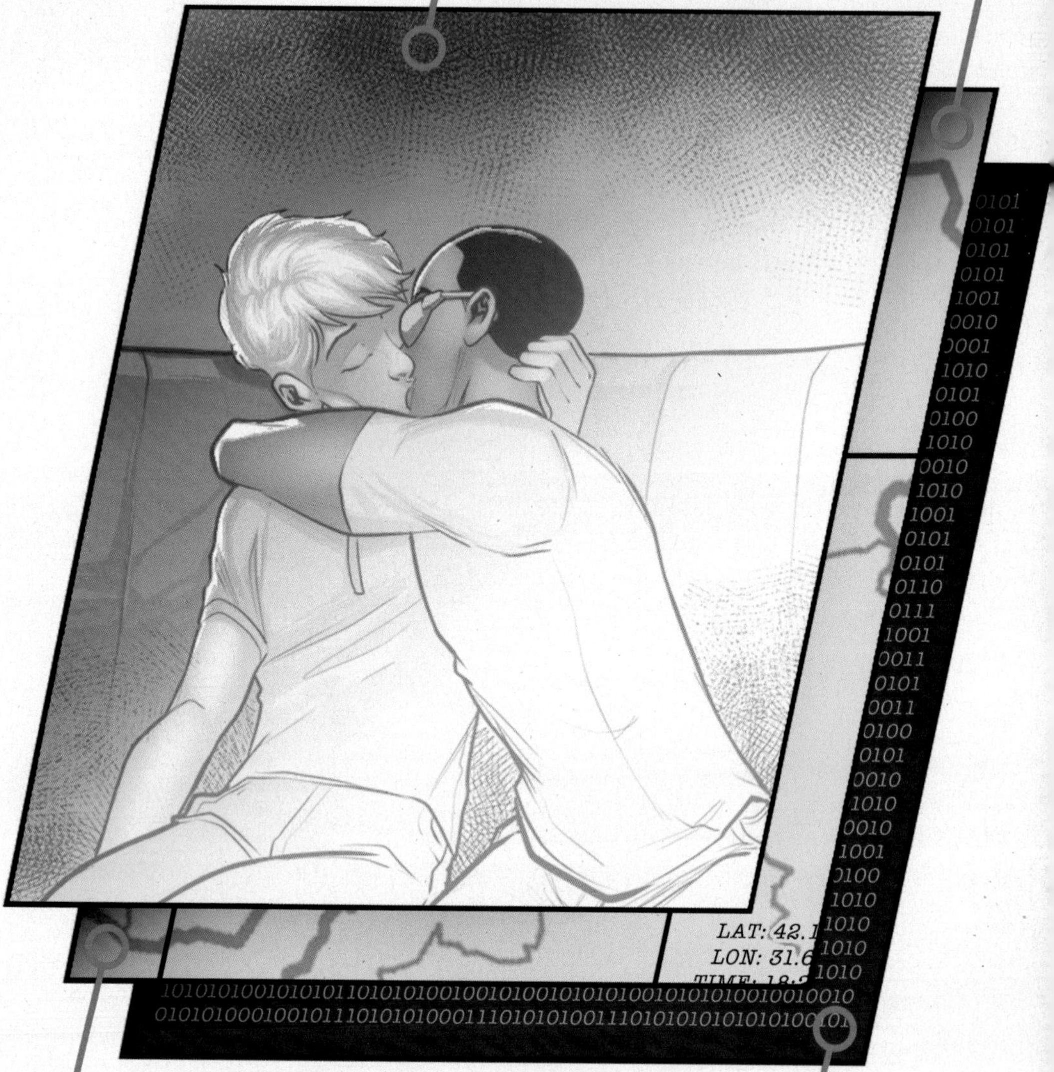

LAT: 42.1
LON: 31.6

iii. Third hidden layer reveals device information -- photo taken and posted from my old phone.

iv. Preliminary hypothesis: I both edited and posted this photo for myself to find later. Tagging Tommy in it would make him aware of it, and thus able to provide an alibi to my previous assumptions about how I died. (But why--why would I bury probative value like this?)

FINAL ASSESSMENT:

- Metadata supports Tommy's claim that the chronology the Five and I pieced together and the cause of my death were incorrect.
- Photo was not taken at Club Pepper in West Hollywood but was posted from there.
- Photo was posted from my old phone -- have not seen that phone since before my demise, no recollection as to what happened to it upon my death.
- Photo was taken and subsequently posted during a Cerebro backup blind spot -- meaning the week between one backup and the next. (Why?)
- (Note to self: At what point do I involve X-Factor...?)

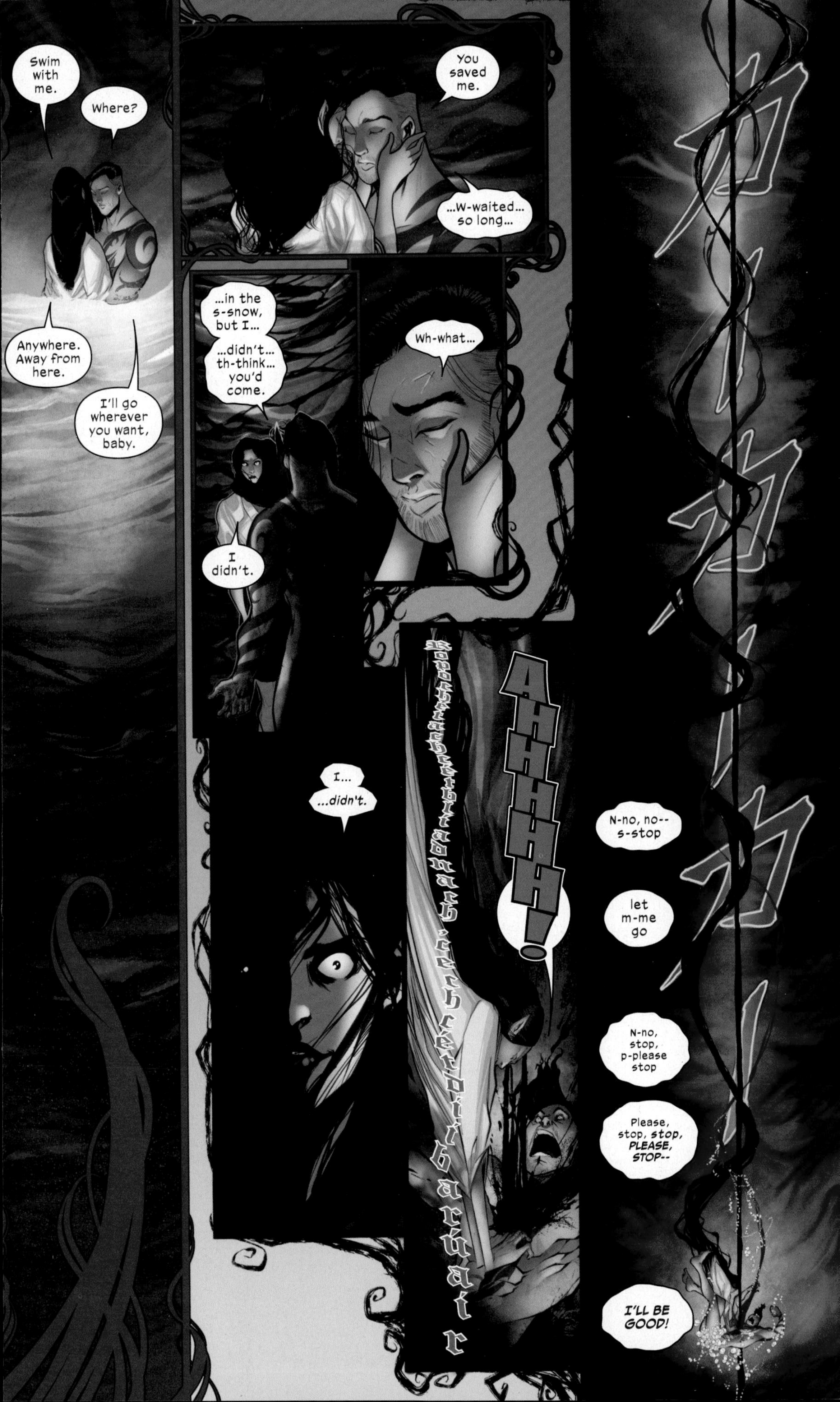

Swim with me.
Where?
Anywhere. Away from here.
I'll go wherever you want, baby.
You saved me.
...W-waited... so long...
...in the s-snow, but I...
...didn't... th-think... you'd come.
I didn't.
Wh-what...
I... ...didn't.
AHHHHHH!
N-no, no-- s-stop
let m-me go
N-no, stop, p-please stop
Please, stop, *stop*, ***PLEASE, STOP--***
I'LL BE GOOD!

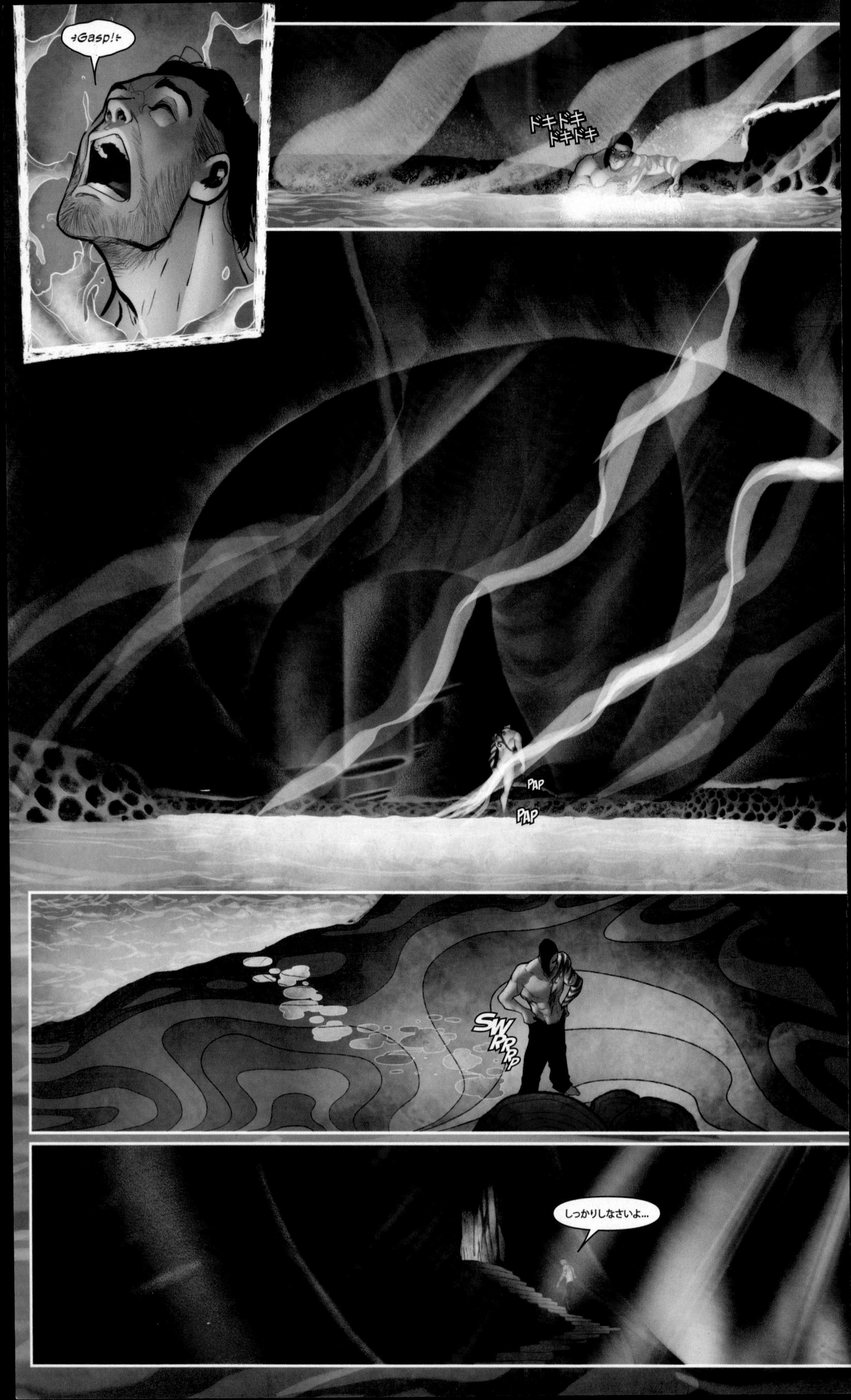

Gasp!
ドキドキ
ドキドキ
PAP
PAP
SWRRRP
しっかりしなさいよ…

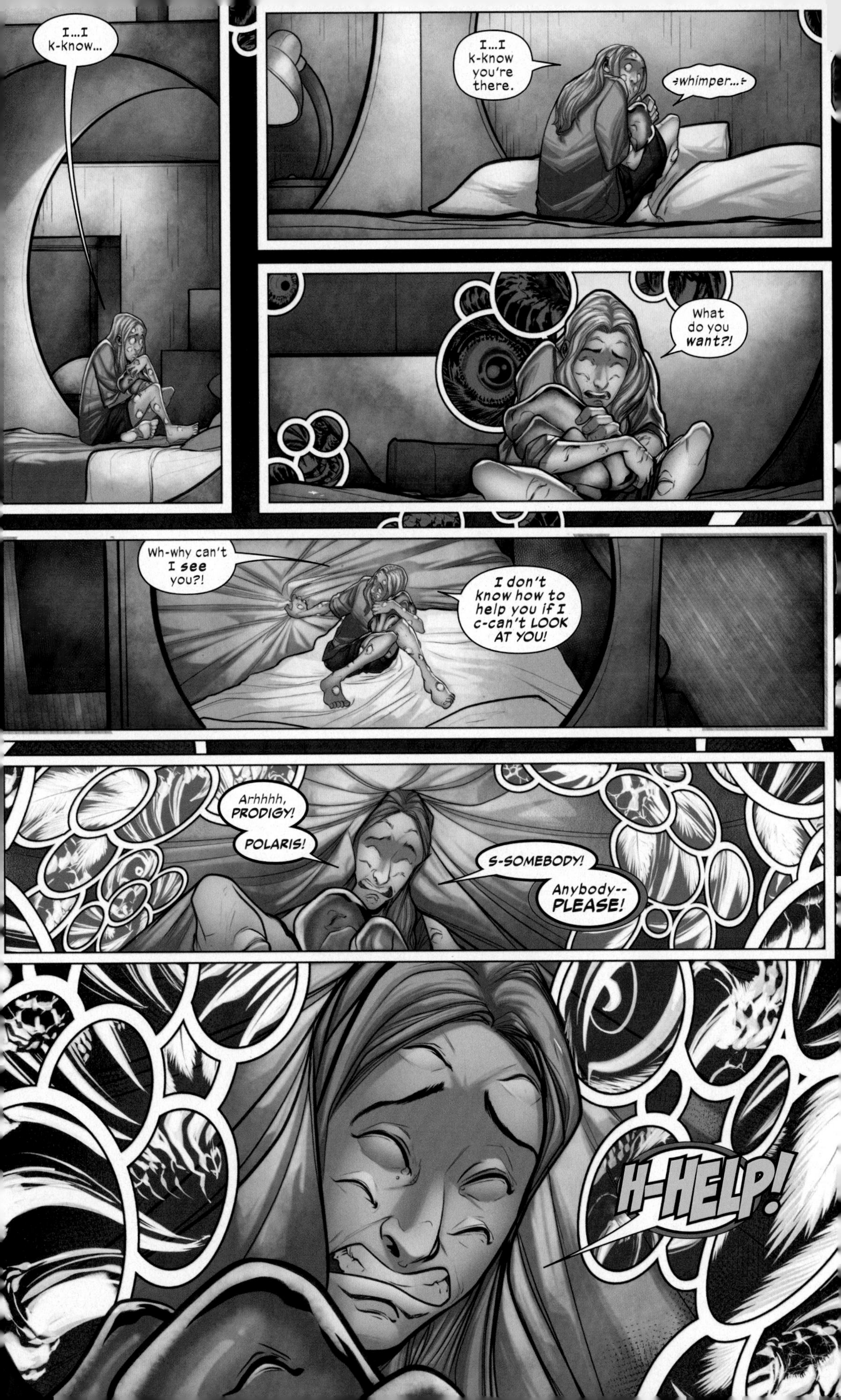
I...I k-know...
I...I k-know you're there.
whimper...
What do you want?!
Wh-why can't I see you?!
I don't know how to help you if I c-can't LOOK AT YOU!
Arhhhh, PRODIGY!
POLARIS!
S-SOMEBODY!
Anybody-- PLEASE!
H-HELP!

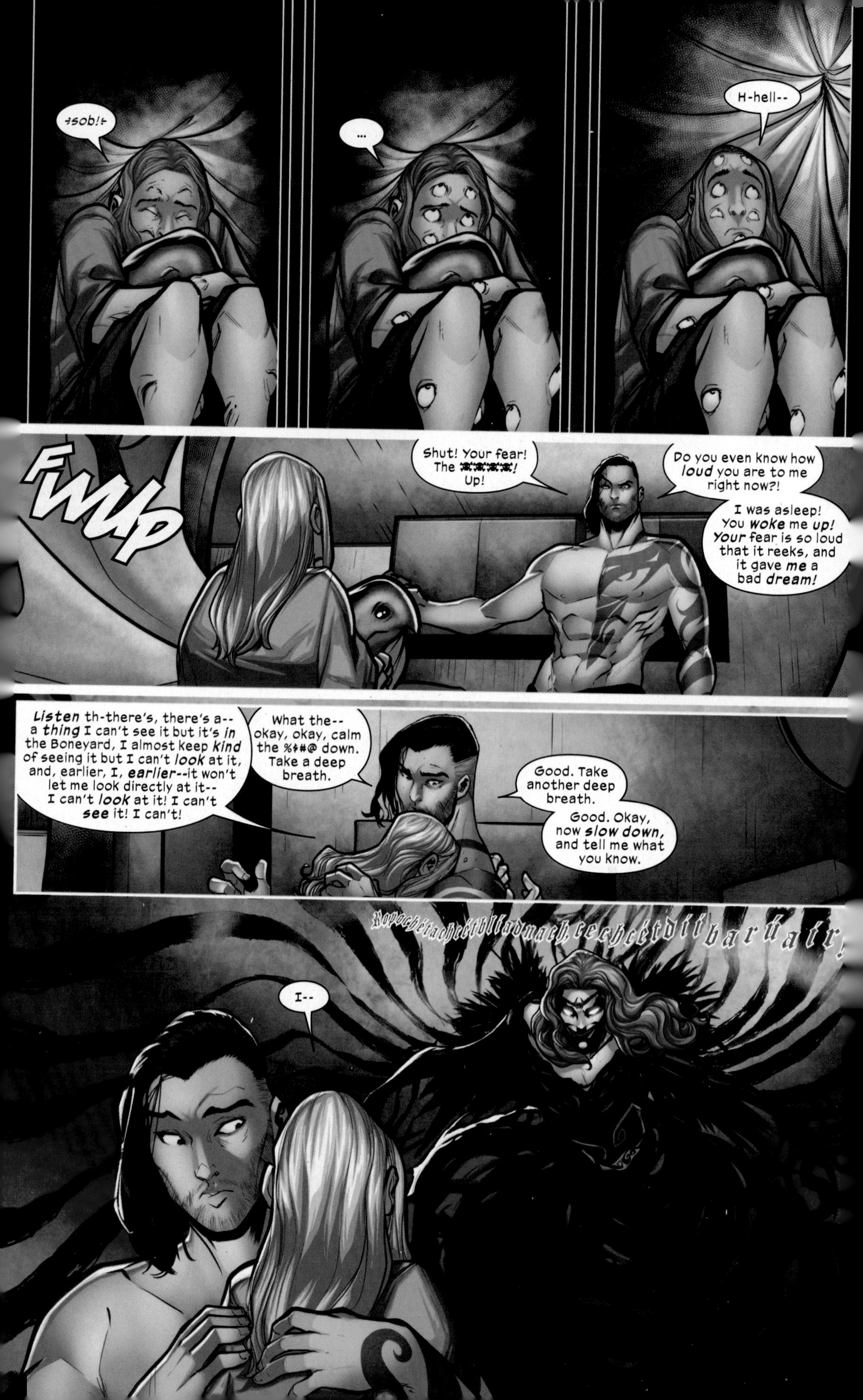

‡sob!‡
...
H-hell--
FWUP
Shut! Your fear! The ☠☠☠☠! Up!
Do you even know how loud you are to me right now?!
I was asleep! You woke me up! Your fear is so loud that it reeks, and it gave me a bad dream!
Listen th-there's, there's a-- a thing I can't see it but it's in the Boneyard, I almost keep kind of seeing it but I can't look at it, and, earlier, I, earlier--it won't let me look directly at it-- I can't look at it! I can't see it! I can't!
What the-- okay, okay, calm the %‡#@ down. Take a deep breath.
Good. Take another deep breath.
Good. Okay, now slow down, and tell me what you know.
I--

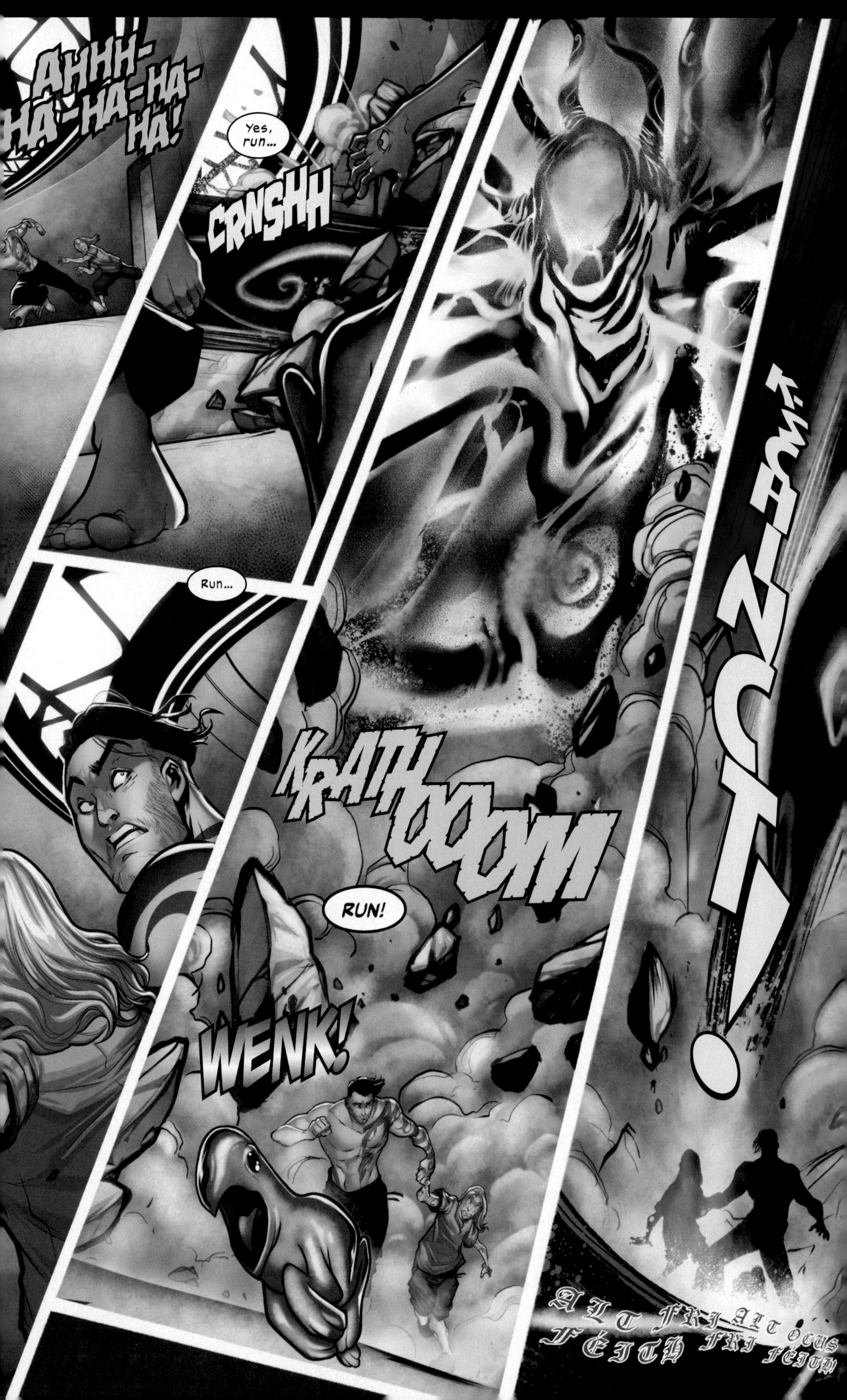
AHHH-HA-HA-HA-HA!
yes, run...
CRNSHH
Run...
KRATHOOOOM
RUN!
WENK!
K'CHANCT!
ALT FRI ALT ÓCUS FÉITH FRI FÉITH!

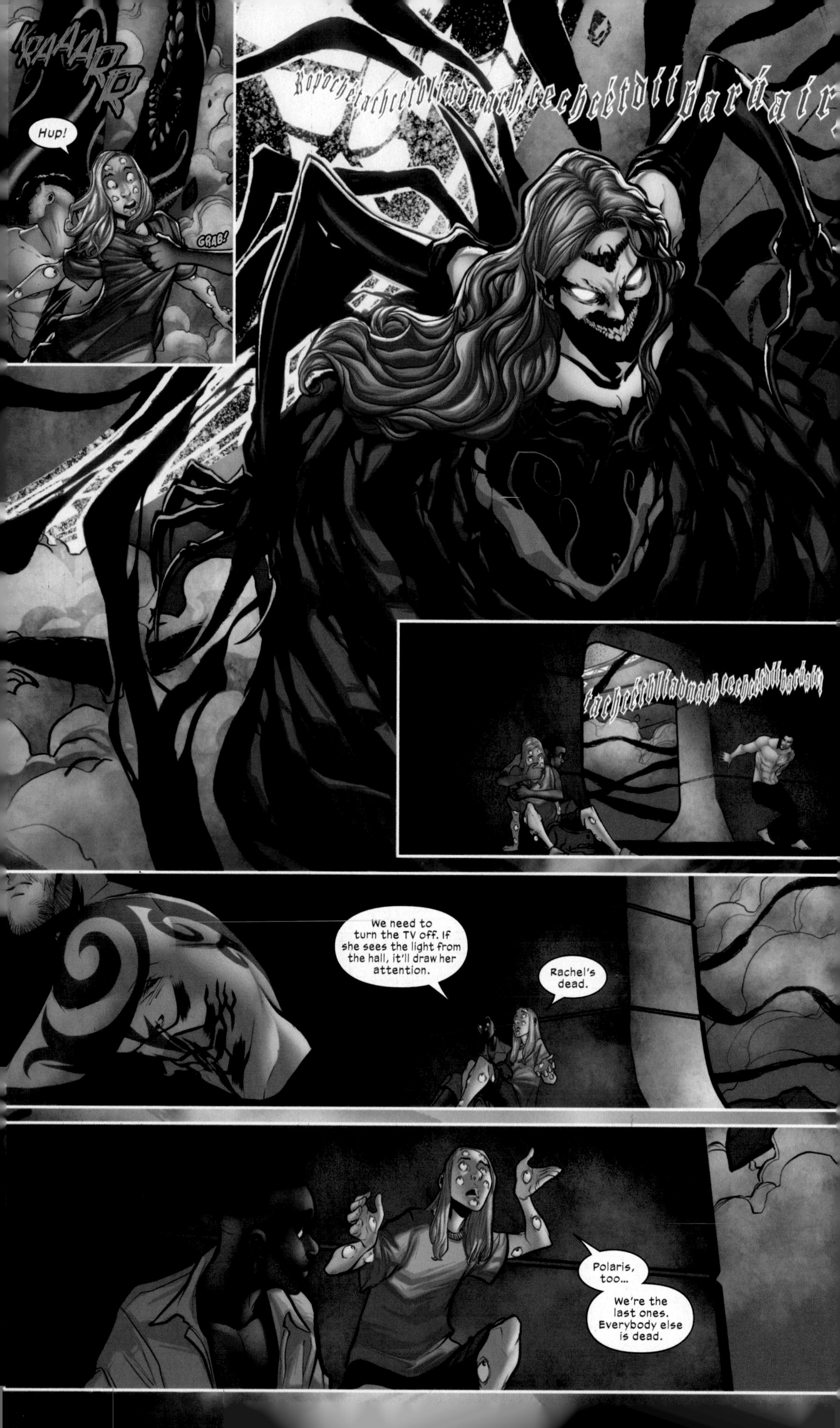
KRAAARRR
Hup!
GRAB!
We need to turn the TV off. If she sees the light from the hall, it'll draw her attention.
Rachel's dead.
Polaris, too...
We're the last ones. Everybody else is dead.

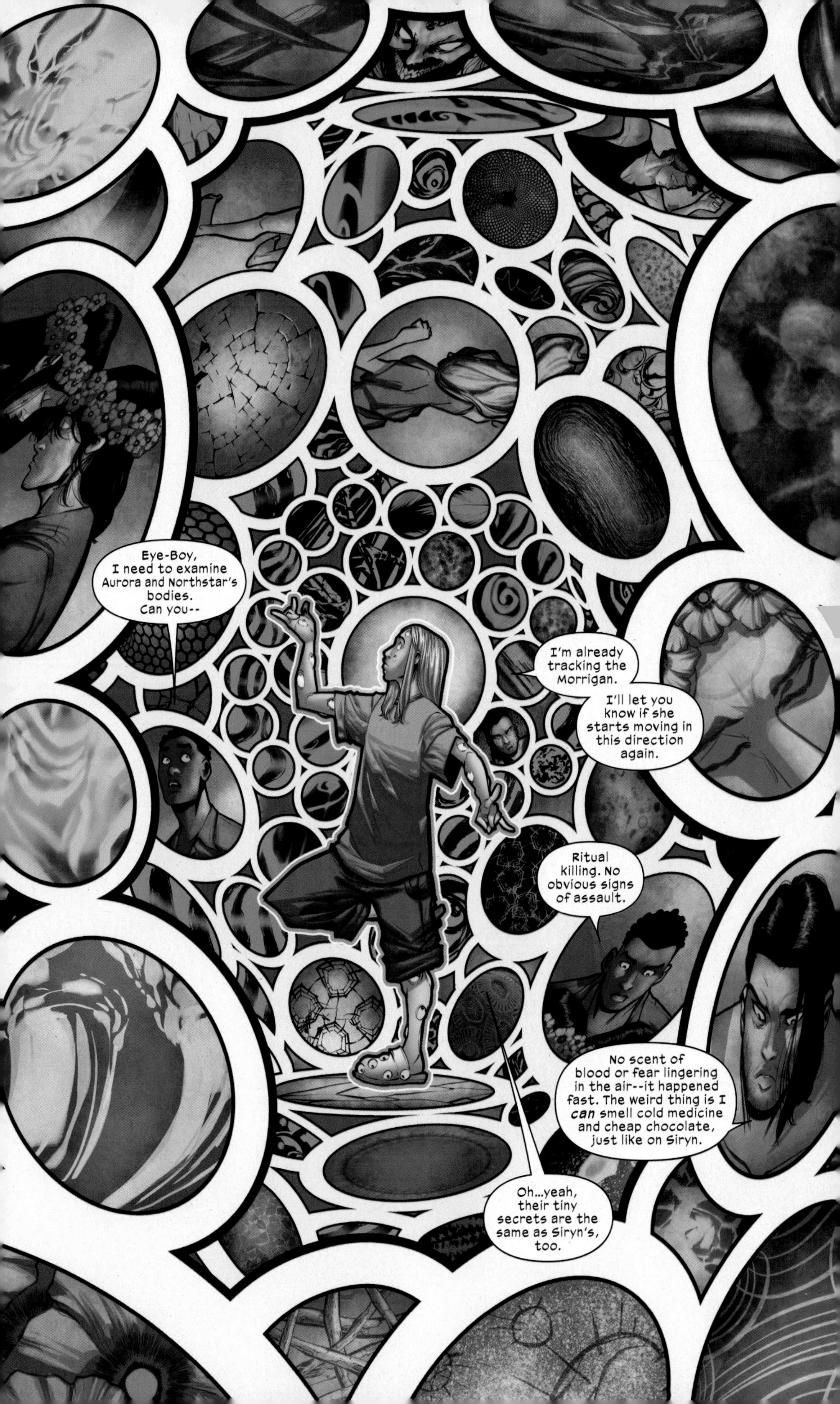
Eye-Boy, I need to examine Aurora and Northstar's bodies. Can you--
I'm already tracking the Morrigan.
I'll let you know if she starts moving in this direction again.
Ritual killing. No obvious signs of assault.
No scent of blood or fear lingering in the air--it happened fast. The weird thing is I *can* smell cold medicine and cheap chocolate, just like on Siryn.
Oh...yeah, their tiny secrets are the same as Siryn's, too.

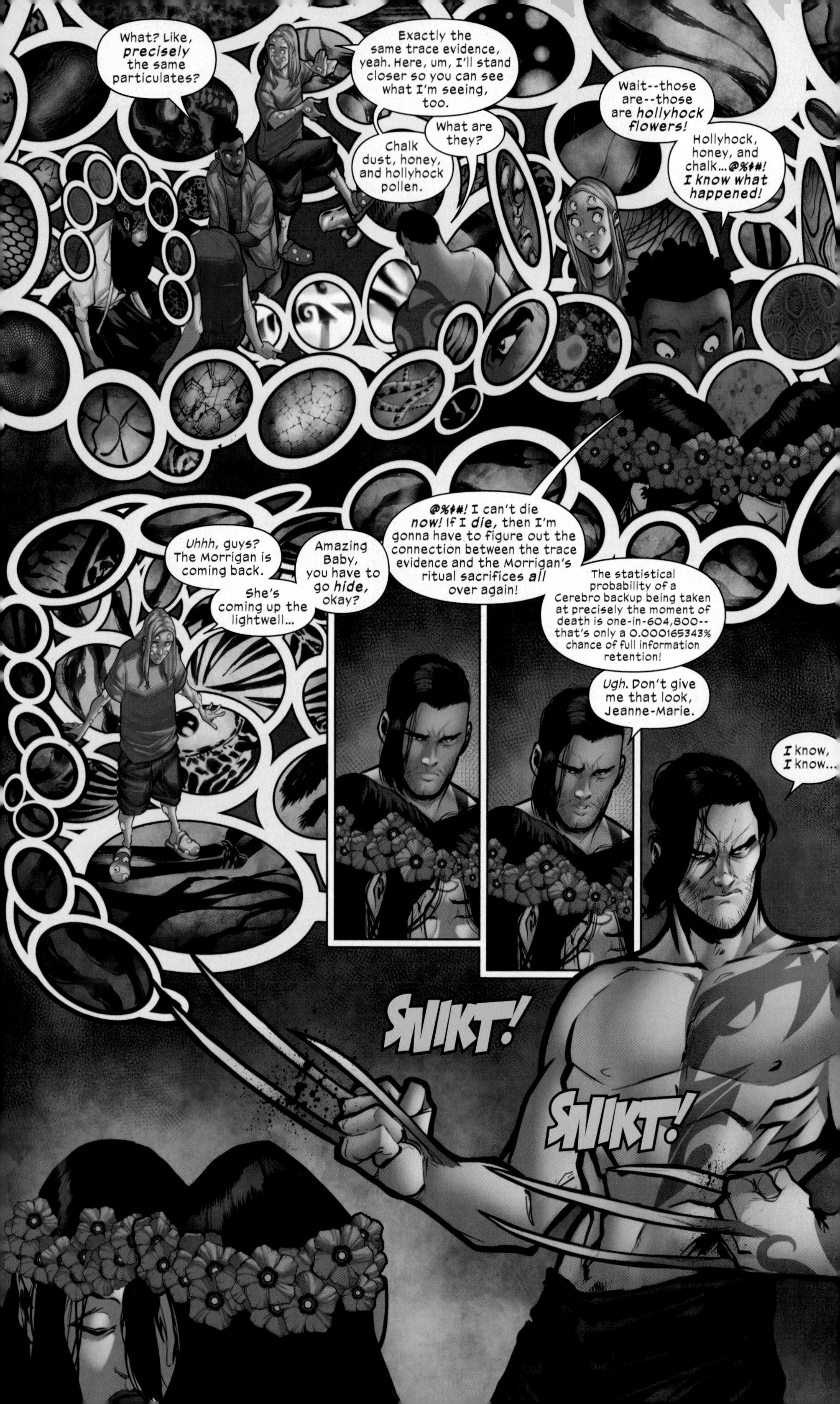

What? Like, *precisely* the same particulates?
Exactly the same trace evidence, yeah. Here, um, I'll stand closer so you can see what I'm seeing, too.
What are they?
Chalk dust, honey, and hollyhock pollen.
Wait--those are--those are *hollyhock flowers!*
Hollyhock, honey, and chalk... @%$#! *I know what happened!*
Uhhh, guys? The Morrigan is coming back.
She's coming up the lightwell...
Amazing Baby, you have to go *hide*, okay?
@%$#! I can't die *now!* If I *die*, then I'm gonna have to figure out the connection between the trace evidence and the Morrigan's ritual sacrifices *all* over again!
The statistical probability of a Cerebro backup being taken at precisely the moment of death is one-in-604,800--that's only a 0.000165343% chance of full information retention!
Ugh. Don't give me that look, Jeanne-Marie.
I know, *I* know...
SNIKT!
SNIKT!

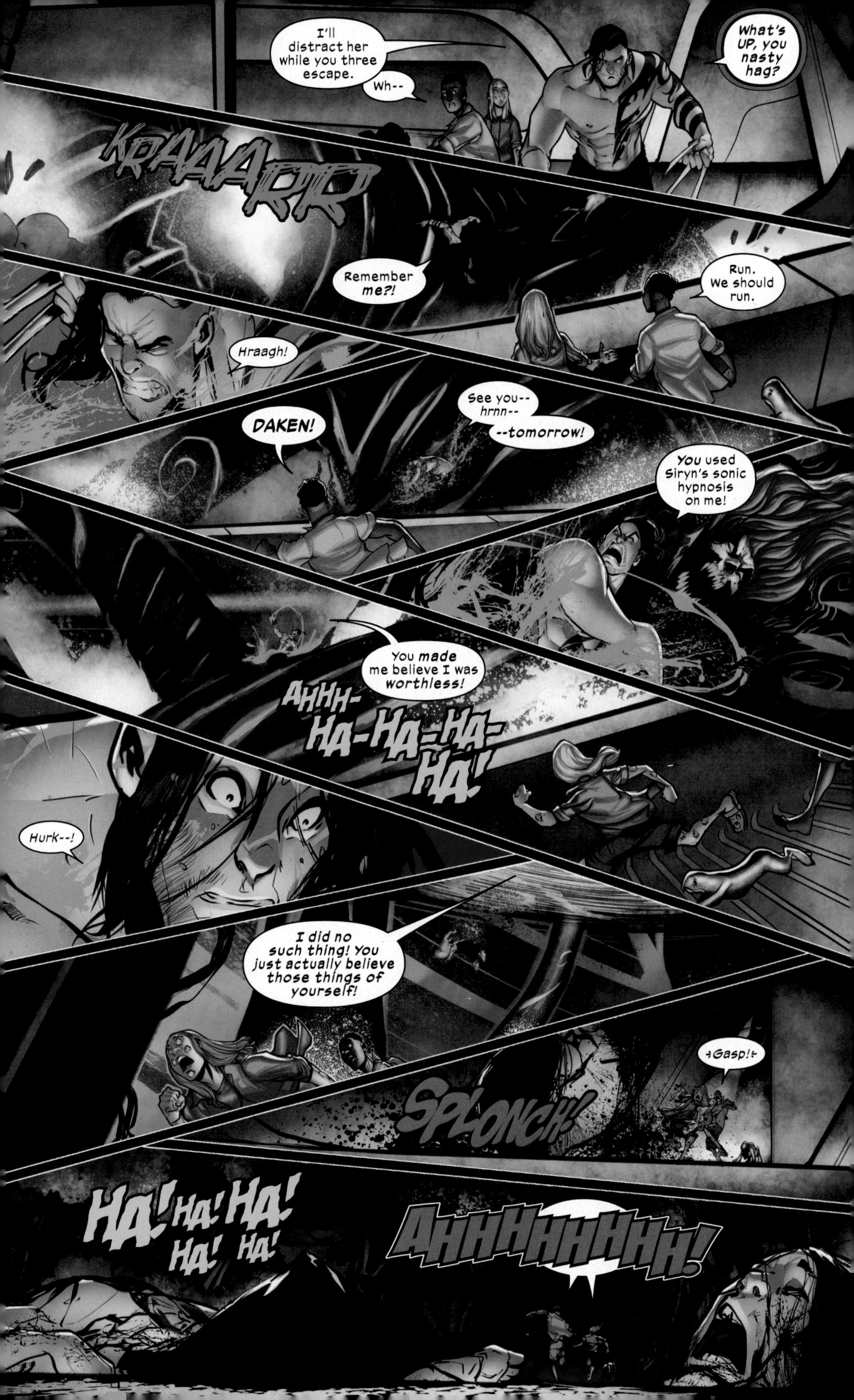
I'll distract her while you three escape.
Wh--
What's UP, you nasty hag?
KRAAARRR
Remember me?!
Run. We should run.
Hraagh!
See you-- hrnn--
--tomorrow!
DAKEN!
You used Siryn's sonic hypnosis on me!
You made me believe I was worthless!
AHHH-HA-HA-HA-HA!
Hurk--!
I did no such thing! You just actually believe those things of yourself!
Gasp!
SPLONCH!
HA! HA! HA! HA! HA!
AHHHHHHHH!

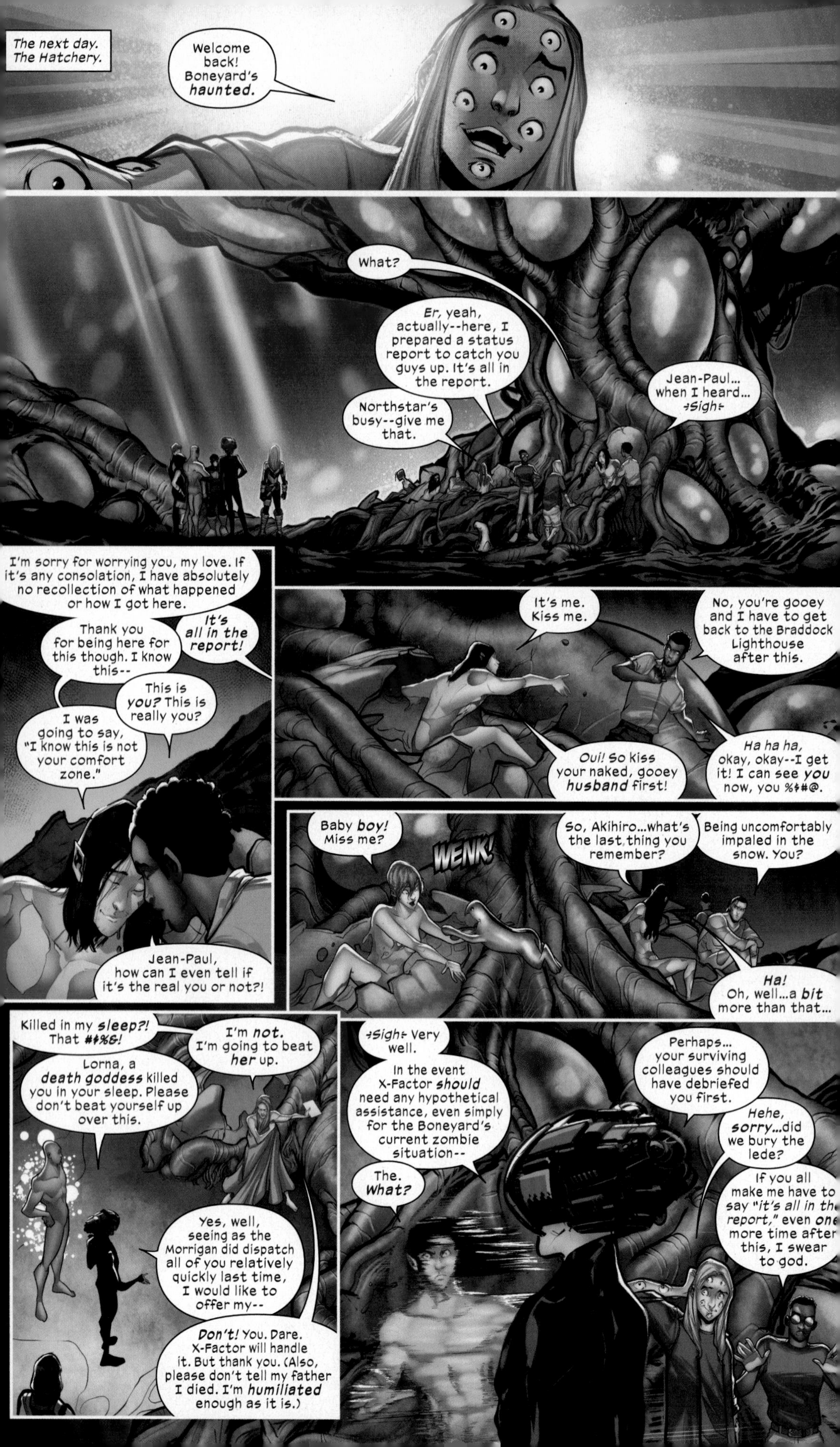
The next day. The Hatchery.
Welcome back! Boneyard's *haunted.*
What?
Er, yeah, actually--here, I prepared a status report to catch you guys up. It's all in the report.
Northstar's busy--give me that.
Jean-Paul... when I heard... ⸗Sigh⸗
I'm sorry for worrying you, my love. If it's any consolation, I have absolutely no recollection of what happened or how I got here.
Thank you for being here for this though. I know this--
It's all in the report!
This is *you?* This is really you?
I was going to say, "I know this is not your comfort zone."
Jean-Paul, how can I even tell if it's the real you or not?!
It's me. Kiss me.
No, you're gooey and I have to get back to the Braddock Lighthouse after this.
Oui! So kiss your naked, gooey *husband* first!
Ha ha ha, okay, okay--I get it! I can see *you* now, you %$#@.
Baby *boy!* Miss me?
WENK!
So, Akihiro...what's the last thing you remember?
Being uncomfortably impaled in the snow. You?
Ha! Oh, well...a *bit* more than that...
Killed in my *sleep?!* That #$%&!
I'm *not.* I'm going to beat *her* up.
Lorna, a *death goddess* killed you in your sleep. Please don't beat yourself up over this.
Yes, well, seeing as the Morrigan did dispatch all of you relatively quickly last time, I would like to offer my--
Don't! You. Dare. X-Factor will handle it. But thank you. (Also, please don't tell my father I died. I'm *humiliated* enough as it is.)
⸗Sigh⸗ Very well.
In the event X-Factor *should* need any hypothetical assistance, even simply for the Boneyard's current zombie situation--
The. *What?*
Perhaps... your surviving colleagues should have debriefed you first.
Hehe, *sorry*...did we bury the lede?
If you all make me have to say *"it's all in the report,"* even *one* more time after this, I swear to god.

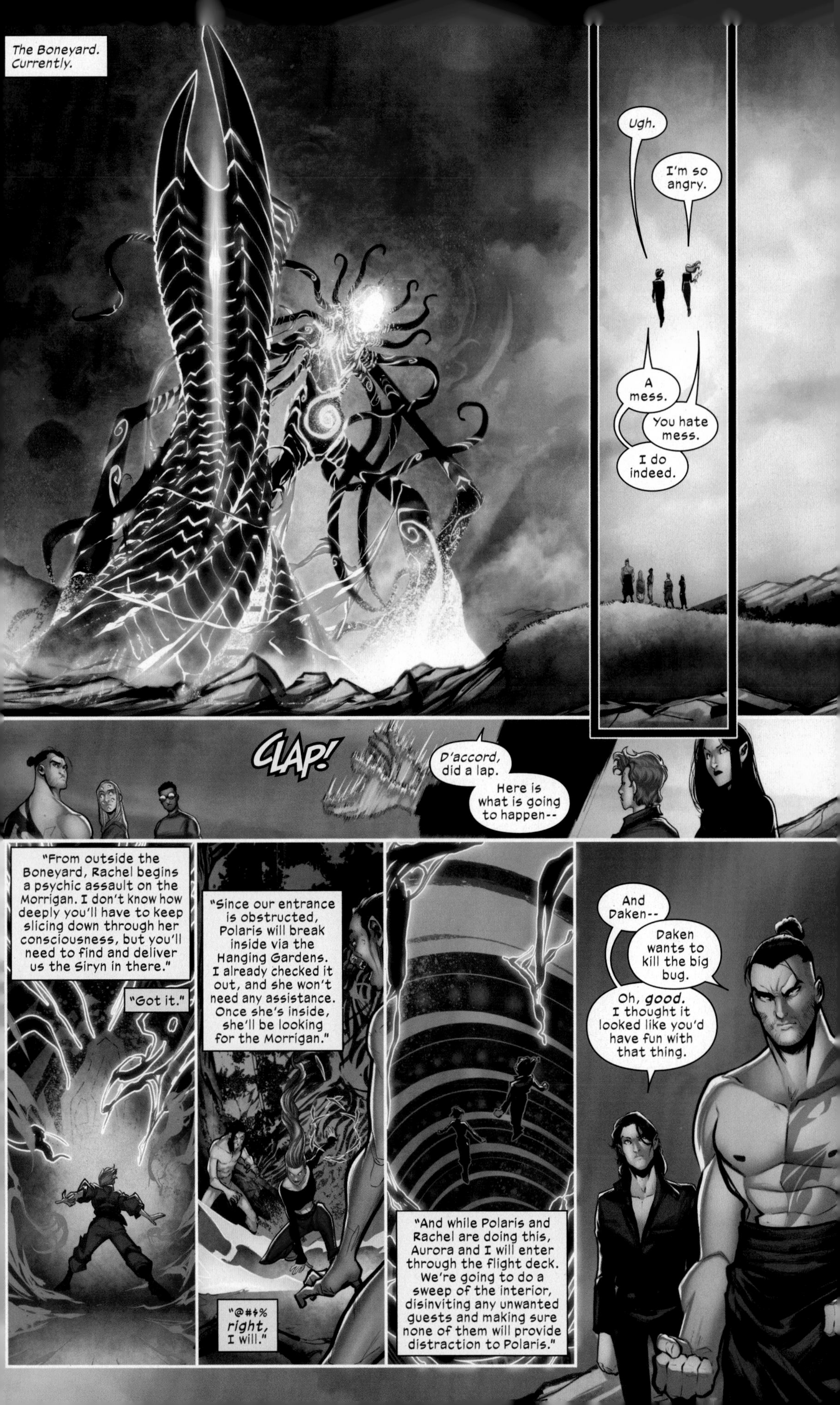

The Boneyard. Currently.
Ugh.
I'm so angry.
A mess.
You hate mess.
I do indeed.
CLAP!
D'accord, did a lap.
Here is what is going to happen--
"From outside the Boneyard, Rachel begins a psychic assault on the Morrigan. I don't know how deeply you'll have to keep slicing down through her consciousness, but you'll need to find and deliver us the Siryn in there."
"Got it."
"Since our entrance is obstructed, Polaris will break inside via the Hanging Gardens. I already checked it out, and she won't need any assistance. Once she's inside, she'll be looking for the Morrigan."
"@#$% right, I will."
"And while Polaris and Rachel are doing this, Aurora and I will enter through the flight deck. We're going to do a sweep of the interior, disinviting any unwanted guests and making sure none of them will provide distraction to Polaris."
And Daken--
Daken wants to kill the big bug.
Oh, good. I thought it looked like you'd have fun with that thing.

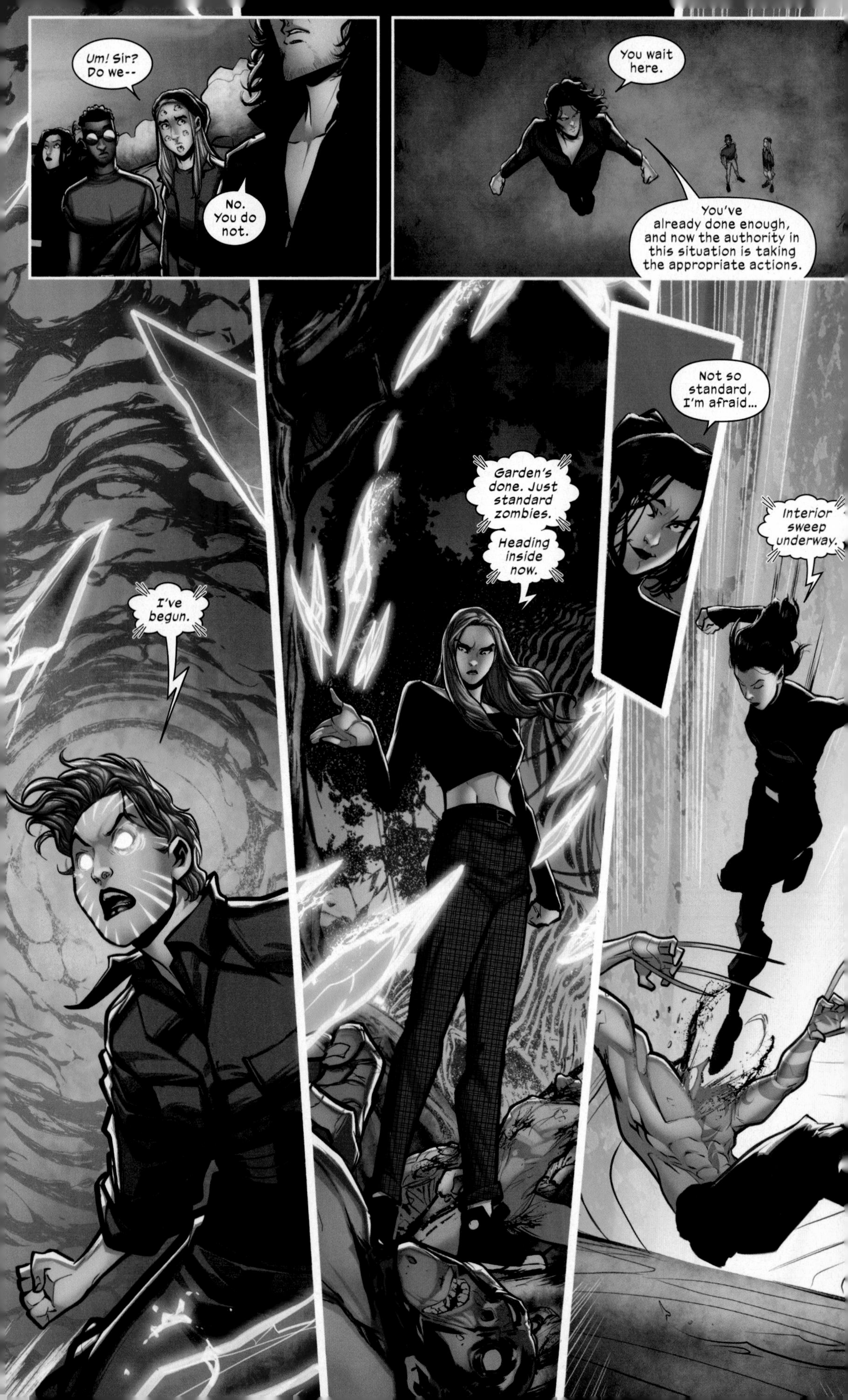

Um! Sir? Do we--
No. You do not.
You wait here.
You've already done enough, and now the authority in this situation is taking the appropriate actions.
I've begun.
Garden's done. Just standard zombies.
Heading inside now.
Not so standard, I'm afraid...
Interior sweep underway.

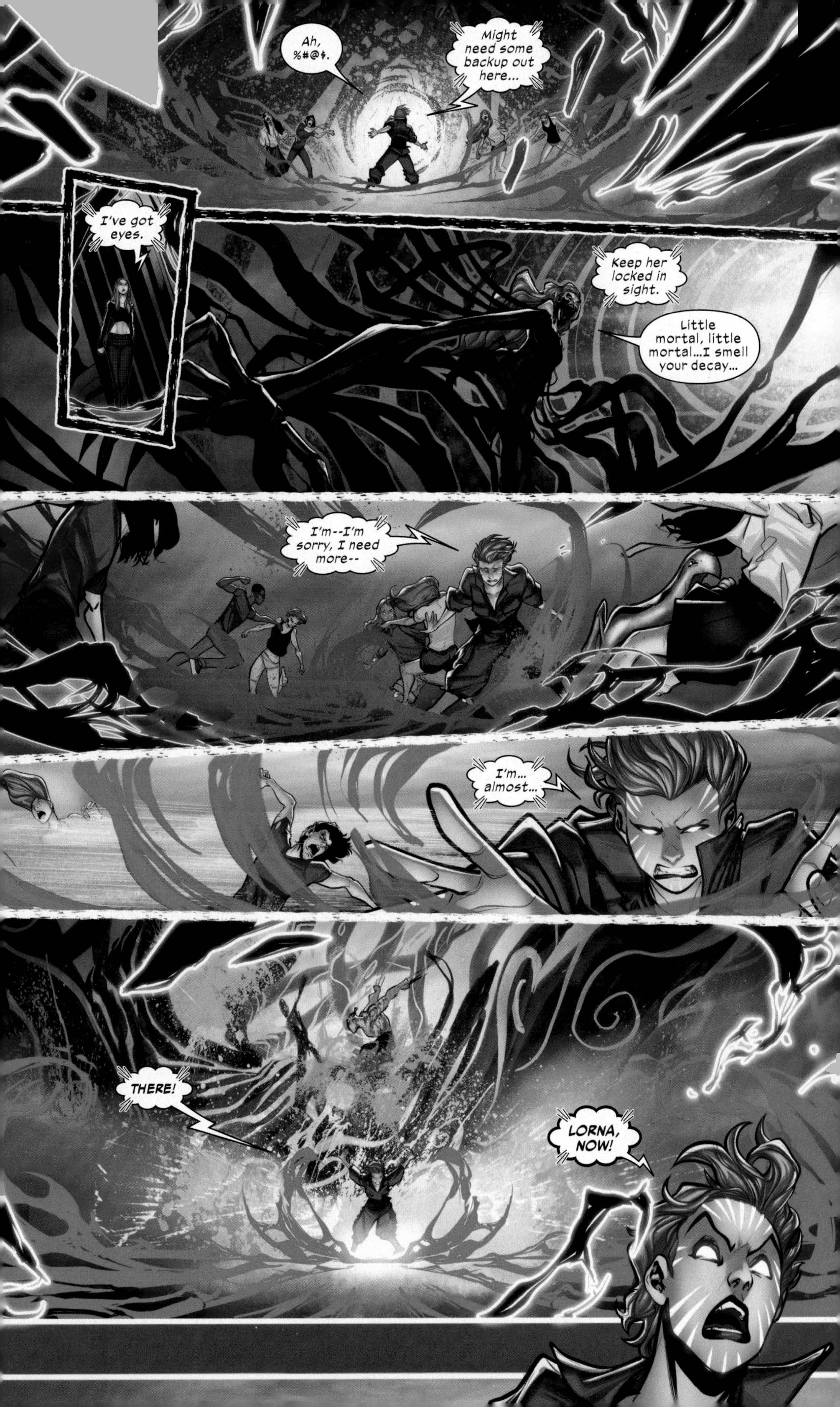
Ah, %#@$.
Might need some backup out here...
I've got eyes.
Keep her locked in sight.
Little mortal, little mortal...I smell your decay...
I'm--I'm sorry, I need more--
I'm... almost...
THERE!
LORNA, NOW!

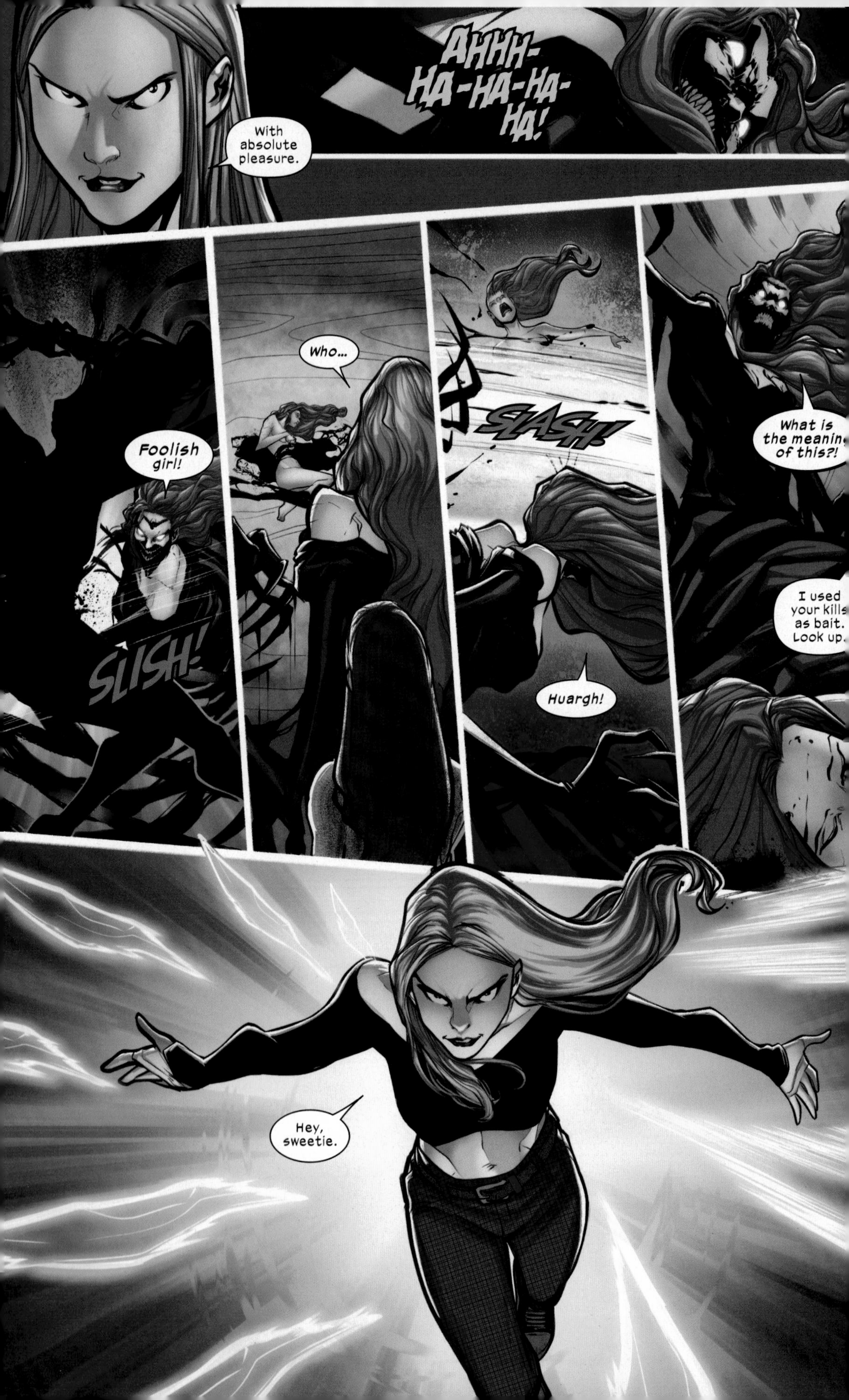

With absolute pleasure.
AHHH-HA-HA-HA-HA!
Foolish girl!
SLISH!
Who...
SLASH!
Huargh!
What is the meanin of this?!
I used your kills as bait. Look up.
Hey, sweetie.

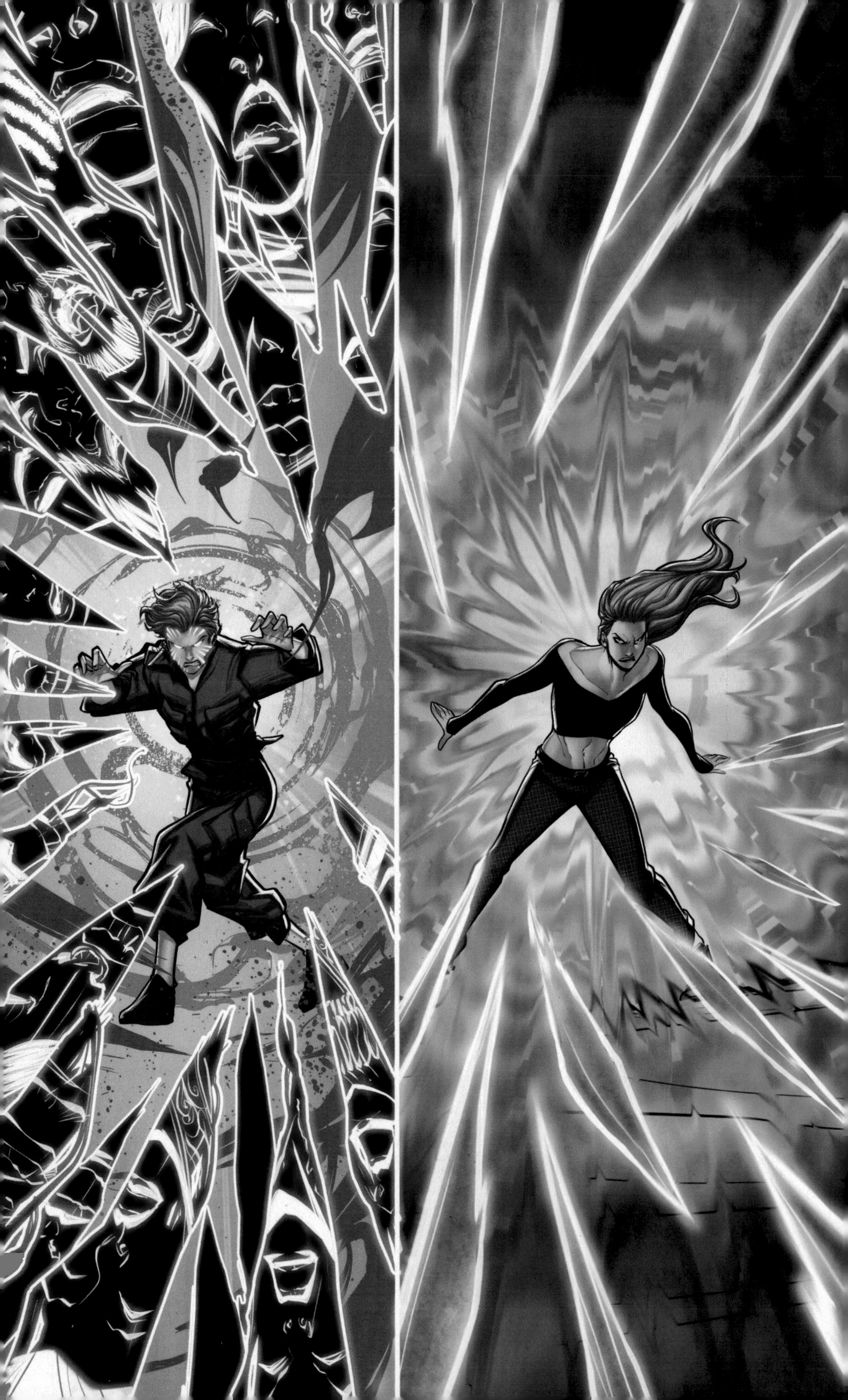

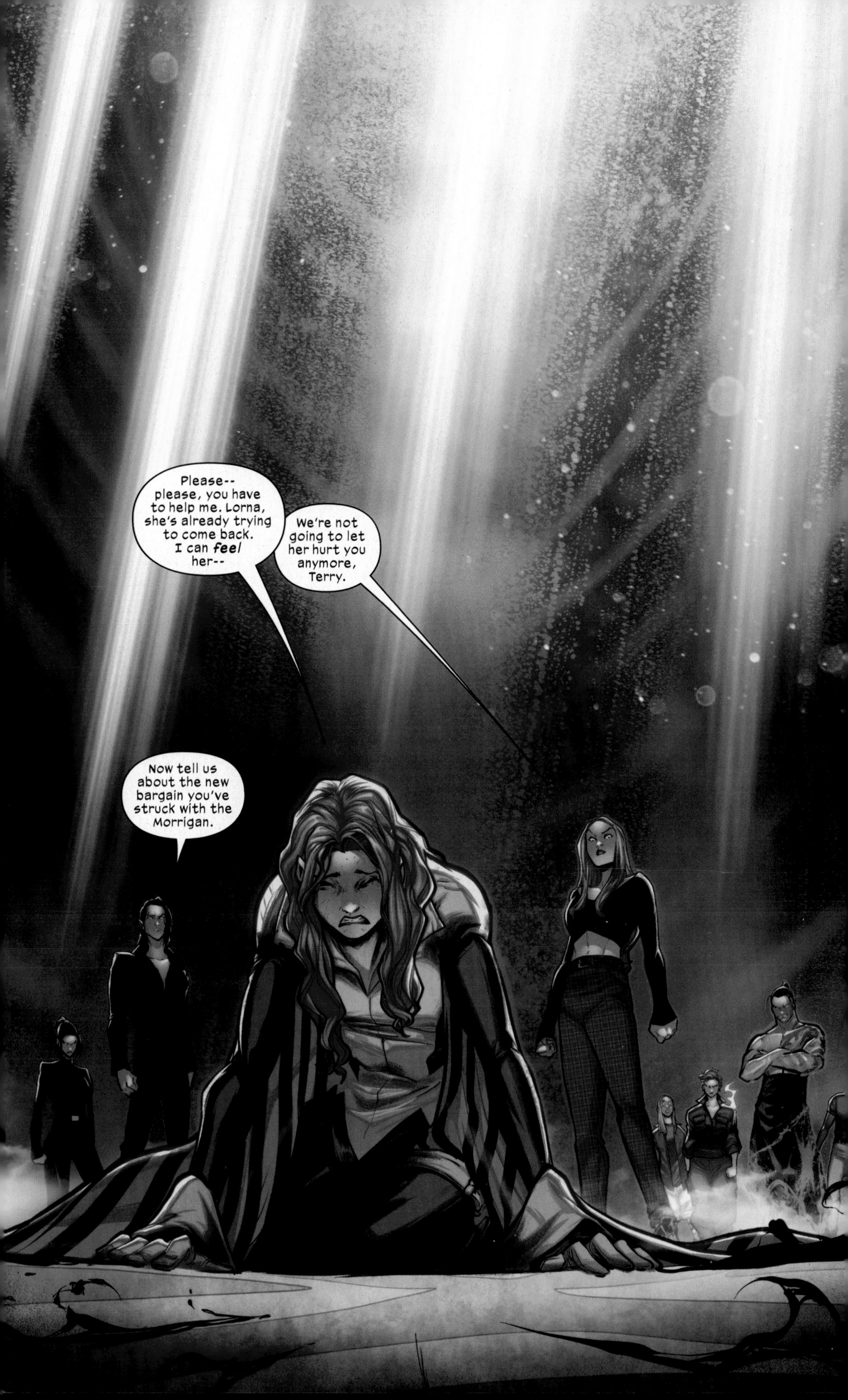
Please-- please, you have to help me. Lorna, she's already trying to come back. I can *feel* her--
We're not going to let her hurt you anymore, Terry.
Now tell us about the new bargain you've struck with the Morrigan.

From: Charles Xavier

To: Jean-Paul Beaubier

Subject: Inquiry about Eye-Boy's Abilities

Northstar,

Firstly, we congratulate you and your X-Factor compatriots on a successful de-haunting of the Boneyard. We knew you were capable, and eagerly await an update on your handling of saving Siryn from the Morrigan. Secondly, it has been brought to the Quiet Council's attention that there have been some very interesting developments regarding Trevor's mutation. Please keep us apprised of this young man's extraordinary sight development.

All the best,

Charles

From: Jean-Paul Beaubier

To: Charles Xavier

Subject: RE: Inquiry about Eye-Boy's Abilities

No. -- Northstar

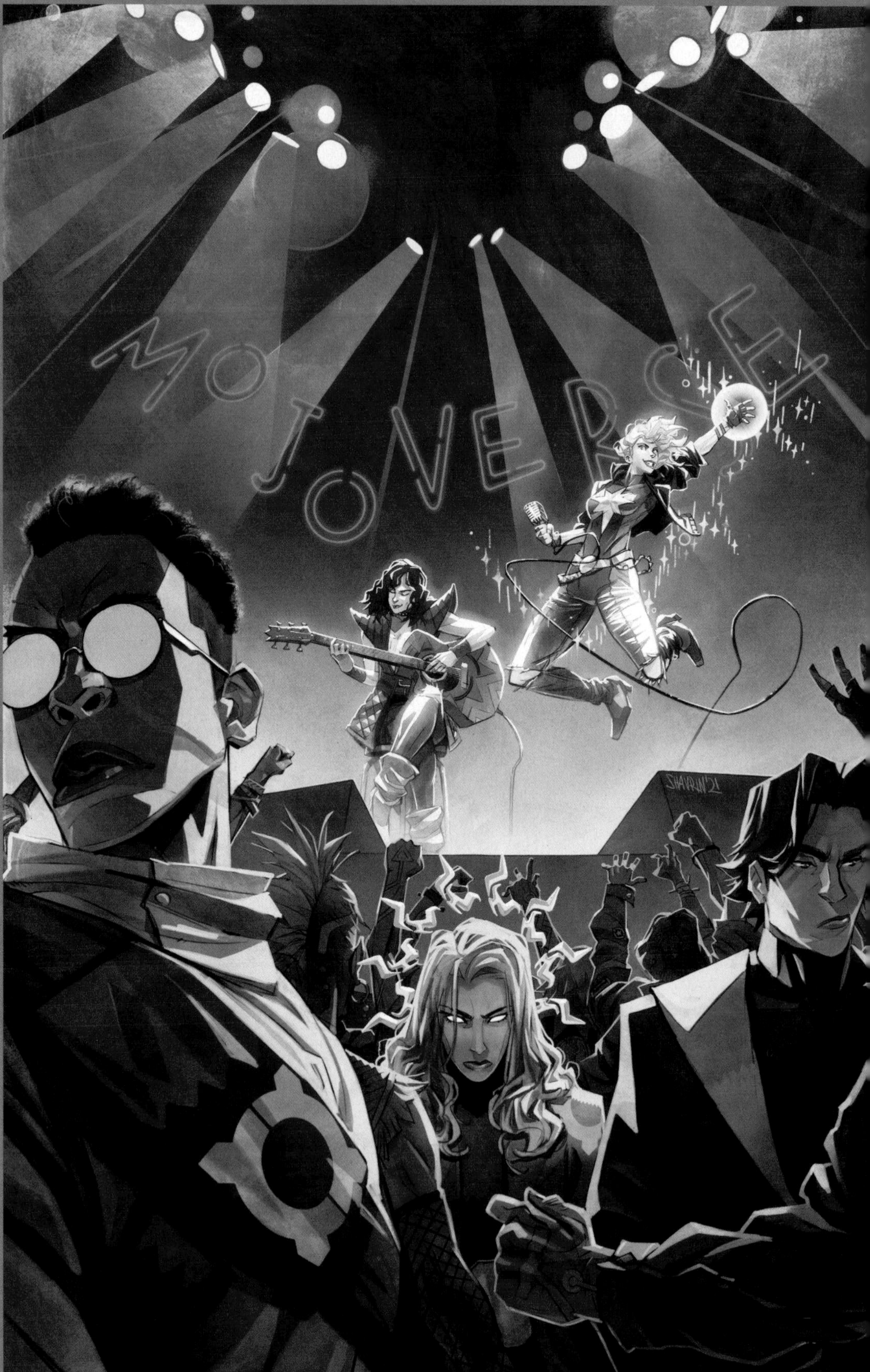
MOJOVERSE

Suite N°9:
DJ Mark's Mixtape
of Mojoverse Beats
to Make Out To

[reign_of_x]

[kra_]
[koa_]

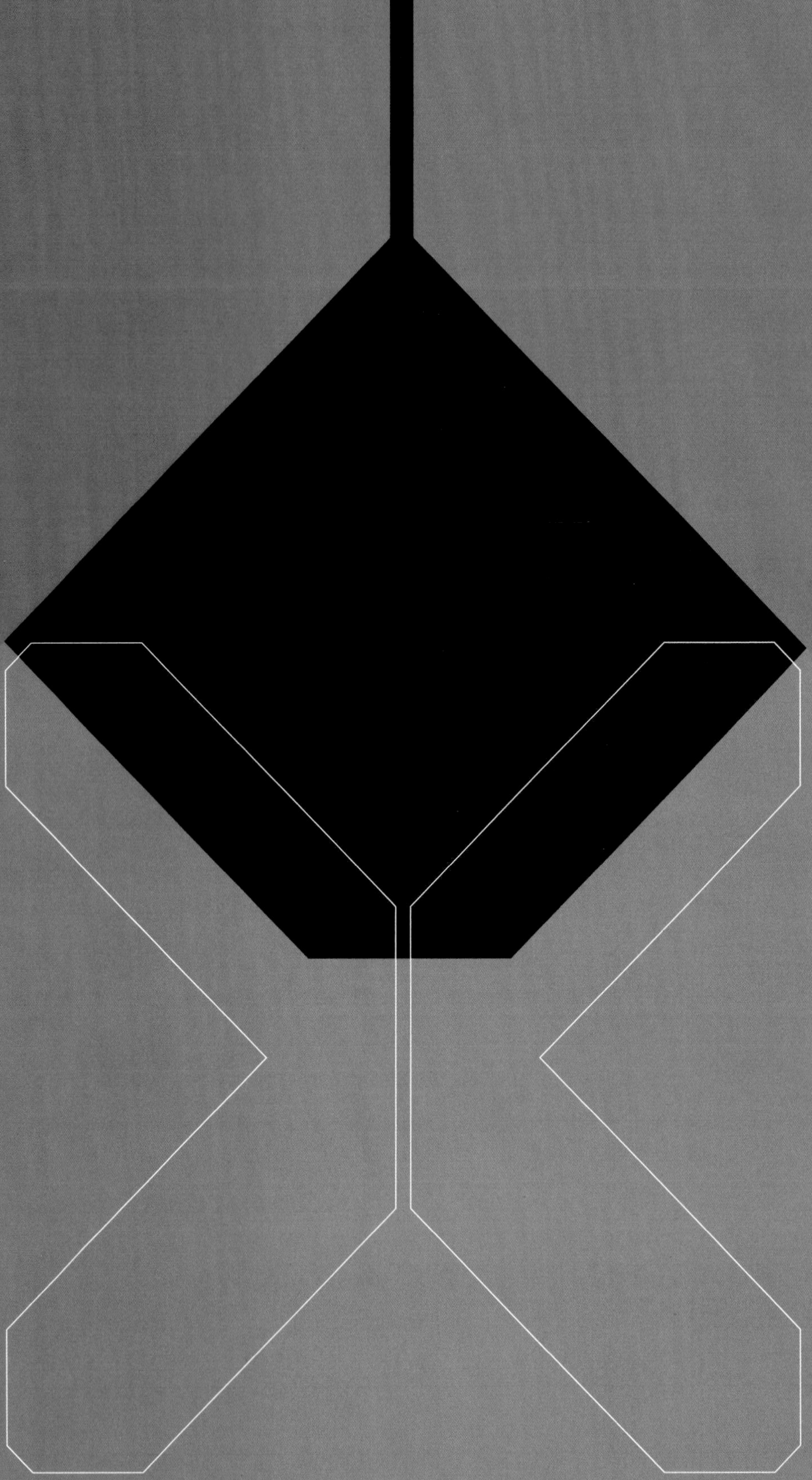

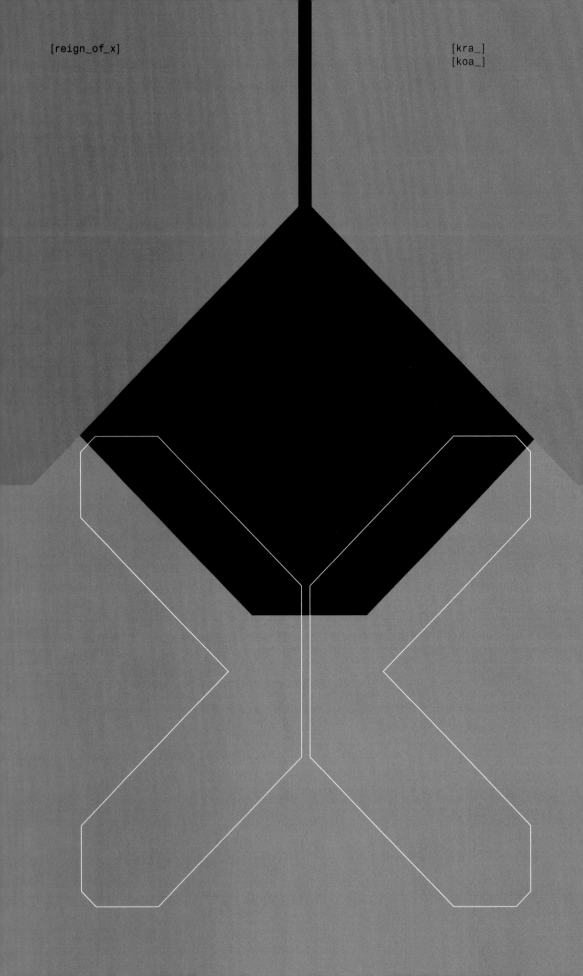

[x-factor_[0.9]
[x-factor_[0.9]

"I -- actually, um, I would describe my role more as a democratically nominated but contractually obligated...babysitter. Yeah, I'm more like the babysitter of the Mojoverse now. Not the regent."

-- SOFÍA MANTEGA
WIND DANCER

[x-factor_[0.X]
[x-factor_[0.X]

[x-factor_[0.9].]
[x-factor_[0.9].]

[x-factor_alpha.]

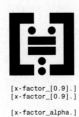

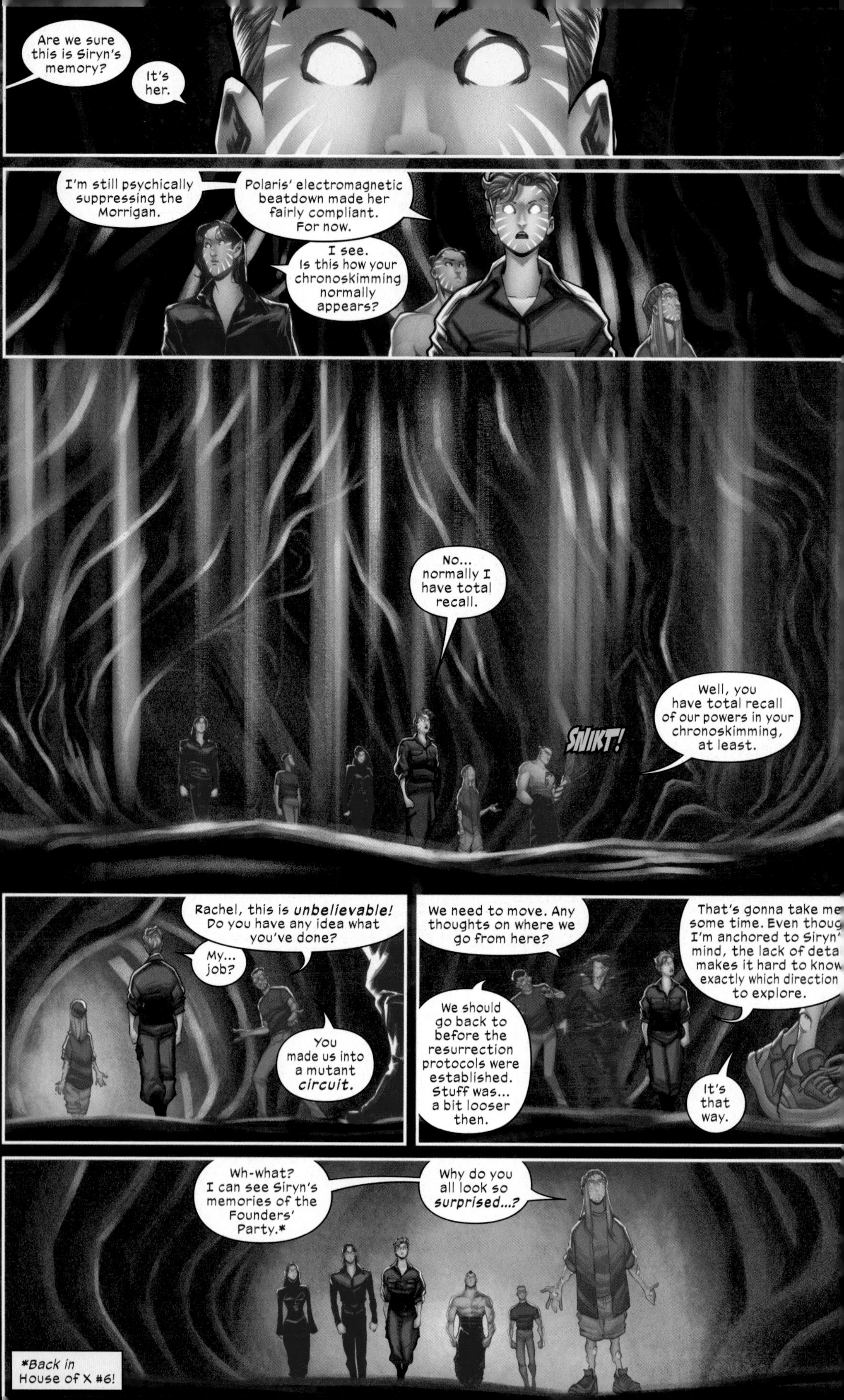

Are we sure this is Siryn's memory?
It's her.
I'm still psychically suppressing the Morrigan.
Polaris' electromagnetic beatdown made her fairly compliant. For now.
I see. Is this how your chronoskimming normally appears?
No... normally I have total recall.
SNIKT!
Well, you have total recall of our powers in your chronoskimming, at least.
Rachel, this is *unbelievable!* Do you have any idea what you've done?
My... job?
You made us into a mutant *circuit.*
We need to move. Any thoughts on where we go from here?
We should go back to before the resurrection protocols were established. Stuff was... a bit looser then.
That's gonna take me some time. Even thoug I'm anchored to Siryn' mind, the lack of deta makes it hard to know exactly which direction to explore.
It's that way.
Wh-what? I can see Siryn's memories of the Founders' Party.*
Why do you all look so *surprised...?*
*Back in House of X #6!

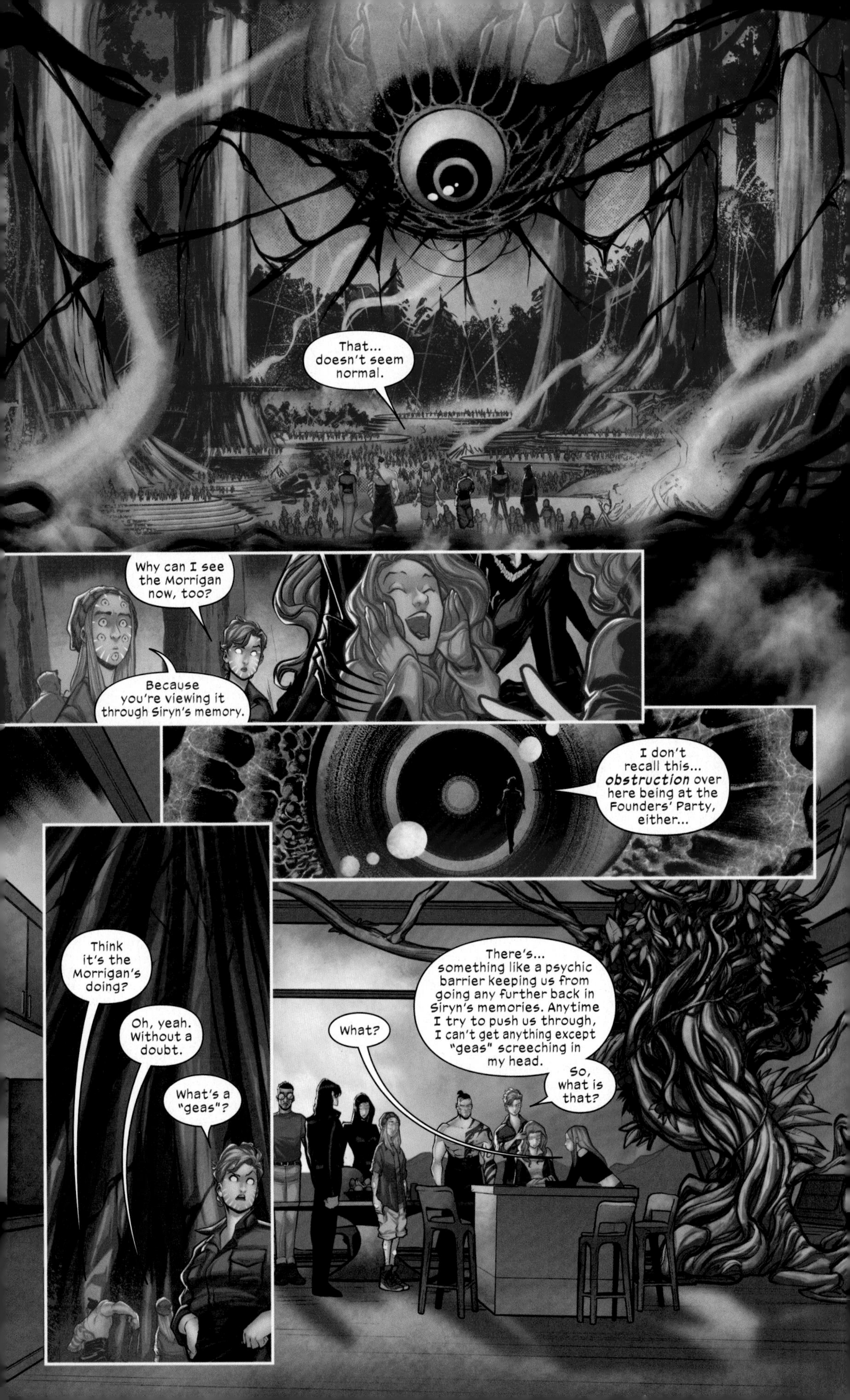
That... doesn't seem normal.
Why can I see the Morrigan now, too?
Because you're viewing it through Siryn's memory.
I don't recall this... *obstruction* over here being at the Founders' Party, either...
Think it's the Morrigan's doing?
Oh, yeah. Without a doubt.
What's a "geas"?
There's... something like a psychic barrier keeping us from going any further back in Siryn's memories. Anytime I try to push us through, I can't get anything except "geas" screeching in my head.
What?
So, what is that?

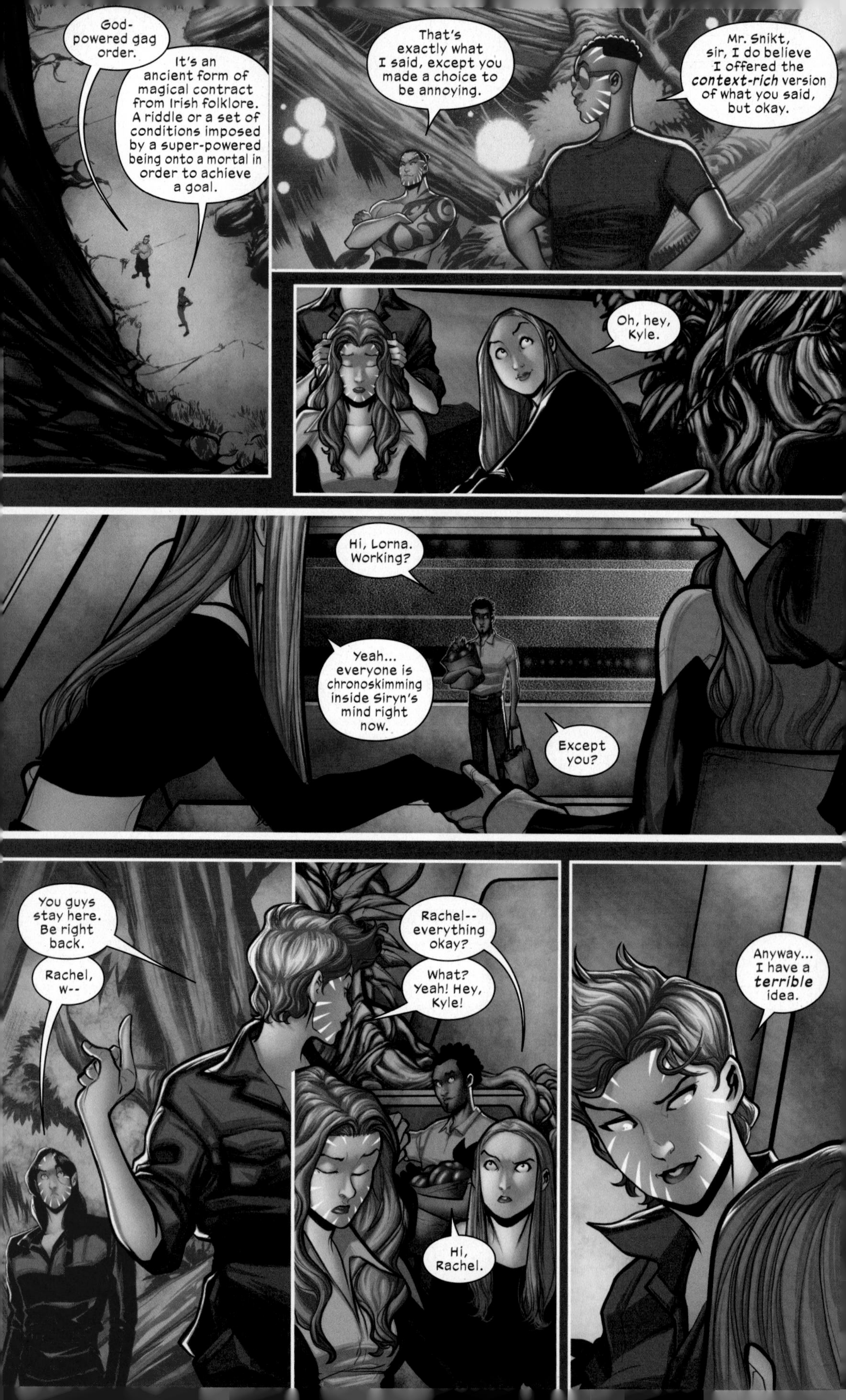
God-powered gag order.
It's an ancient form of magical contract from Irish folklore. A riddle or a set of conditions imposed by a super-powered being onto a mortal in order to achieve a goal.
That's exactly what I said, except you made a choice to be annoying.
Mr. Snikt, sir, I do believe I offered the *context-rich* version of what you said, but okay.
Oh, hey, Kyle.
Hi, Lorna. Working?
Yeah... everyone is chronoskimming inside Siryn's mind right now.
Except you?
You guys stay here. Be right back.
Rachel, w--
Rachel--everything okay?
What? Yeah! Hey, Kyle!
Hi, Rachel.
Anyway... I have a *terrible* idea.

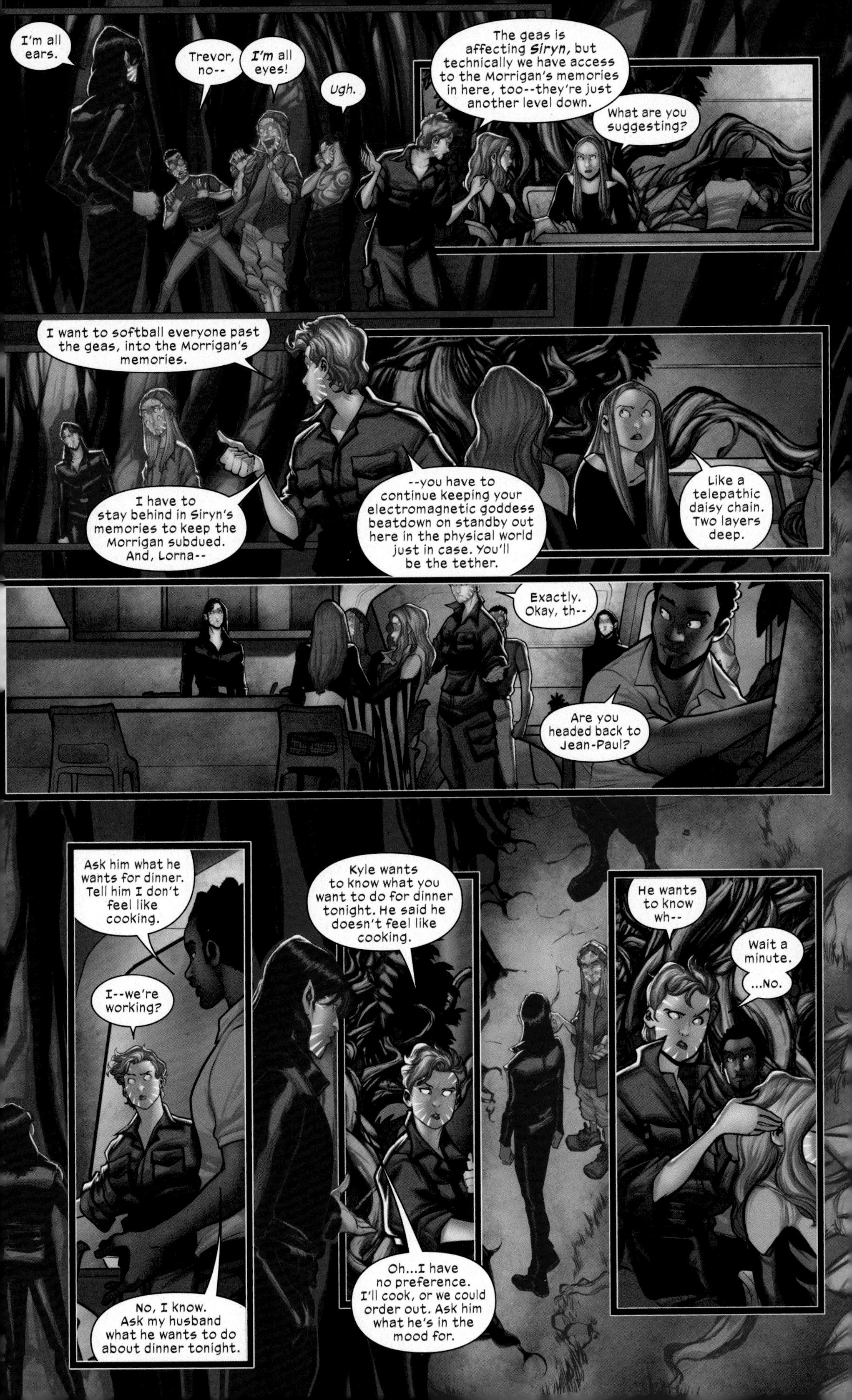

I'm all ears.
Trevor, no--
I'm all eyes!
Ugh.
The geas is affecting Siryn, but technically we have access to the Morrigan's memories in here, too--they're just another level down.
What are you suggesting?
I want to softball everyone past the geas, into the Morrigan's memories.
I have to stay behind in Siryn's memories to keep the Morrigan subdued. And, Lorna--
--you have to continue keeping your electromagnetic goddess beatdown on standby out here in the physical world just in case. You'll be the tether.
Like a telepathic daisy chain. Two layers deep.
Exactly. Okay, th--
Are you headed back to Jean-Paul?
Ask him what he wants for dinner. Tell him I don't feel like cooking.
I--we're working?
No, I know. Ask my husband what he wants to do about dinner tonight.
Kyle wants to know what you want to do for dinner tonight. He said he doesn't feel like cooking.
Oh...I have no preference. I'll cook, or we could order out. Ask him what he's in the mood for.
He wants to know wh--
Wait a minute.
...No.

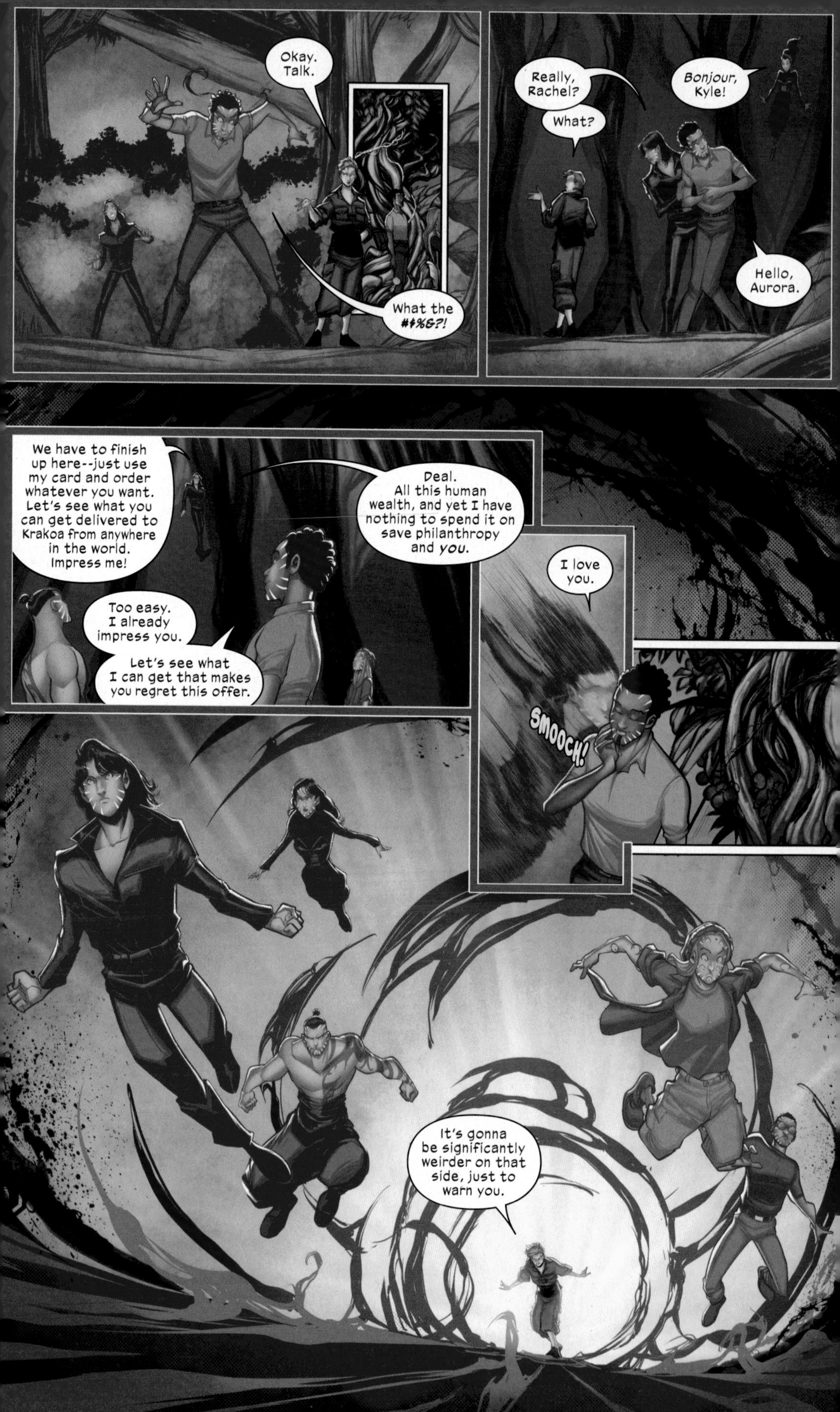

Okay. Talk.
What the #$%&?!
Really, Rachel?
What?
Bonjour, Kyle!
Hello, Aurora.
We have to finish up here--just use my card and order whatever you want. Let's see what you can get delivered to Krakoa from anywhere in the world. Impress me!
Deal. All this human wealth, and yet I have nothing to spend it on save philanthropy and *you*.
Too easy. I already impress you.
Let's see what I can get that makes you regret this offer.
I love you.
SMOOCH!
It's gonna be significantly weirder on that side, just to warn you.

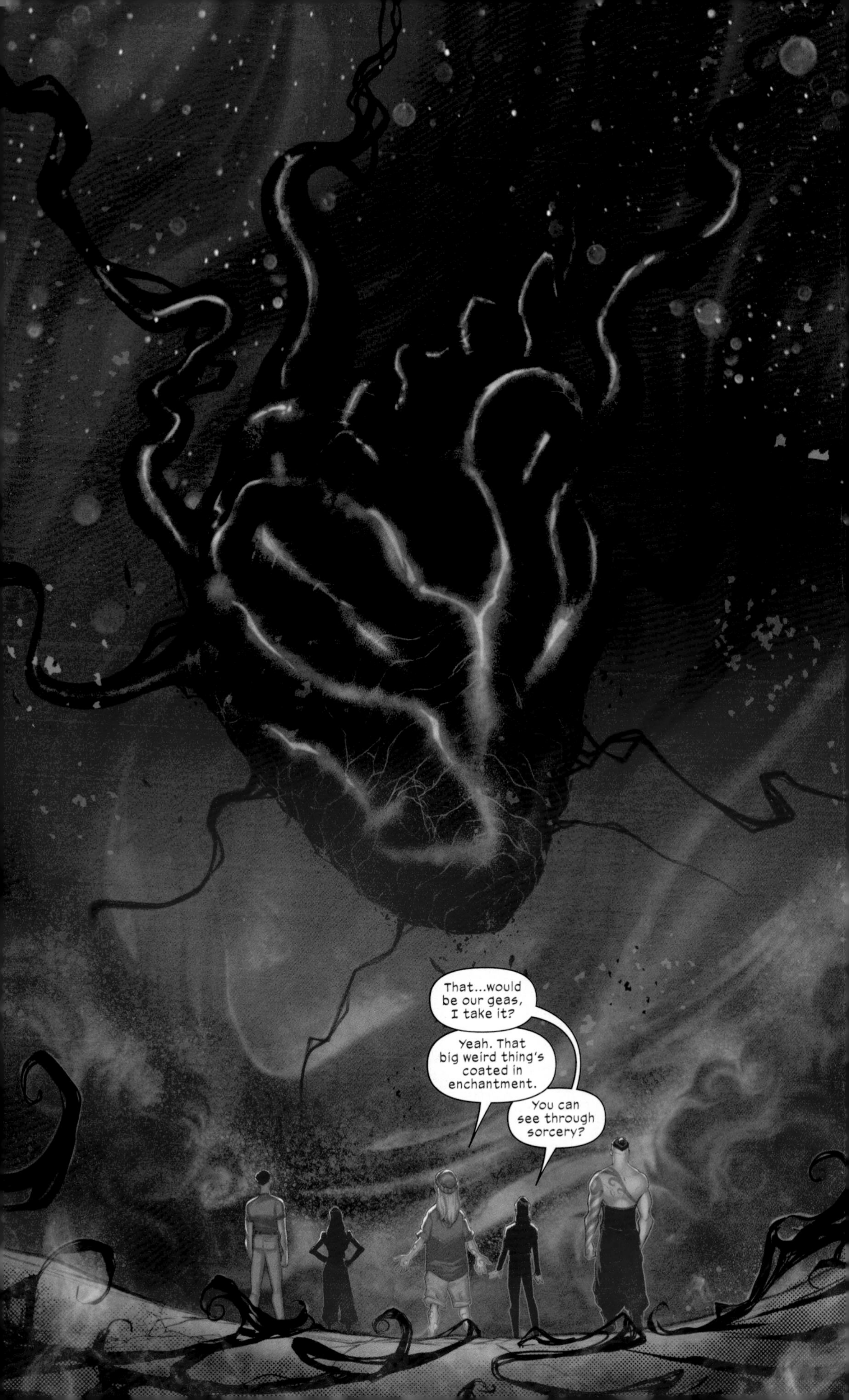
That...would be our geas, I take it?
Yeah. That big weird thing's coated in enchantment.
You can see through sorcery?

I have a question. Do you keep secrets from the Quiet Council?

Haha. Hi, Northstar. Is this us catching up?

Yes. Hello, Dani. How many secrets kept from the Quiet Council do you think is a healthy amount of subterfuge?

Tell me your reasoning here, Jean-Paul.

I've learned that members of my squad are more powerful than even the Council is aware of, and now I am terrified of the misappropriation of their skills because I do not trust leadership to leave well enough alone.

They're probably going to look at these young people in my care and just see all the ways in which their developing abilities could be weaponized.

OK.

I just checked with Xi'an and she's free tonight too.

So how about you grab Kyle and let's all go out to dinner?

That...sounds perfect. Thank you, Dani.

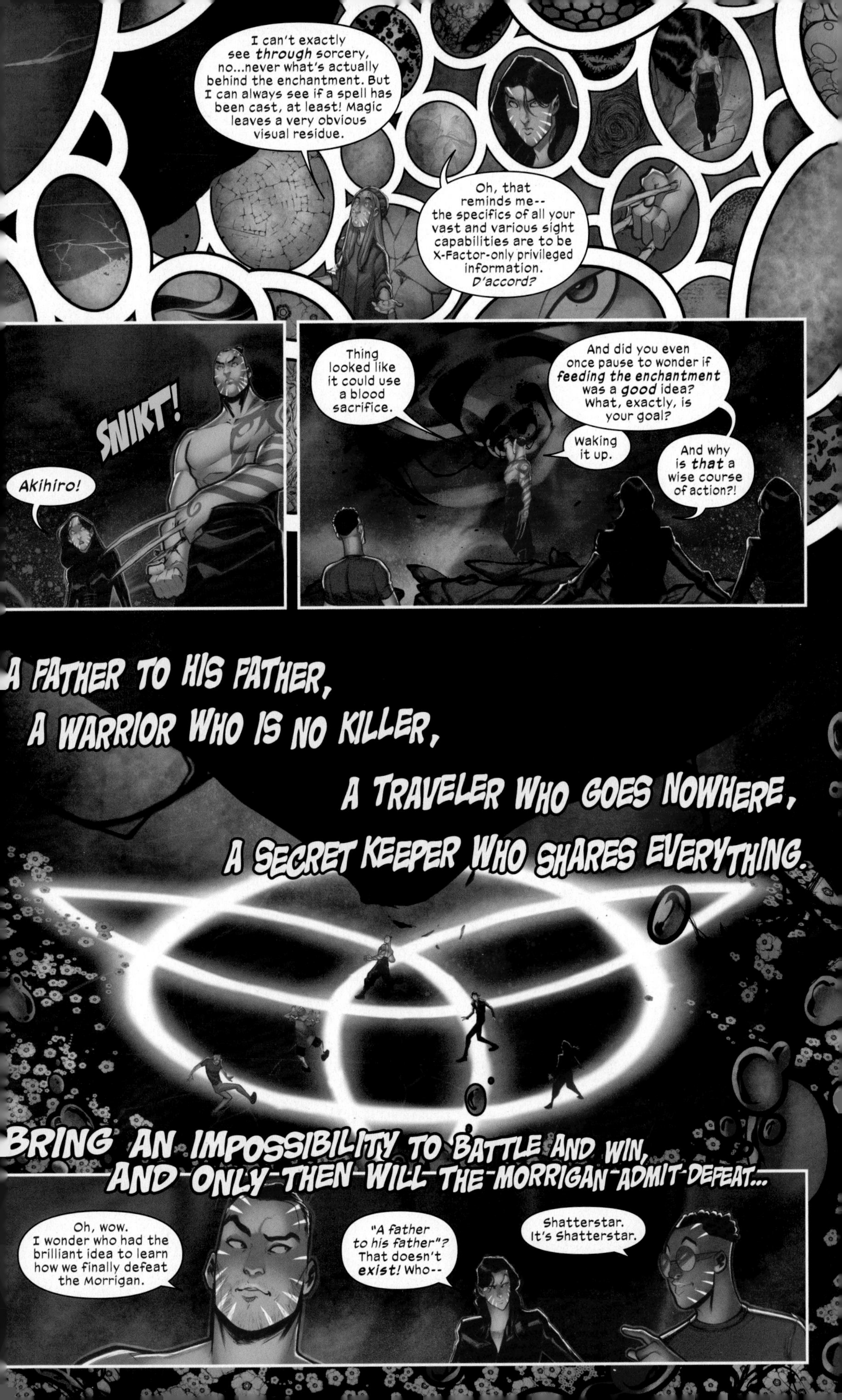
I can't exactly see through sorcery, no...never what's actually behind the enchantment. But I can always see if a spell has been cast, at least! Magic leaves a very obvious visual residue.
Oh, that reminds me-- the specifics of all your vast and various sight capabilities are to be X-Factor-only privileged information. D'accord?
SNIKT!
Akihiro!
Thing looked like it could use a blood sacrifice.
And did you even once pause to wonder if feeding the enchantment was a good idea? What, exactly, is your goal?
Waking it up.
And why is that a wise course of action?!
A FATHER TO HIS FATHER,
A WARRIOR WHO IS NO KILLER,
A TRAVELER WHO GOES NOWHERE,
A SECRET KEEPER WHO SHARES EVERYTHING.
BRING AN IMPOSSIBILITY TO BATTLE AND WIN,
AND ONLY THEN WILL THE MORRIGAN ADMIT DEFEAT...
Oh, wow. I wonder who had the brilliant idea to learn how we finally defeat the Morrigan.
"A father to his father"? That doesn't exist! Who--
Shatterstar. It's Shatterstar.

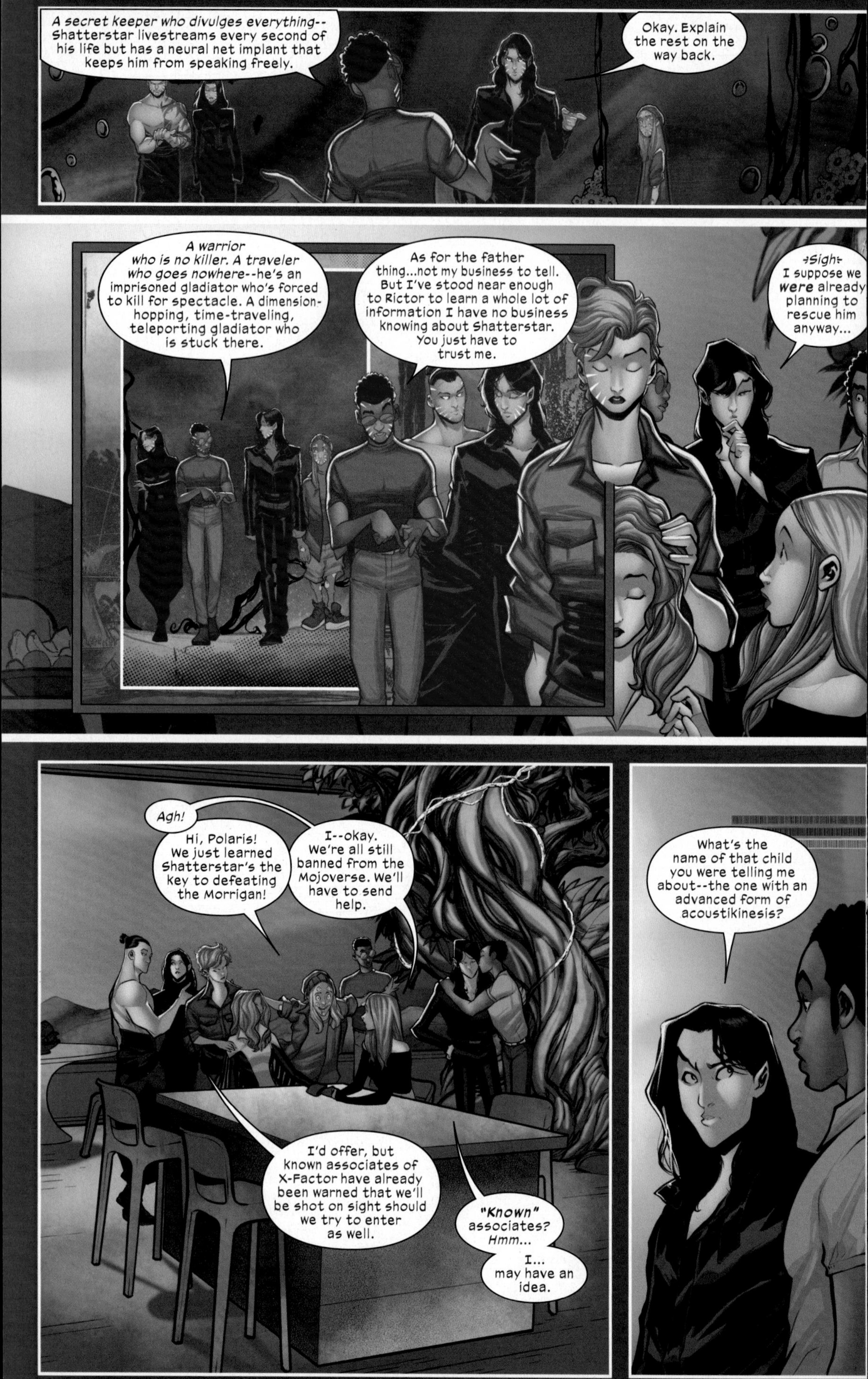
A secret keeper who divulges everything--Shatterstar livestreams every second of his life but has a neural net implant that keeps him from speaking freely.
Okay. Explain the rest on the way back.
A warrior who is no killer. A traveler who goes nowhere--he's an imprisoned gladiator who's forced to kill for spectacle. A dimension-hopping, time-traveling, teleporting gladiator who is stuck there.
As for the father thing...not my business to tell. But I've stood near enough to Rictor to learn a whole lot of information I have no business knowing about Shatterstar. You just have to trust me.
-Sigh- I suppose we were already planning to rescue him anyway...
Agh!
Hi, Polaris! We just learned Shatterstar's the key to defeating the Morrigan!
I--okay. We're all still banned from the Mojoverse. We'll have to send help.
I'd offer, but known associates of X-Factor have already been warned that we'll be shot on sight should we try to enter as well.
"Known" associates? Hmm...
I... may have an idea.
What's the name of that child you were telling me about--the one with an advanced form of acoustikinesis?

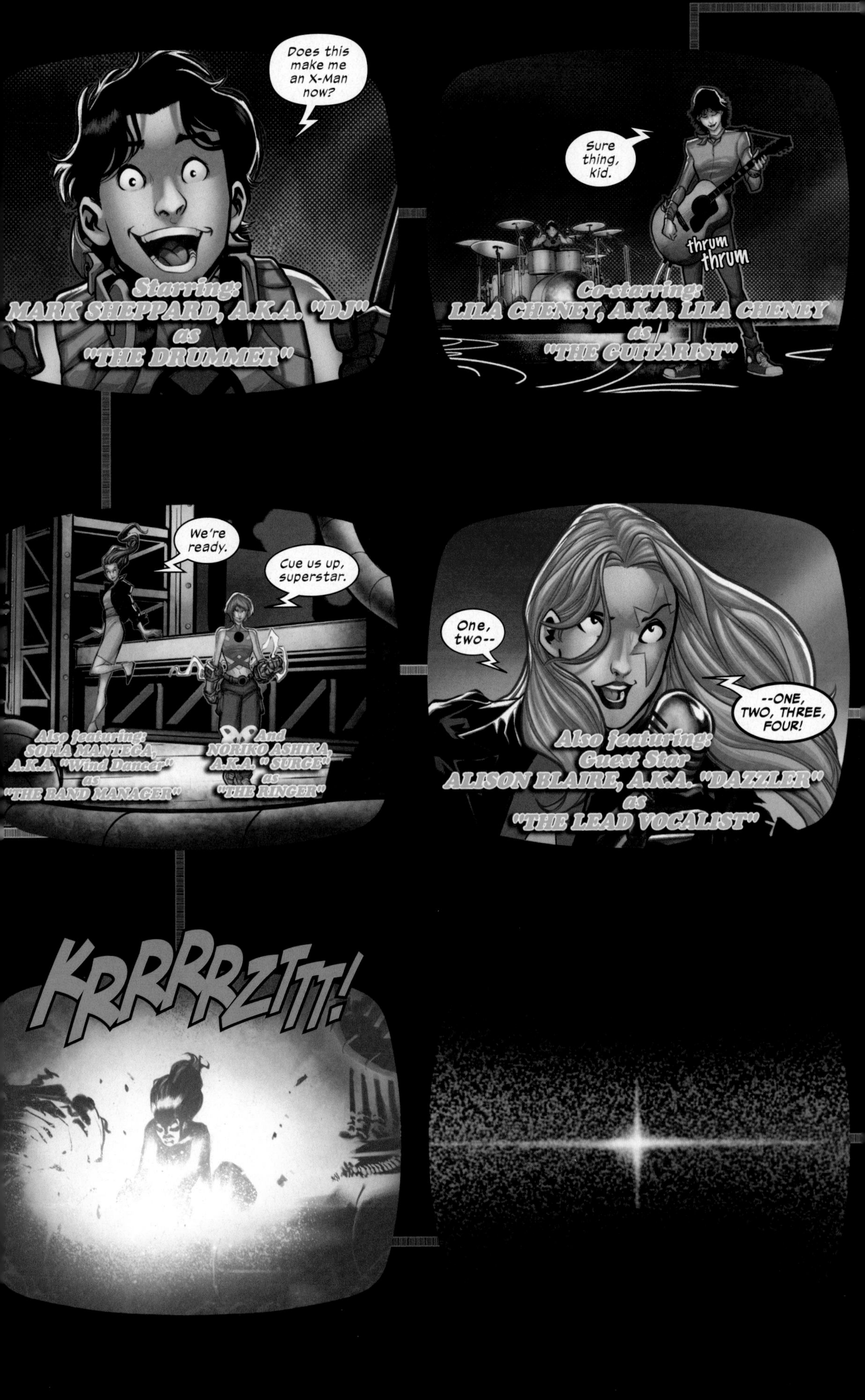
Does this make me an X-Man now?
Starring:
MARK SHEPPARD, A.K.A. "DJ"
as
"THE DRUMMER"
Sure thing, kid.
thrum thrum
Co-starring:
LILA CHENEY, A.K.A. LILA CHENEY
as
"THE GUITARIST"
We're ready.
Cue us up, superstar.
Also featuring:
SOFIA MANTEGA,
A.K.A. "Wind Dancer"
as
"THE BAND MANAGER"
And
NORIKO ASHIKA,
A.K.A. "SURGE"
as
"THE RINGER"
One, two--
--ONE, TWO, THREE, FOUR!
Also featuring:
Guest Star
ALISON BLAIRE, A.K.A. "DAZZLER"
as
"THE LEAD VOCALIST"
KRRRRZTTT!

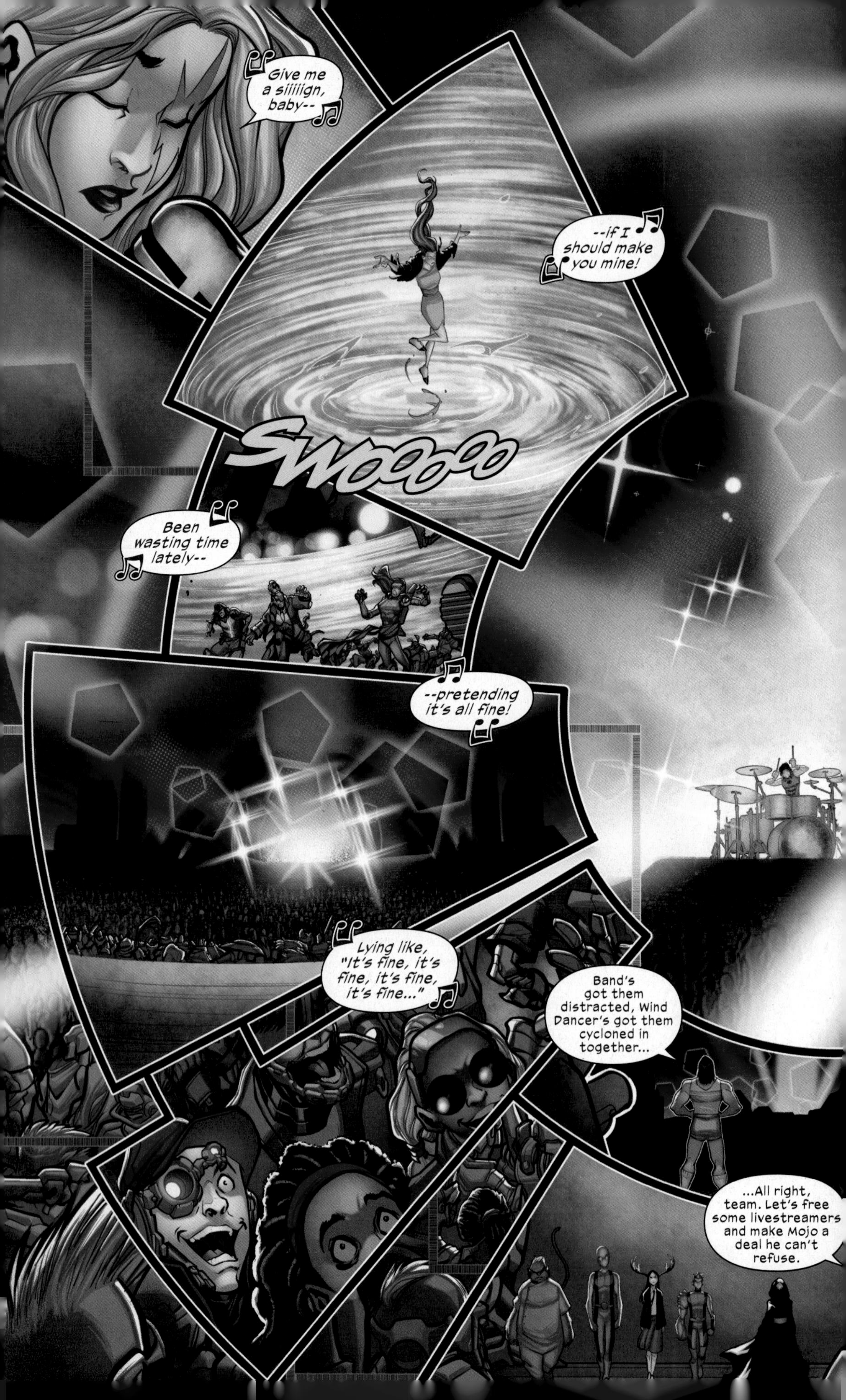
Give me a siiiiign, baby--
--if I should make you mine!
SWOOooo
Been wasting time lately--
--pretending it's all fine!
Lying like, "It's fine, it's fine, it's fine, it's fine..."
Band's got them distracted, Wind Dancer's got them cycloned in together...
...All right, team. Let's free some livestreamers and make Mojo a deal he can't refuse.

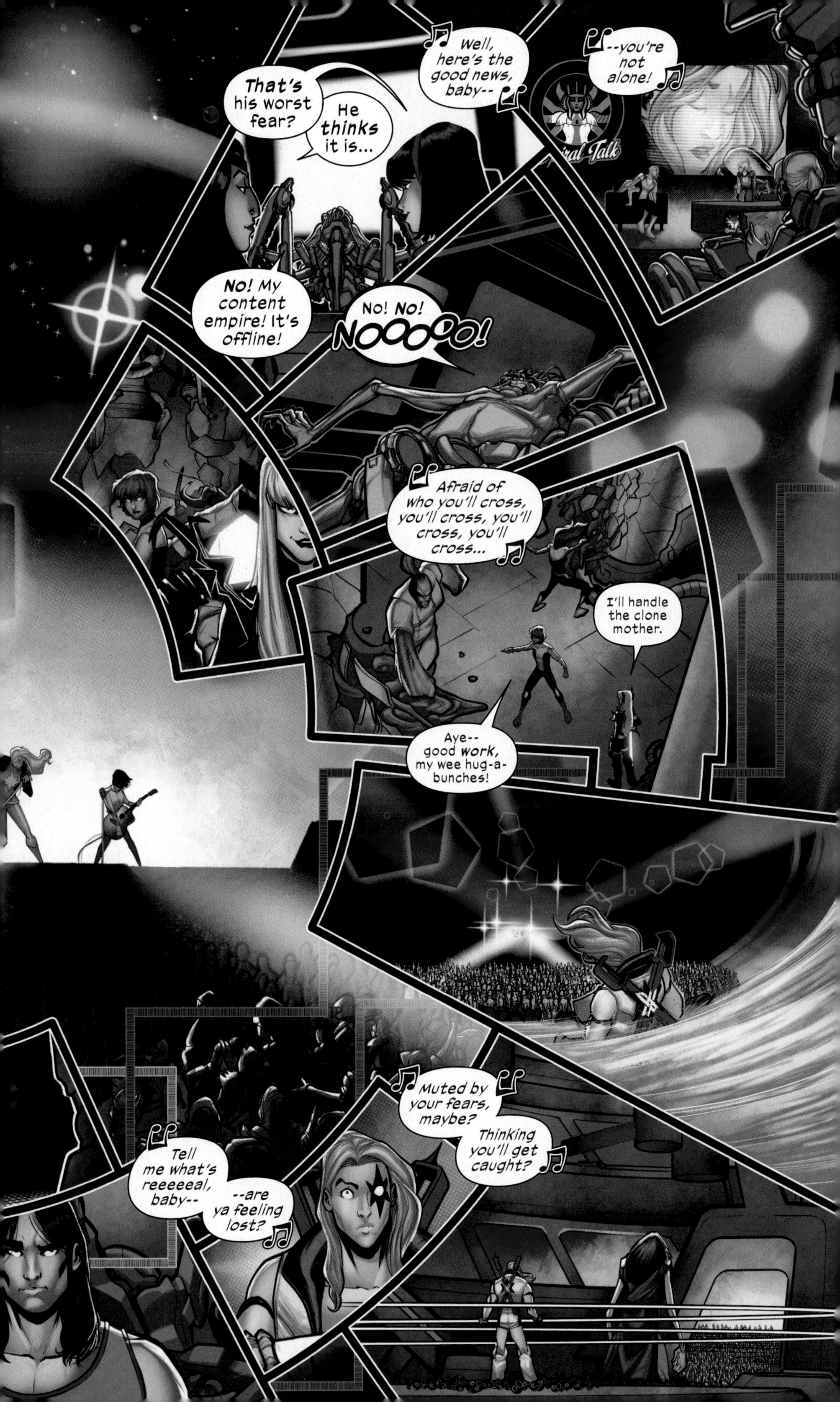
That's his worst fear?
He thinks it is...
Well, here's the good news, baby--
--you're not alone!
No! My content empire! It's offline!
No! No! NOOOOO!
Afraid of who you'll cross, you'll cross, you'll cross, you'll cross...
I'll handle the clone mother.
Aye-- good work, my wee hug-a-bunches!
Tell me what's reeeeeal, baby--
--are ya feeling lost?
Muted by your fears, maybe?
Thinking you'll get caught?

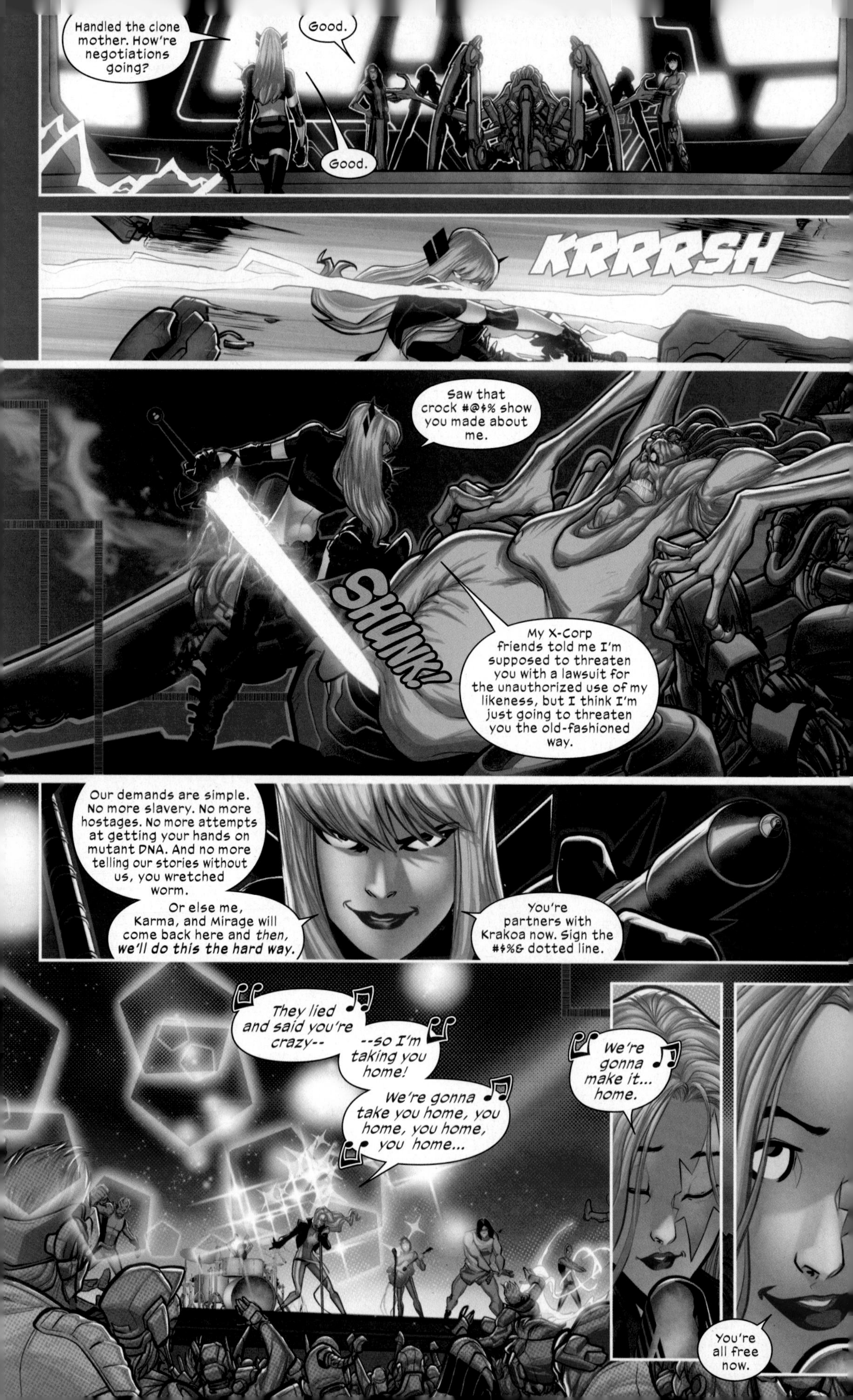

Handled the clone mother. How're negotiations going?
Good.
Good.
KRRRSH
Saw that crock #@$% show you made about me.
SHUNK!
My X-Corp friends told me I'm supposed to threaten you with a lawsuit for the unauthorized use of my likeness, but I think I'm just going to threaten you the old-fashioned way.
Our demands are simple. No more slavery. No more hostages. No more attempts at getting your hands on mutant DNA. And no more telling our stories without us, you wretched worm.
Or else me, Karma, and Mirage will come back here and *then*, **we'll do this the hard way.**
You're partners with Krakoa now. Sign the #$%& dotted line.
They lied and said you're crazy--
--so I'm taking you home!
We're gonna take you home, you home, you home, you home...
We're gonna make it... home.
You're all free now.

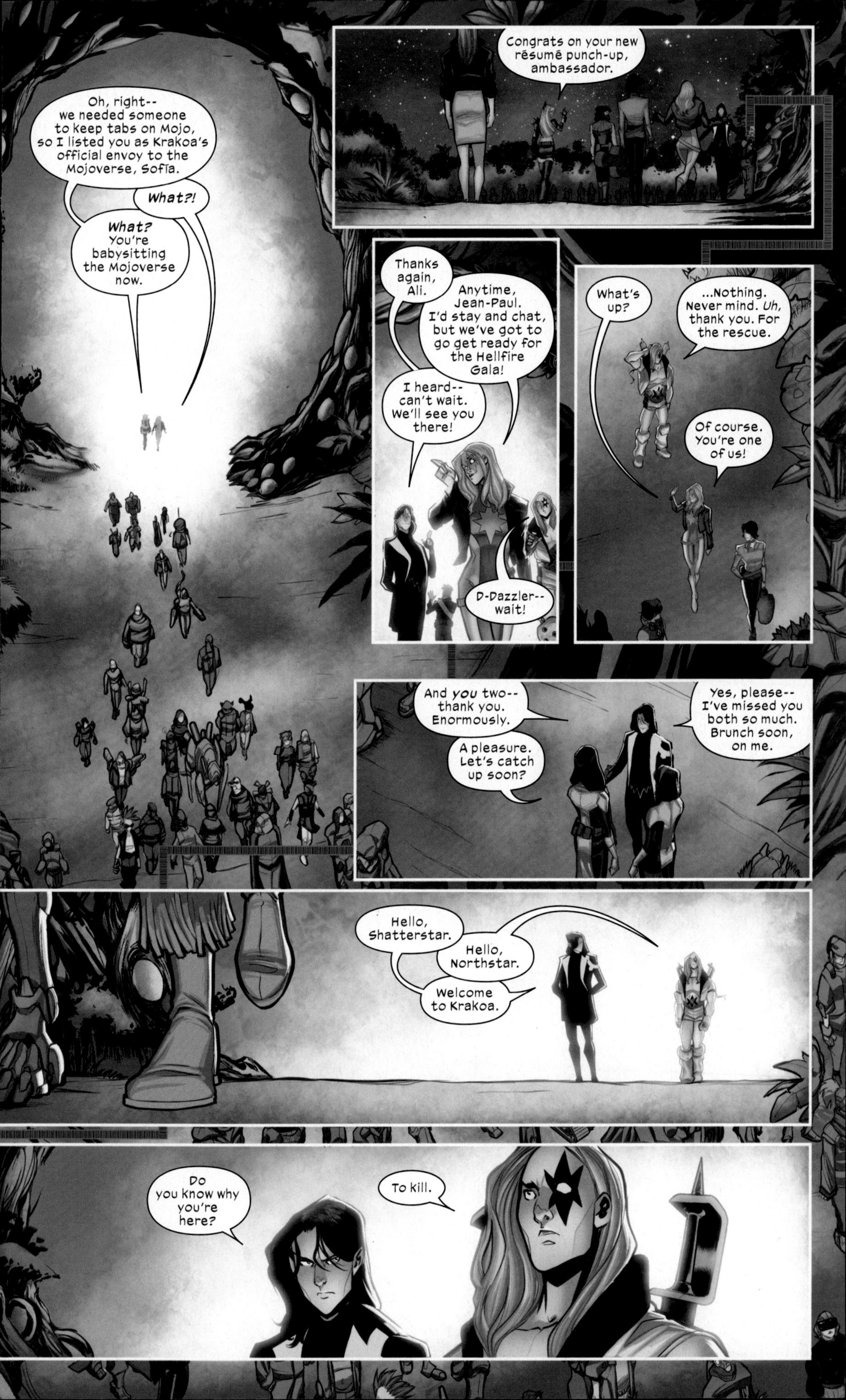
Oh, right--
we needed someone
to keep tabs on Mojo,
so I listed you as Krakoa's
official envoy to the
Mojoverse, Sofía.
What?!
What?
You're
babysitting
the Mojoverse
now.
Congrats on your new
résumé punch-up,
ambassador.
Thanks
again,
Ali.
Anytime,
Jean-Paul.
I'd stay and chat,
but we've got to
go get ready for
the Hellfire
Gala!
I heard--
can't wait.
We'll see you
there!
D-Dazzler--
wait!
What's
up?
...Nothing.
Never mind. Uh,
thank you. For
the rescue.
Of course.
You're one
of us!
And you two--
thank you.
Enormously.
A pleasure.
Let's catch
up soon?
Yes, please--
I've missed you
both so much.
Brunch soon,
on me.
Hello,
Shatterstar.
Hello,
Northstar.
Welcome
to Krakoa.
Do
you know why
you're
here?
To kill.

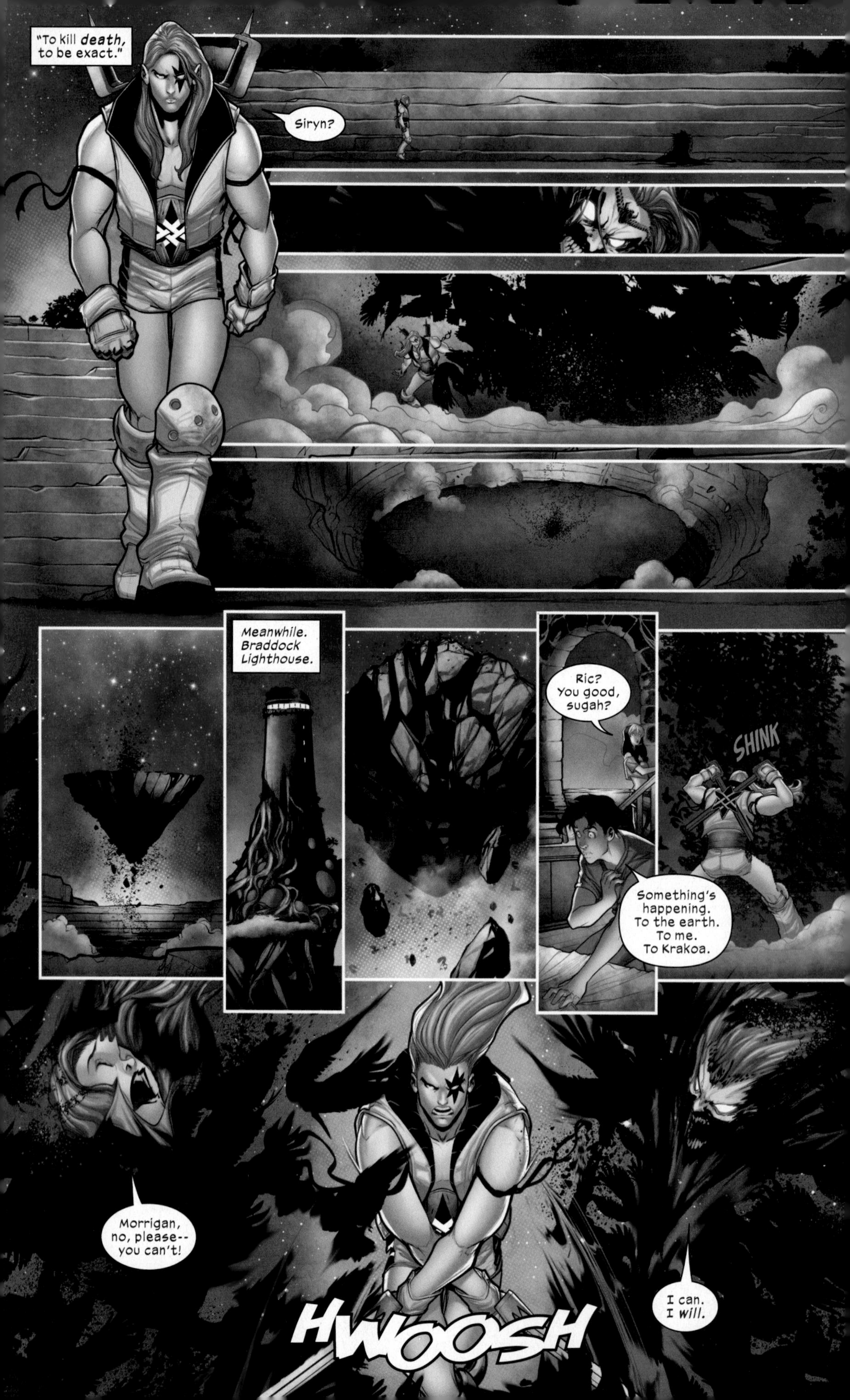
"To kill *death*, to be exact."
Siryn?
Meanwhile. Braddock Lighthouse.
Ric? You good, sugah?
SHINK
Something's happening. To the earth. To me. To Krakoa.
Morrigan, no, please--you can't!
HWOOSH
I can. I *will*.

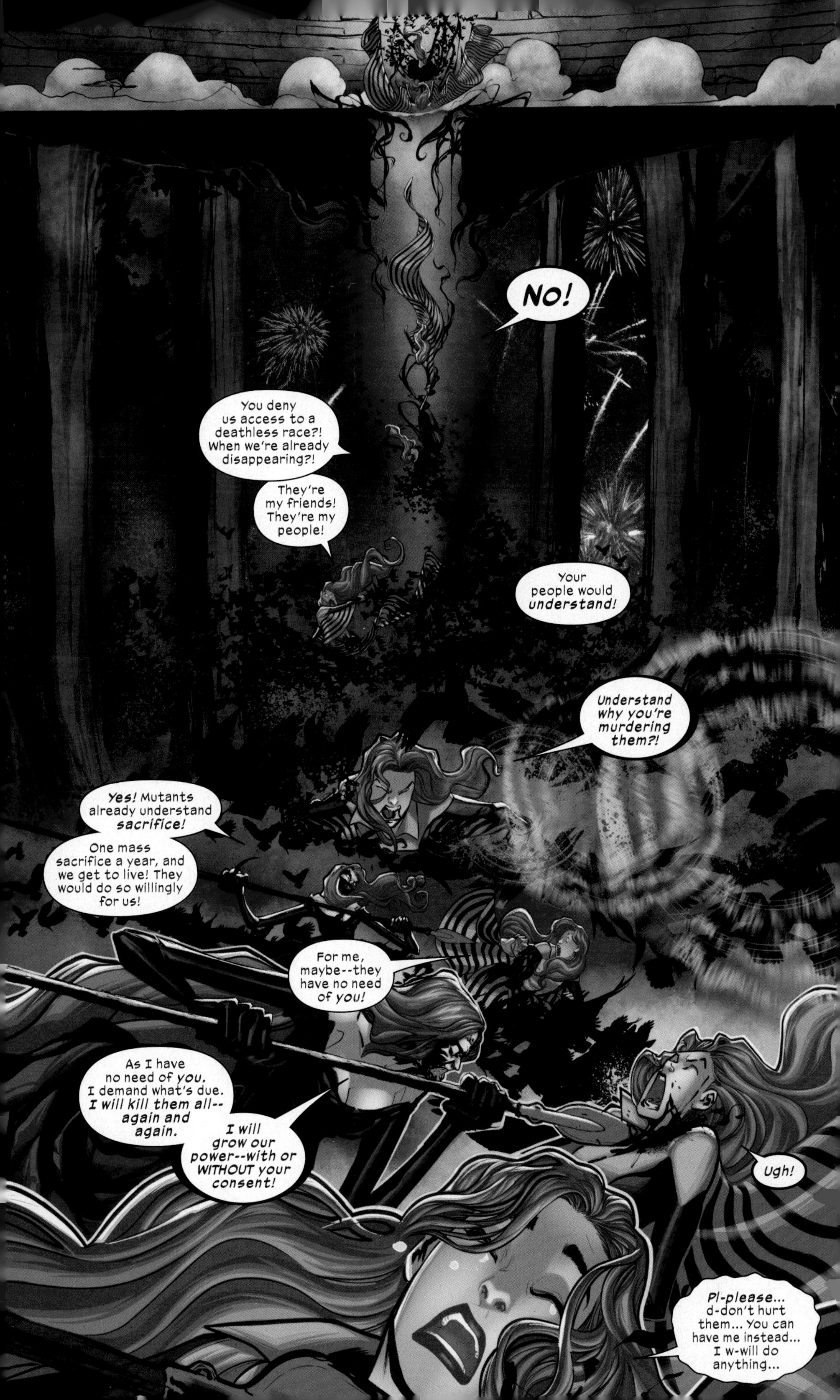
NO!
You deny us access to a deathless race?! When we're already disappearing?!
They're my friends! They're my people!
Your people would understand!
Understand why you're murdering them?!
Yes! Mutants already understand sacrifice!
One mass sacrifice a year, and we get to live! They would do so willingly for us!
For me, maybe--they have no need of you!
As I have no need of you. I demand what's due. I will kill them all--again and again.
I will grow our power--with or WITHOUT your consent!
Ugh!
Pl-please... d-don't hurt them... You can have me instead... I w-will do anything...

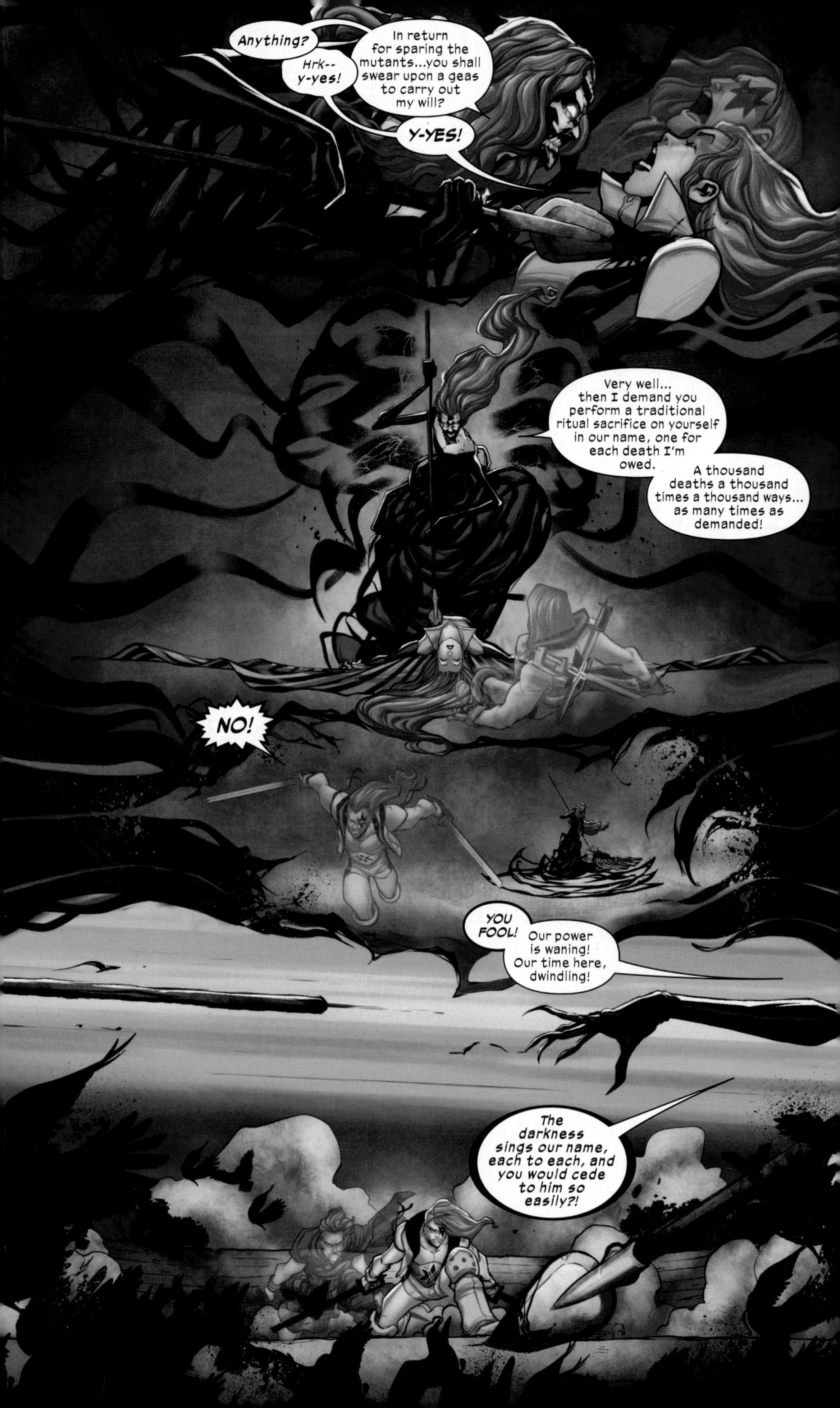
Anything?
In return for sparing the mutants...you shall swear upon a geas to carry out my will?
Hrk-- y-yes!
Y-YES!
Very well... then I demand you perform a traditional ritual sacrifice on yourself in our name, one for each death I'm owed.
A thousand deaths a thousand times a thousand ways... as many times as demanded!
NO!
YOU FOOL!
Our power is waning! Our time here, dwindling!
The darkness sings our name, each to each, and you would cede to him so easily?!

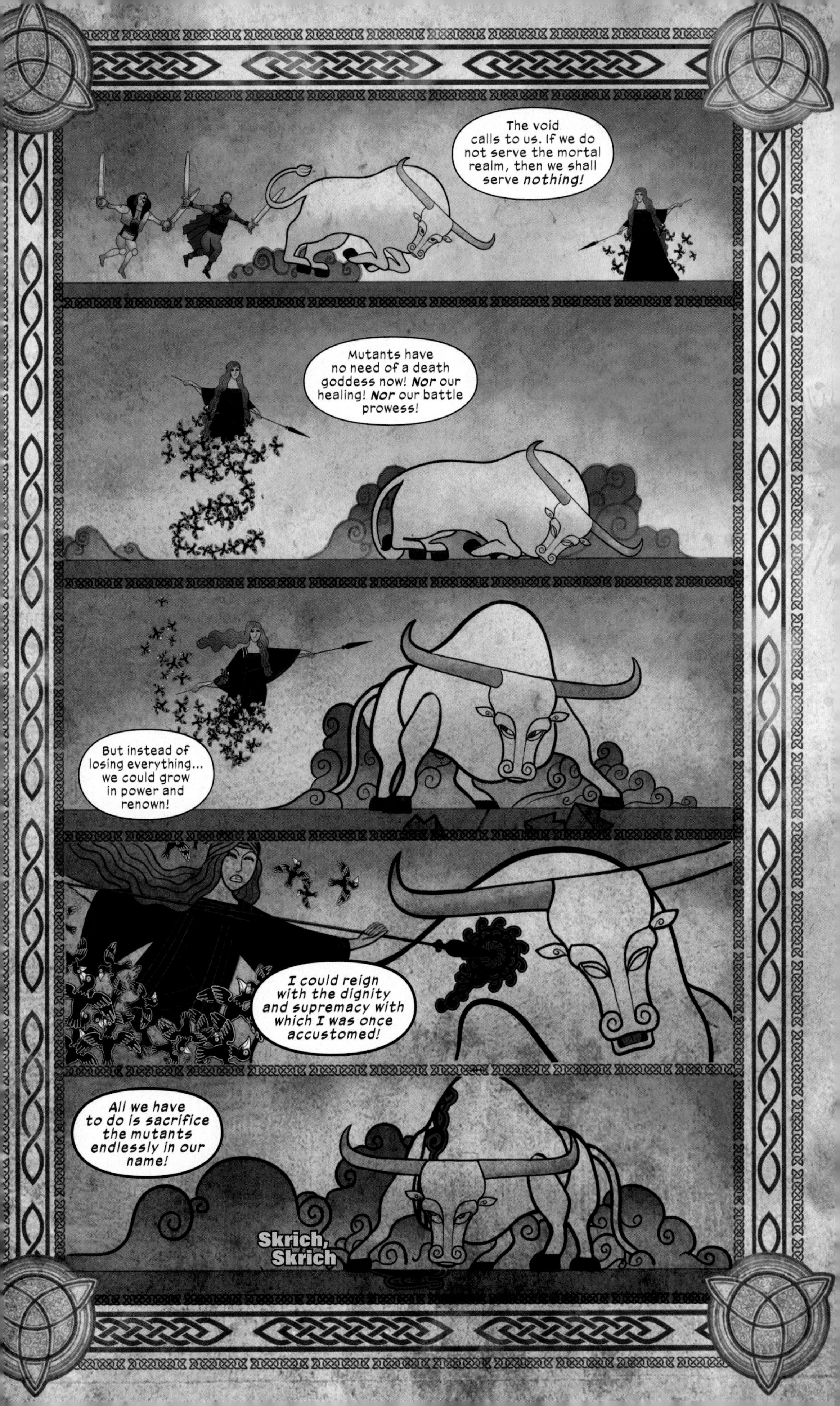
The void calls to us. If we do not serve the mortal realm, then we shall serve *nothing!*
Mutants have no need of a death goddess now! *Nor* our healing! *Nor* our battle prowess!
But instead of losing everything... we could grow in power and renown!
I could reign with the dignity and supremacy with which I was once accustomed!
All we have to do is sacrifice the mutants endlessly in our name!
Skrich, Skrich

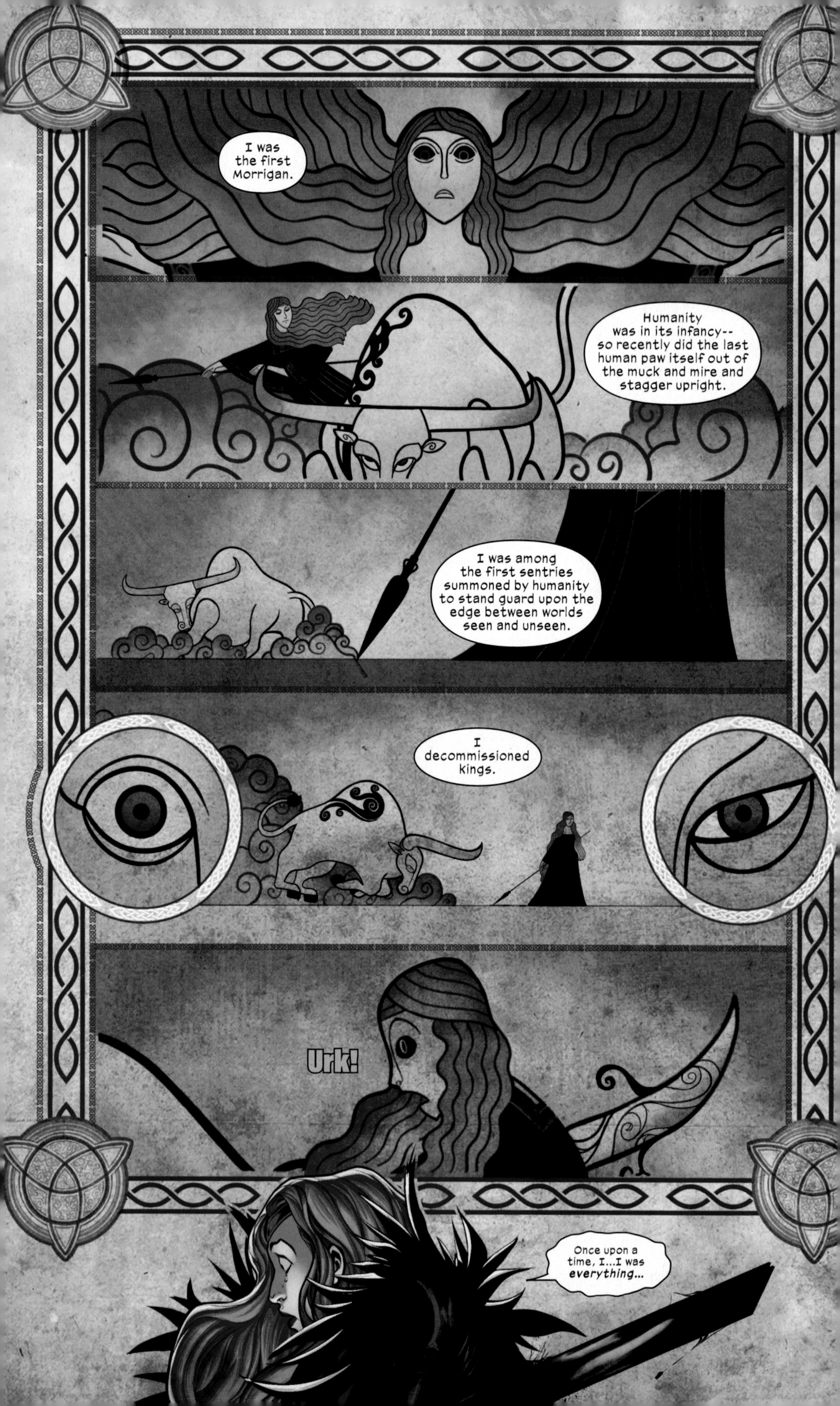
I was the first Morrigan.
Humanity was in its infancy--so recently did the last human paw itself out of the muck and mire and stagger upright.
I was among the first sentries summoned by humanity to stand guard upon the edge between worlds seen and unseen.
I decommissioned kings.
Urk!
Once upon a time, I...I was *everything*...

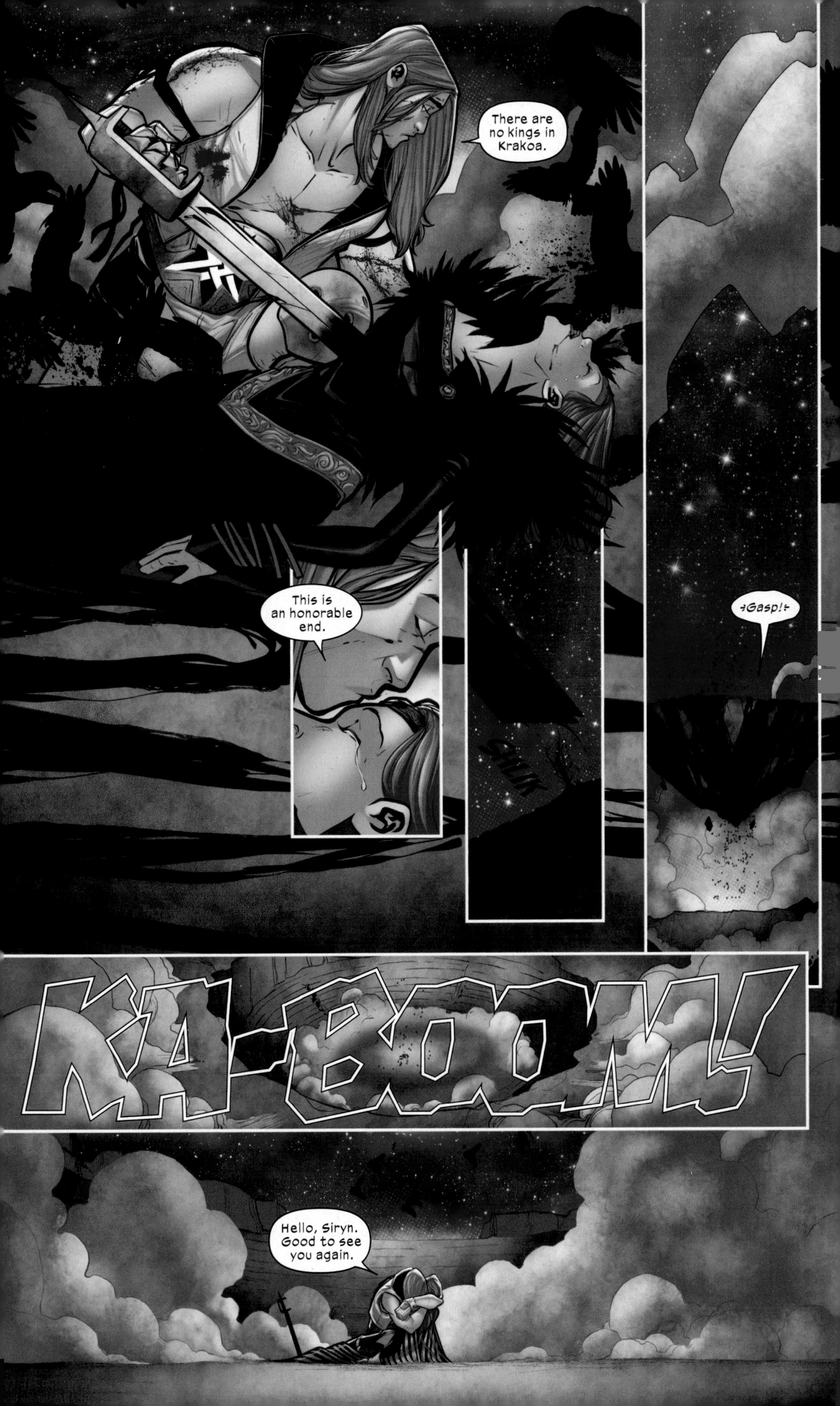
There are no kings in Krakoa.
This is an honorable end.
SHLIK
-Gasp!-
KA-BOOM!
Hello, Siryn. Good to see you again.

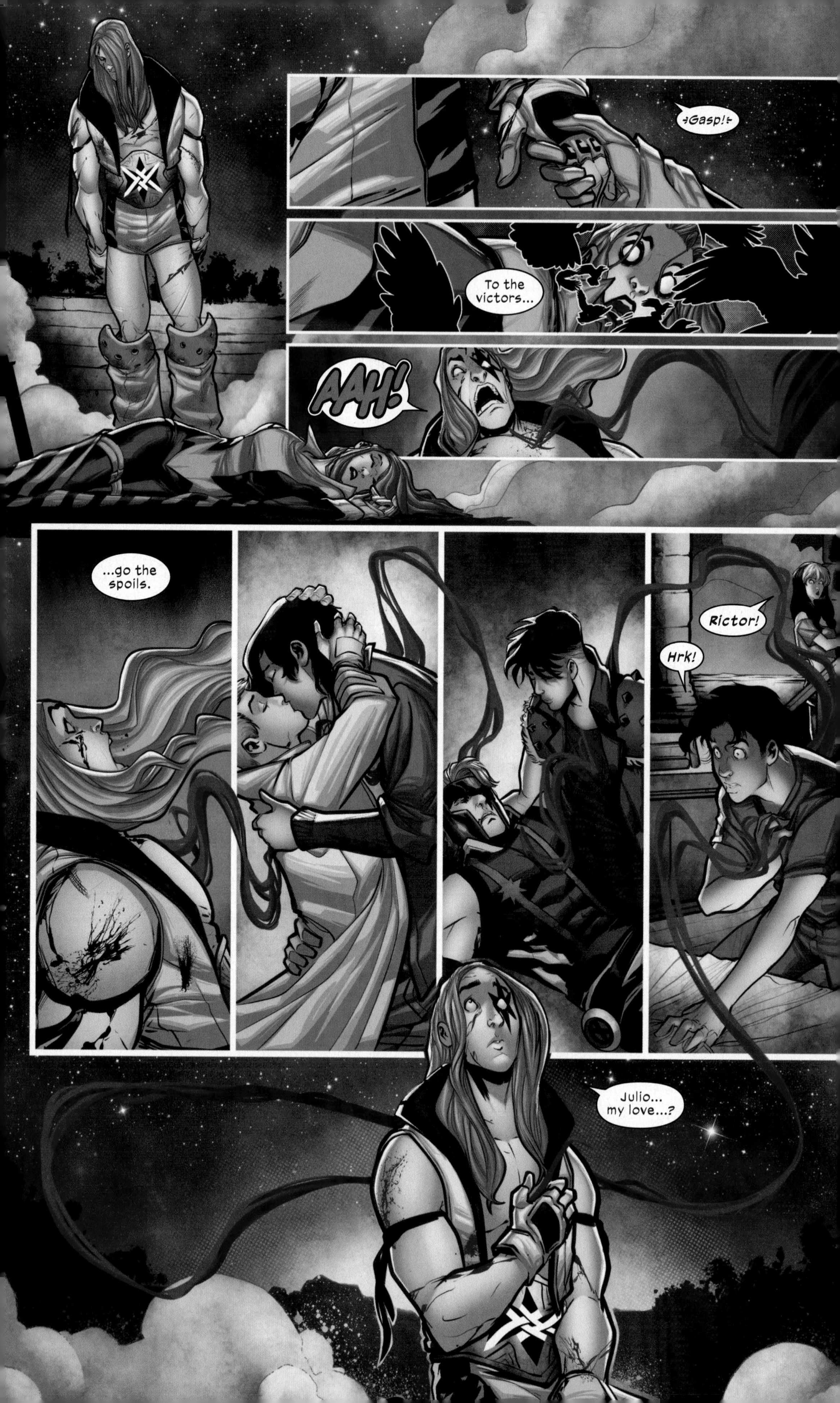

-Gasp!-
To the victors...
AAH!
...go the spoils.
Rictor!
Hrk!
Julio... my love...?

[reign_of_x]

[proof_X]
[death_X]

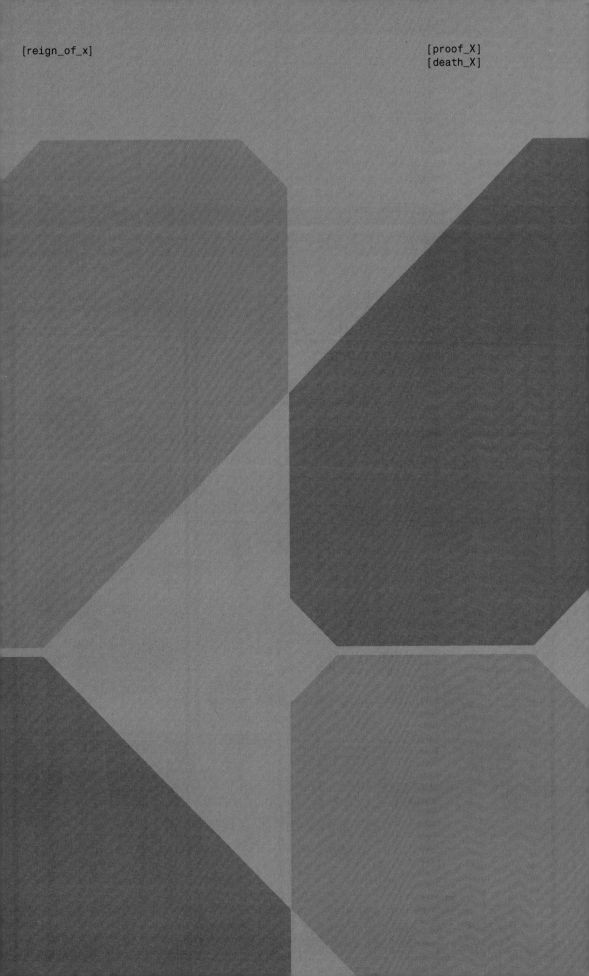

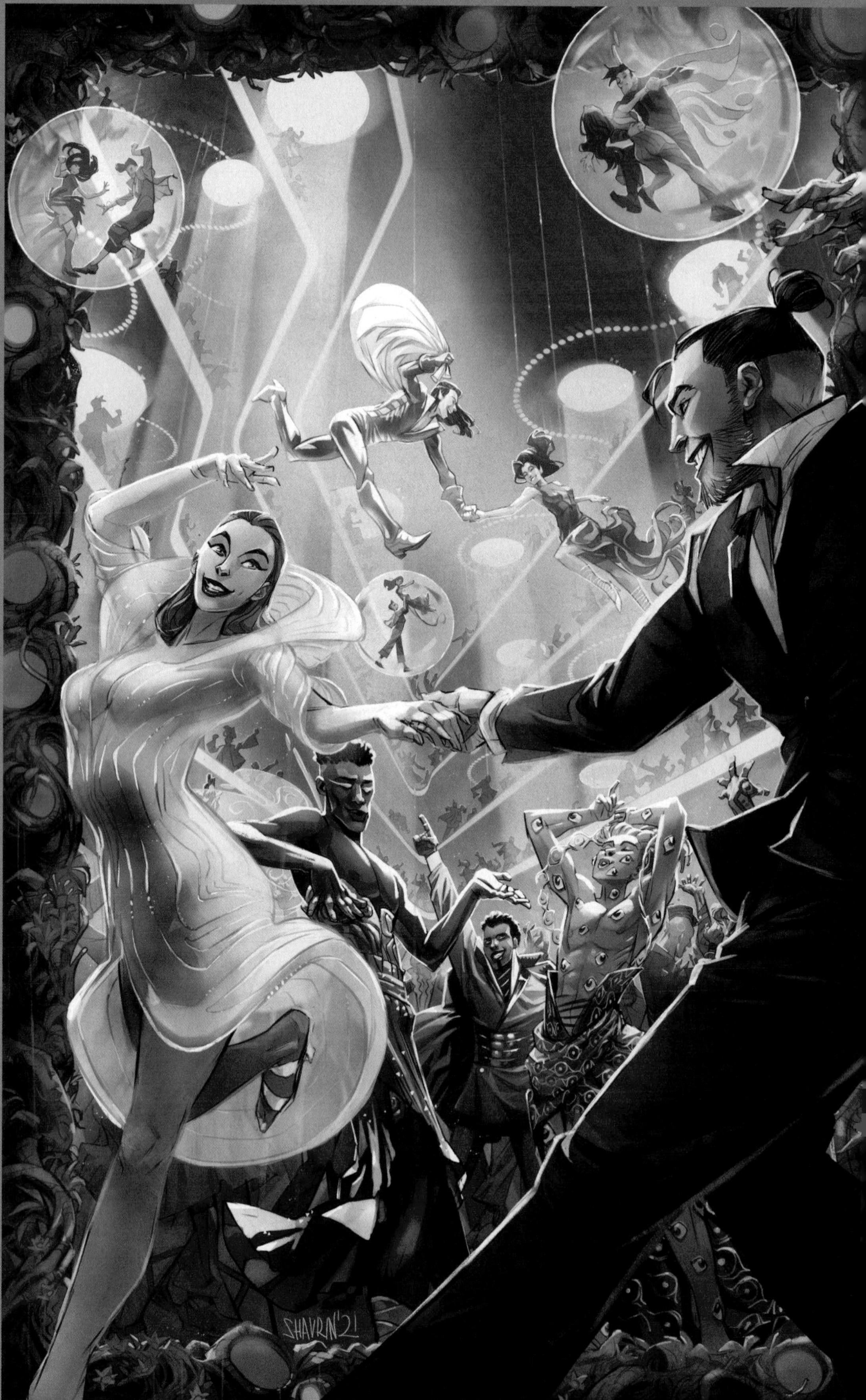

Finale

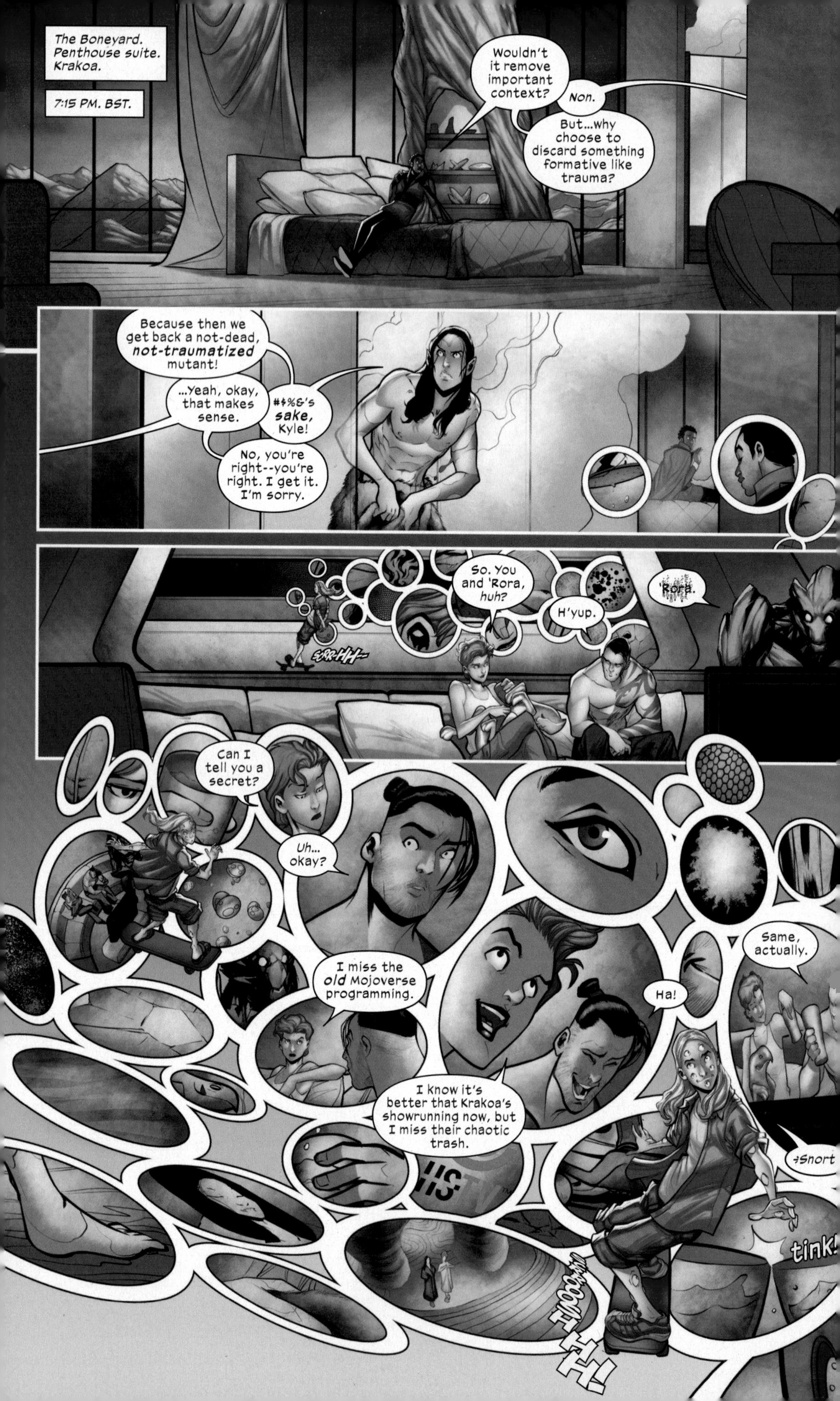
The Boneyard.
Penthouse suite.
Krakoa.
7:15 PM. BST.
Wouldn't it remove important context?
Non.
But...why choose to discard something formative like trauma?
Because then we get back a not-dead, ***not-traumatized*** mutant!
#$%&'s ***sake,*** Kyle!
...Yeah, okay, that makes sense.
No, you're right--you're right. I get it. I'm sorry.
So. You and 'Rora, *huh?*
H'yup.
'Rora.
Can I tell you a secret?
Uh... okay?
I miss the ***old*** Mojoverse programming.
Ha!
Same, actually.
I know it's better that Krakoa's showrunning now, but I miss their chaotic trash.
Snort
tink!

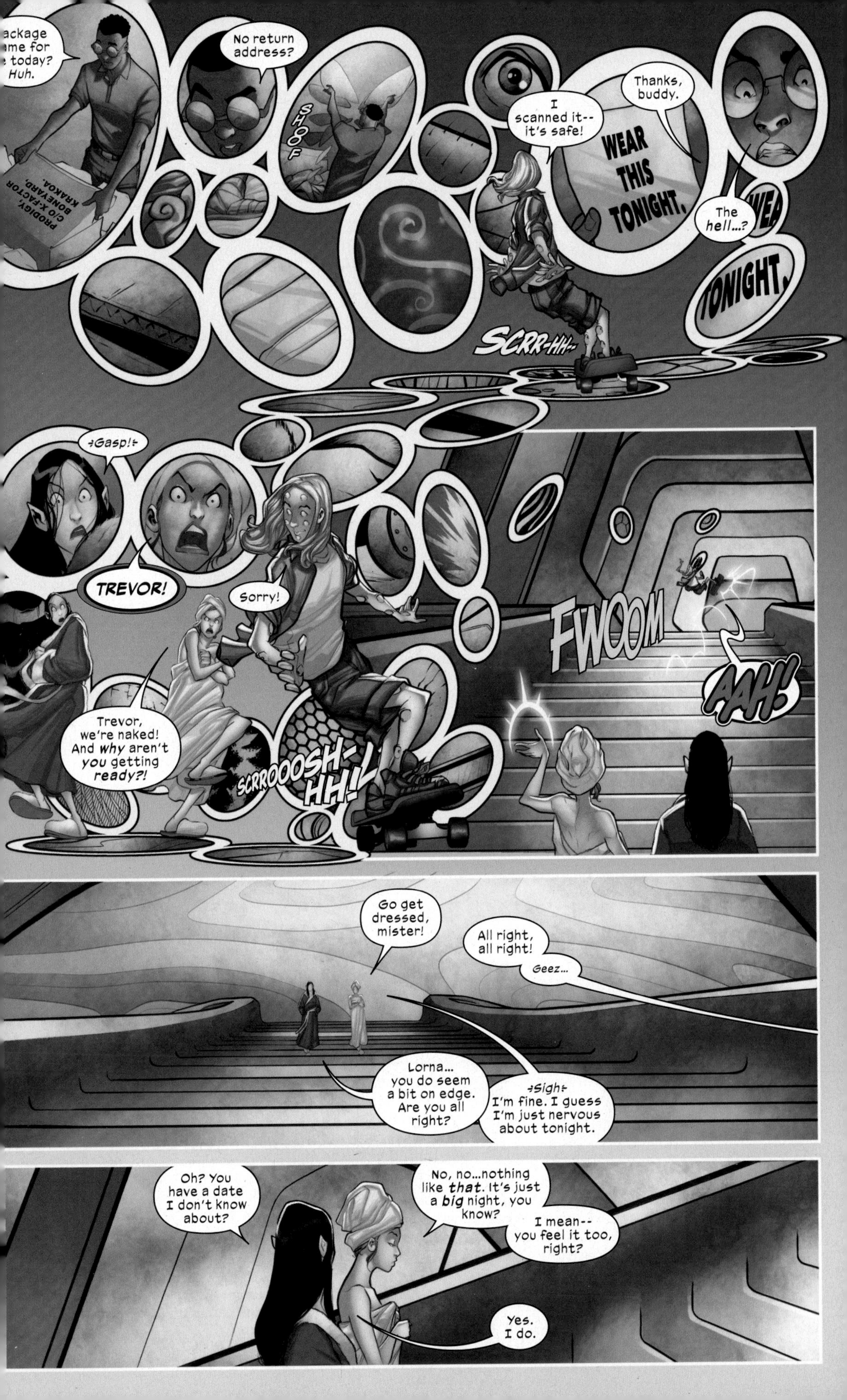
...ackage ...ame for ... today? Huh.
PRODIGY, C/O X-FACTOR BONEYARD, KRAKOA.
No return address?
SHOOF
I scanned it-- it's safe!
Thanks, buddy.
WEAR THIS TONIGHT.
The hell...?
WEAR TONIGHT.
SCRR-HH--
÷Gasp!÷
TREVOR!
Sorry!
FWOOM
AAH!
Trevor, we're naked! And why aren't you getting ready?!
SCRROOOSH-HH!!
Go get dressed, mister!
All right, all right!
Geez...
Lorna... you do seem a bit on edge. Are you all right?
÷Sigh÷ I'm fine. I guess I'm just nervous about tonight.
Oh? You have a date I don't know about?
No, no...nothing like that. It's just a big night, you know?
I mean-- you feel it too, right?
Yes. I do.

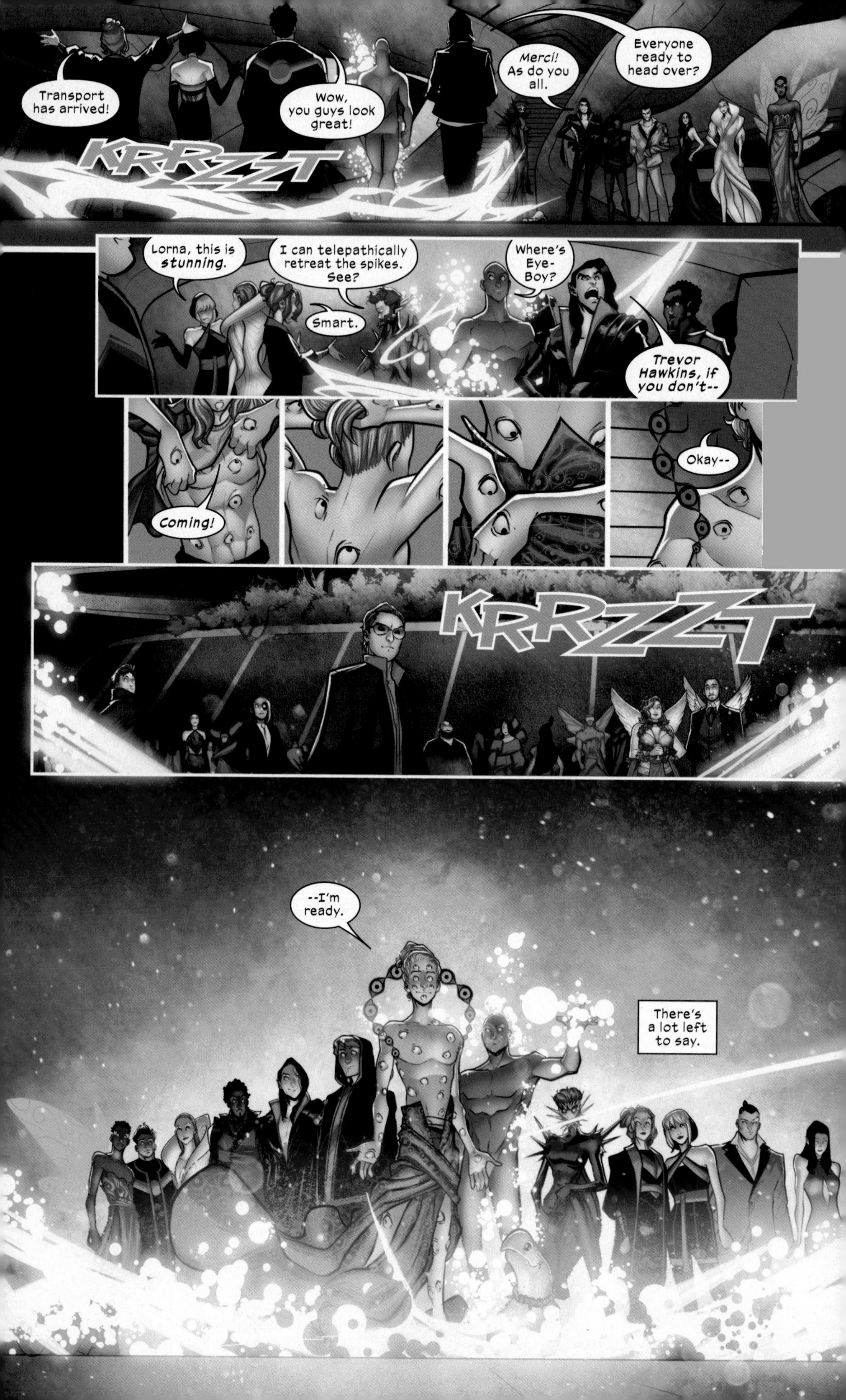
Transport has arrived!
Wow, you guys look great!
Merci! As do you all.
Everyone ready to head over?
KRRZZZT
Lorna, this is *stunning*.
I can telepathically retreat the spikes. See?
Smart.
Where's Eye-Boy?
Trevor Hawkins, if you don't--
Coming!
Okay--
KRRZZZT
--I'm ready.
There's a lot left to say.

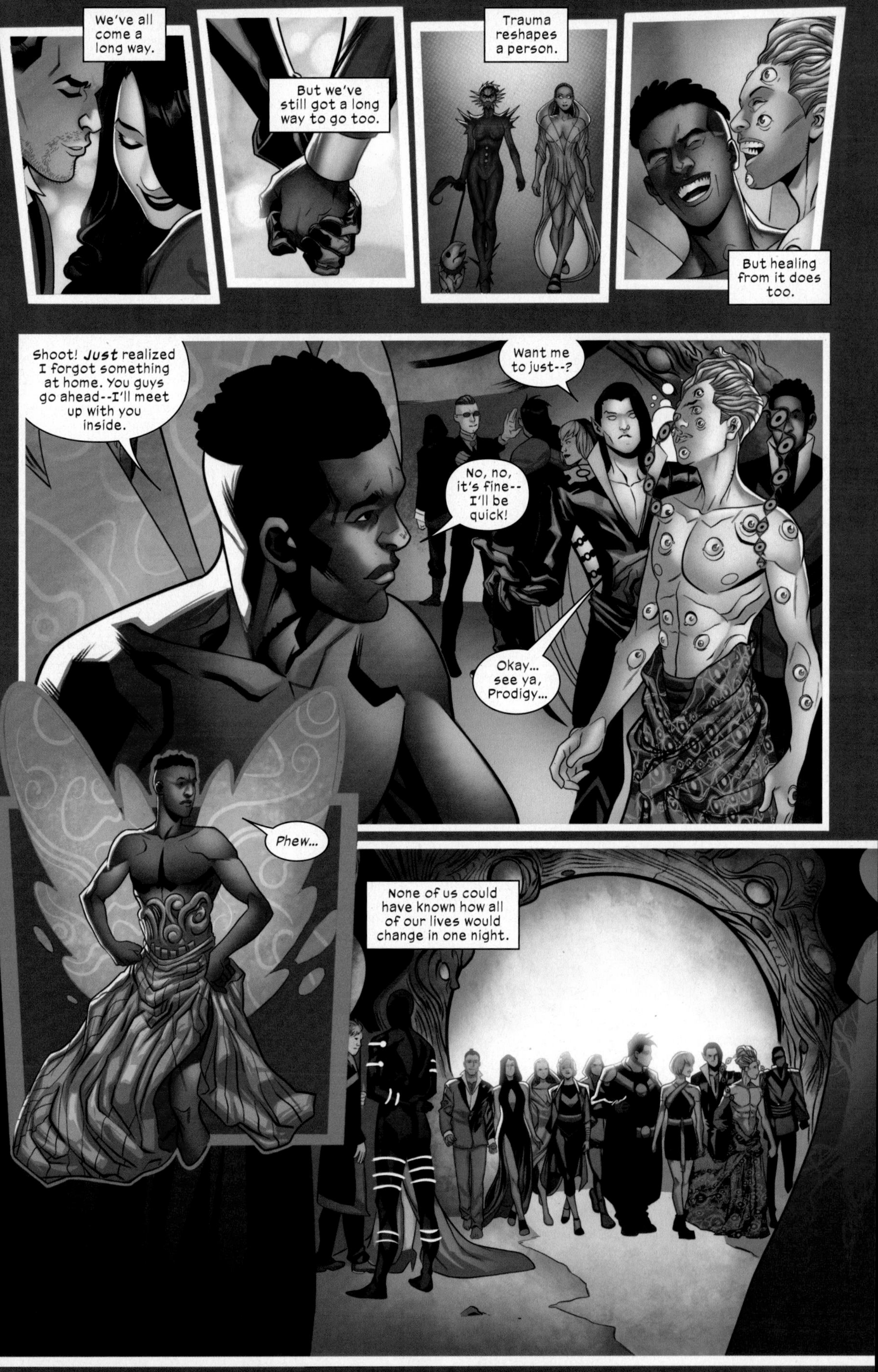
We've all come a long way.
But we've still got a long way to go too.
Trauma reshapes a person.
But healing from it does too.
Shoot! Just realized I forgot something at home. You guys go ahead--I'll meet up with you inside.
Want me to just--?
No, no, it's fine-- I'll be quick!
Okay... see ya, Prodigy...
Phew...
None of us could have known how all of our lives would change in one night.

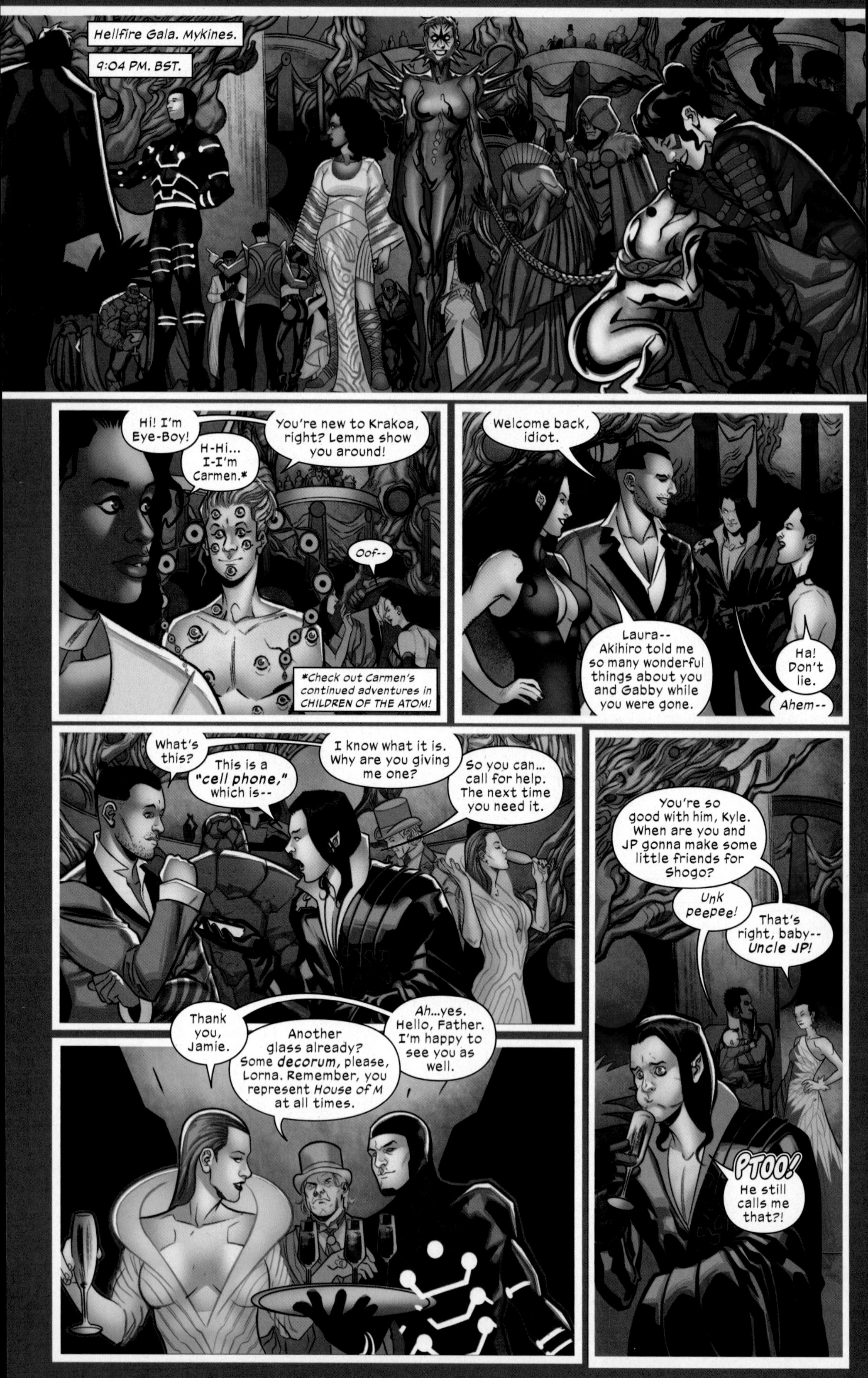

Hellfire Gala. MyKines.
9:04 PM. BST.
Hi! I'm Eye-Boy!
You're new to Krakoa, right? Lemme show you around!
H-Hi... I-I'm Carmen.*
Oof--
*Check out Carmen's continued adventures in CHILDREN OF THE ATOM!
Welcome back, idiot.
Laura-- Akihiro told me so many wonderful things about you and Gabby while you were gone.
Ha! Don't lie.
Ahem--
What's this?
This is a "cell phone," which is--
I know what it is. Why are you giving me one?
So you can... call for help. The next time you need it.
You're so good with him, Kyle. When are you and JP gonna make some little friends for Shogo?
Unk peepee!
That's right, baby-- Uncle JP!
PTOO!
He still calls me that?!
Thank you, Jamie.
Another glass already? Some decorum, please, Lorna. Remember, you represent House of M at all times.
Ah...yes. Hello, Father. I'm happy to see you as well.

THE HELLFIRE GALA

X-FACTOR has been investigating dead and missing mutants, thus ensuring their resurrections. More recently, that included Siryn's multiple, unusual deaths at the hands of the Morrigan, the goddess of death. With the aid of Shatterstar -- now freed from the Mojoverse -- the Morrigan was defeated. But before she departed, she bestowed upon Shatterstar a strange gift...

Meanwhile, Prodigy has been working in secret to solve a murder: his own! But now, it's time for the party of the year...

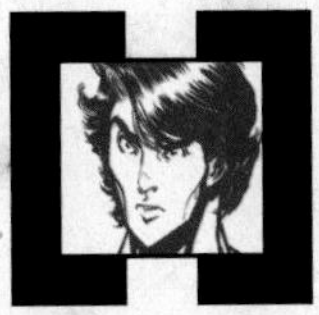
Northstar

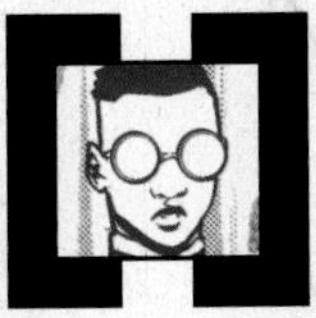
Prodigy

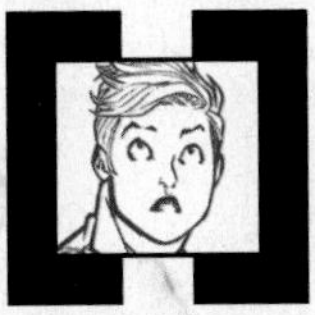
Prestige

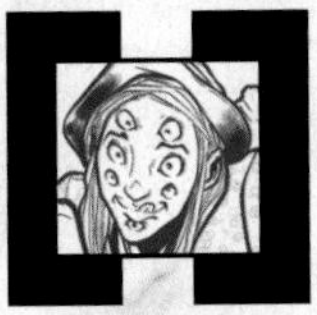
Eye-Boy

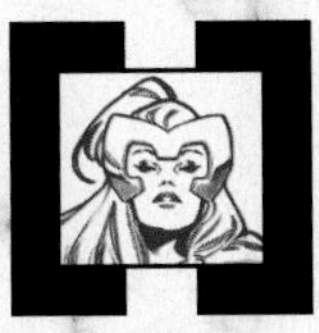
Polaris

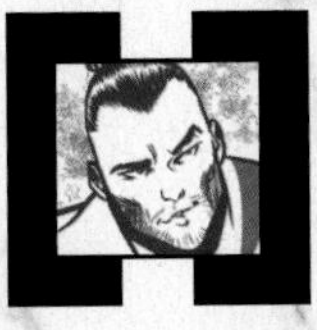
Daken

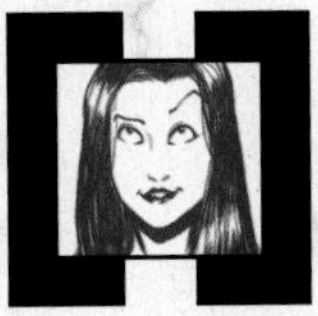
Aurora

Hellfire Gala

The Hellfire Trading Company

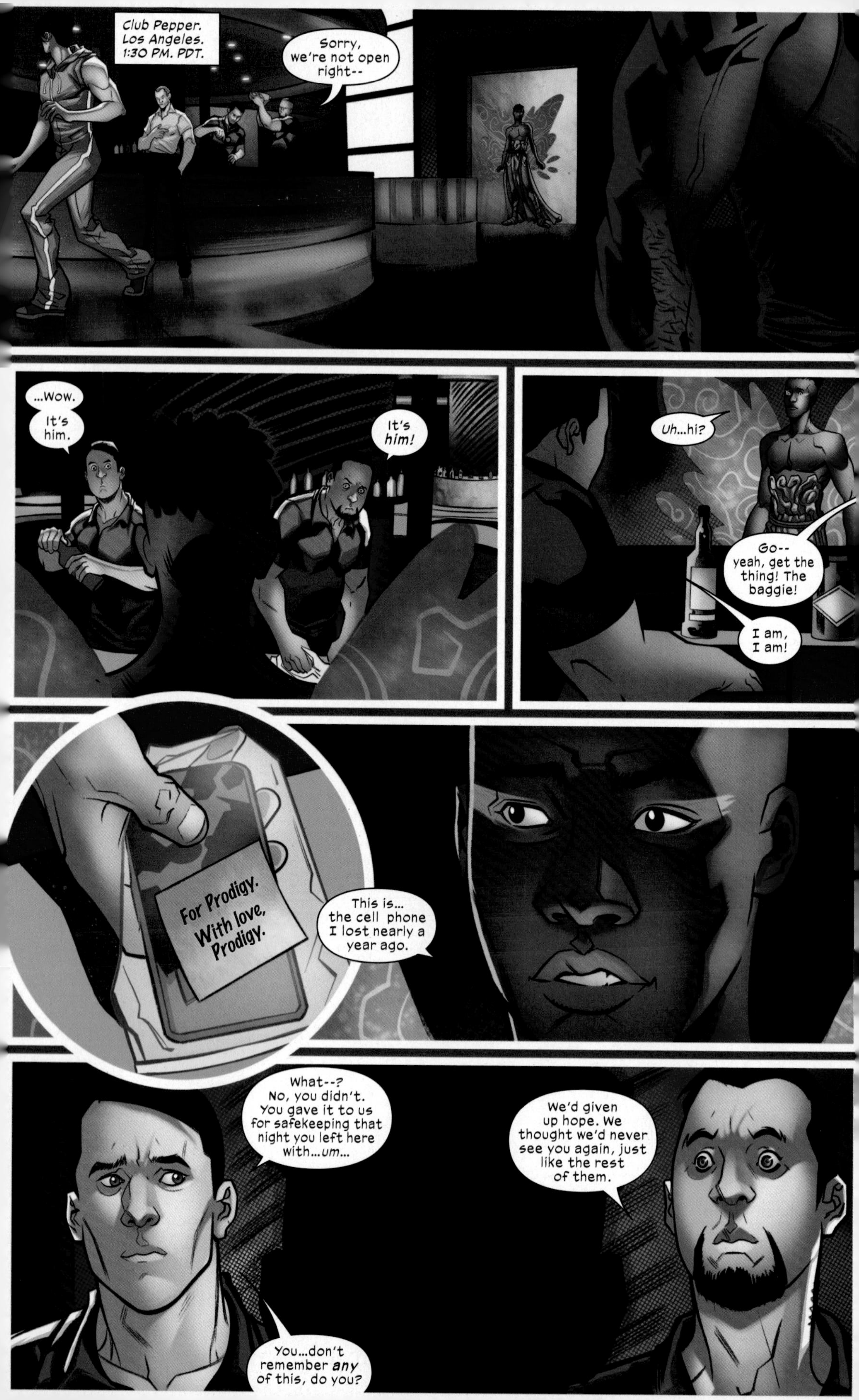
Club Pepper.
Los Angeles.
1:30 PM. PDT.
Sorry, we're not open right--
...Wow.
It's him.
It's *him!*
Uh...hi?
Go-- yeah, get the thing! The baggie!
I am, I am!
For Prodigy.
With love,
Prodigy.
This is... the cell phone I lost nearly a year ago.
What--? No, you didn't. You gave it to us for safekeeping that night you left here with...*um*...
We'd given up hope. We thought we'd never see you again, just like the rest of them.
You...don't remember *any* of this, do you?

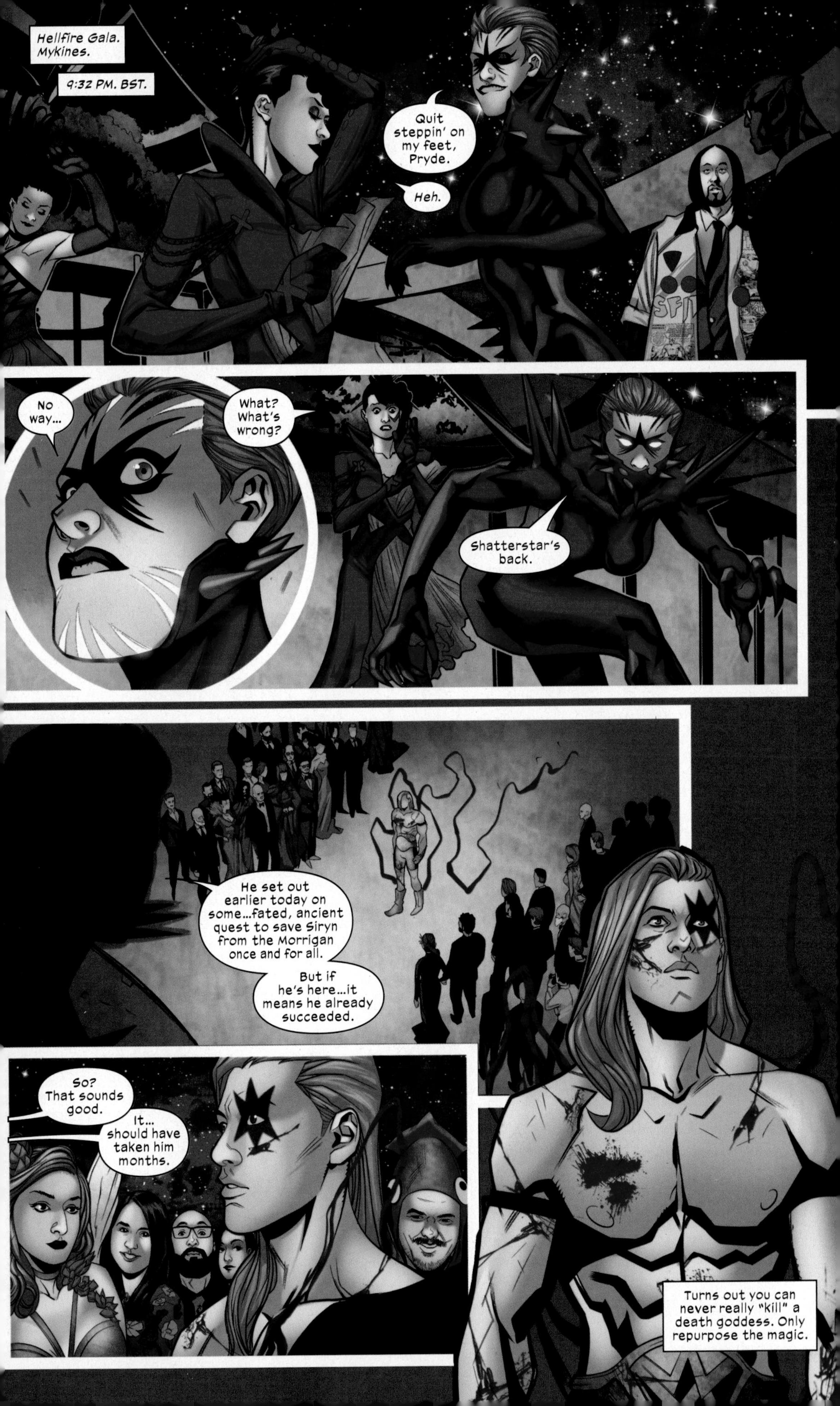

Hellfire Gala. Mykines.
9:32 PM. BST.
Quit steppin' on my feet, Pryde.
Heh.
No way...
What? What's wrong?
Shatterstar's back.
He set out earlier today on some...fated, ancient quest to save Siryn from the Morrigan once and for all.
But if he's here...it means he already succeeded.
So? That sounds good.
It... should have taken him months.
Turns out you can never really "kill" a death goddess. Only repurpose the magic.

Much, much later--we finally had to sit Shatterstar down and ask him to repeat every word the Morrigan said before her defeat.

The Morrigan was correct in saying mutants have no need of a death goddess.

But we *do* die.

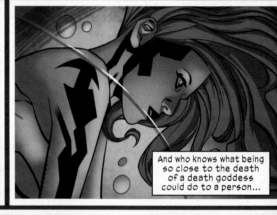

And who knows what being so close to the death of a death goddess could do to a person...

The Morrigan's last words: "To the victor go the spoils."

To see Rictor's perspective of this reunion, check out EXCALIBUR #21!

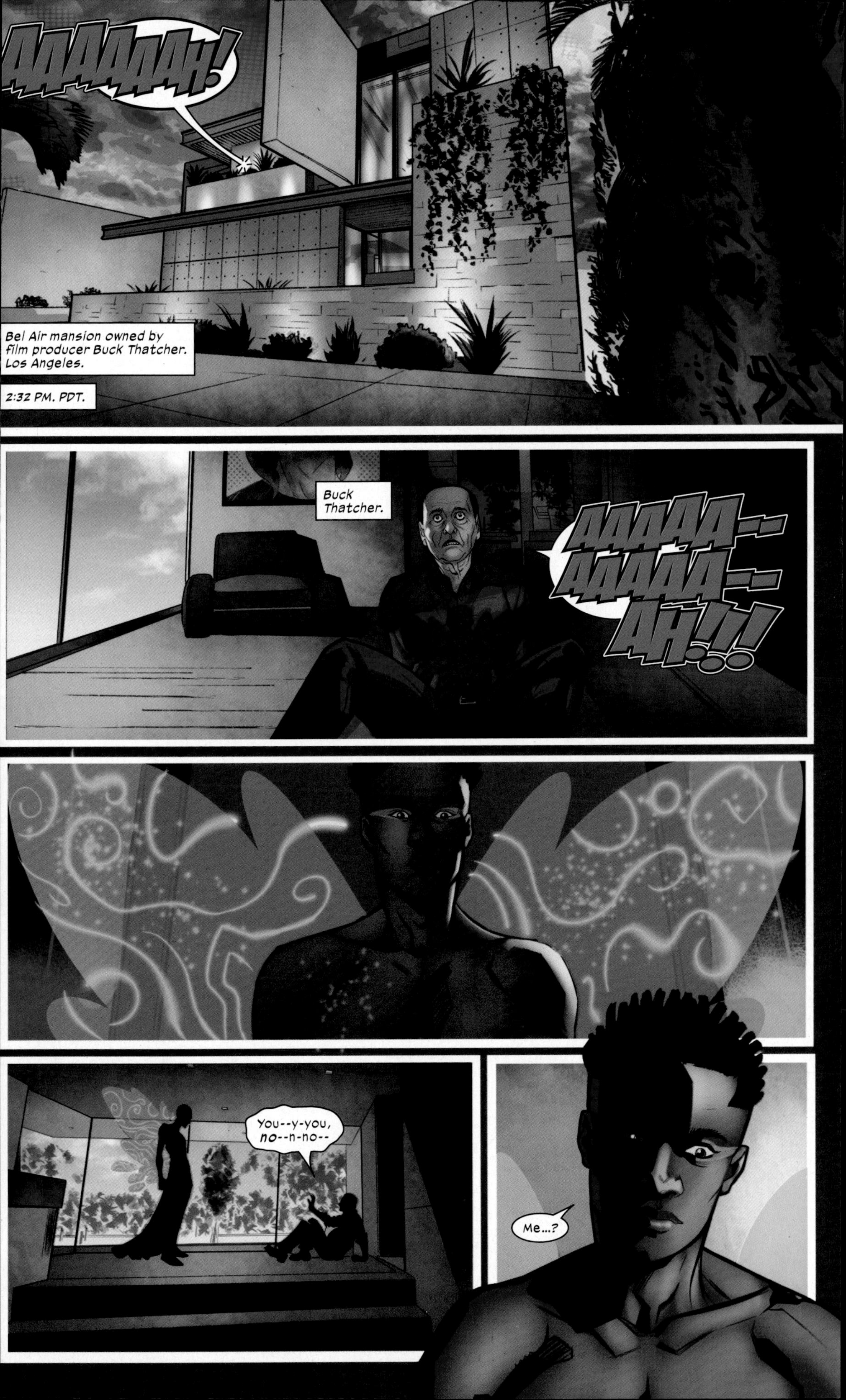
AAAAAAAH!
Bel Air mansion owned by film producer Buck Thatcher. Los Angeles.
2:32 PM. PDT.
Buck Thatcher.
AAAAA--AAAAA--AH!!!
You--y-you, no--n-no--
Me...?

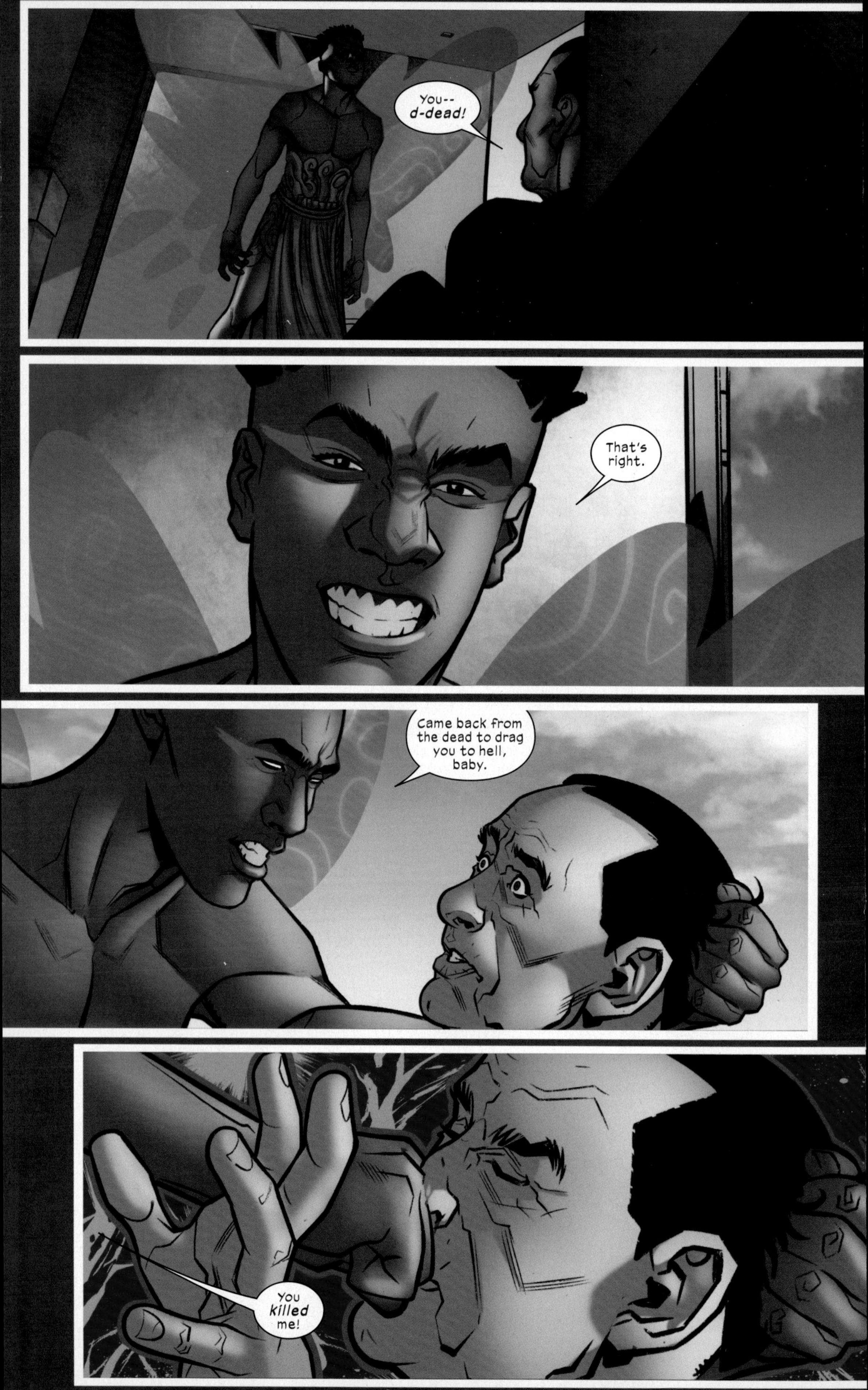
You--
d-dead!
That's right.
Came back from the dead to drag you to hell, baby.
You killed me!

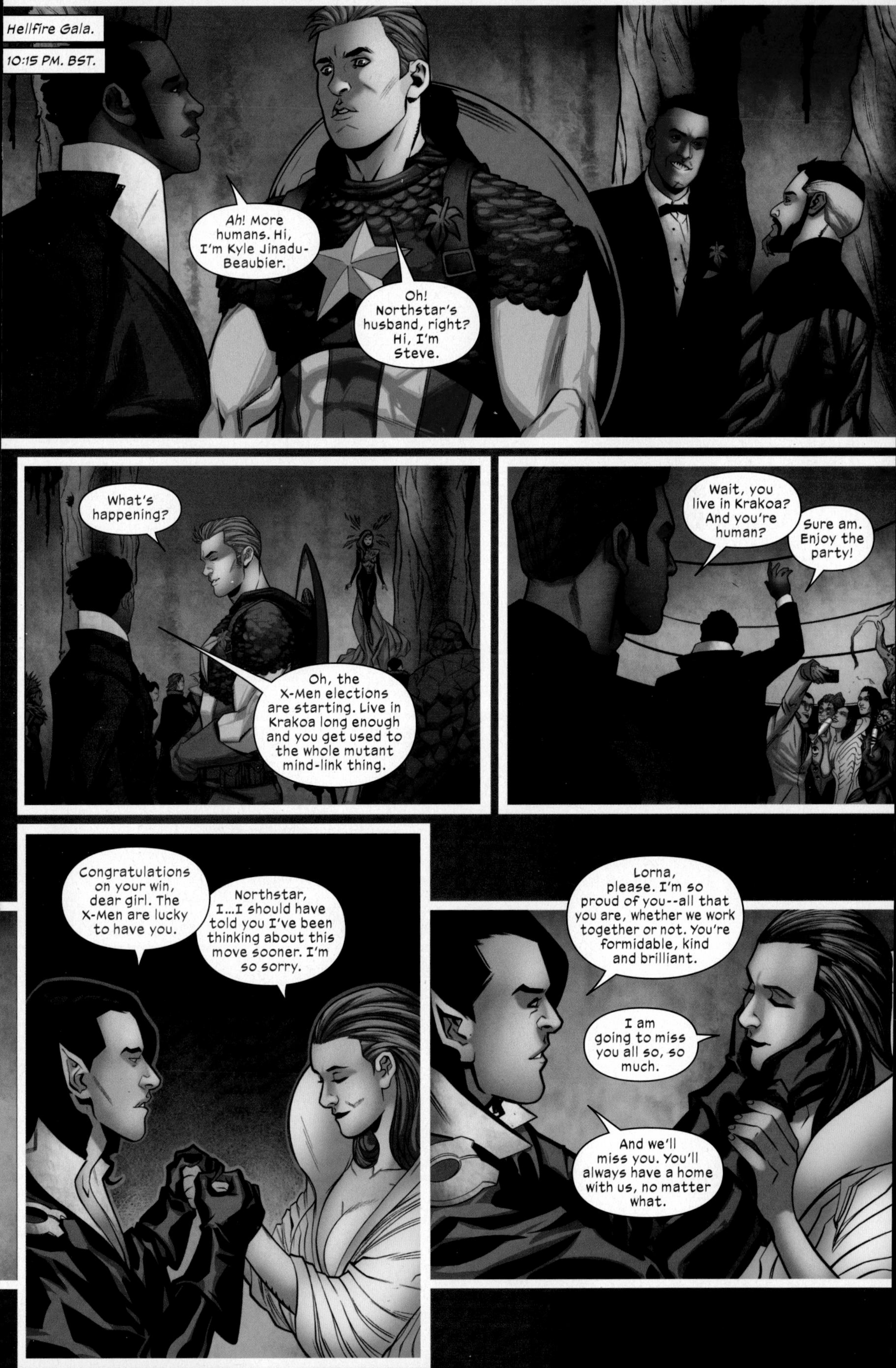
Hellfire Gala.
10:15 PM. BST.
Ah! More humans. Hi, I'm Kyle Jinadu-Beaubier.
Oh! Northstar's husband, right? Hi, I'm Steve.
What's happening?
Oh, the X-Men elections are starting. Live in Krakoa long enough and you get used to the whole mutant mind-link thing.
Wait, you live in Krakoa? And you're human?
Sure am. Enjoy the party!
Congratulations on your win, dear girl. The X-Men are lucky to have you.
Northstar, I...I should have told you I've been thinking about this move sooner. I'm so sorry.
Lorna, please. I'm so proud of you--all that you are, whether we work together or not. You're formidable, kind and brilliant.
I am going to miss you all so, so much.
And we'll miss you. You'll always have a home with us, no matter what.

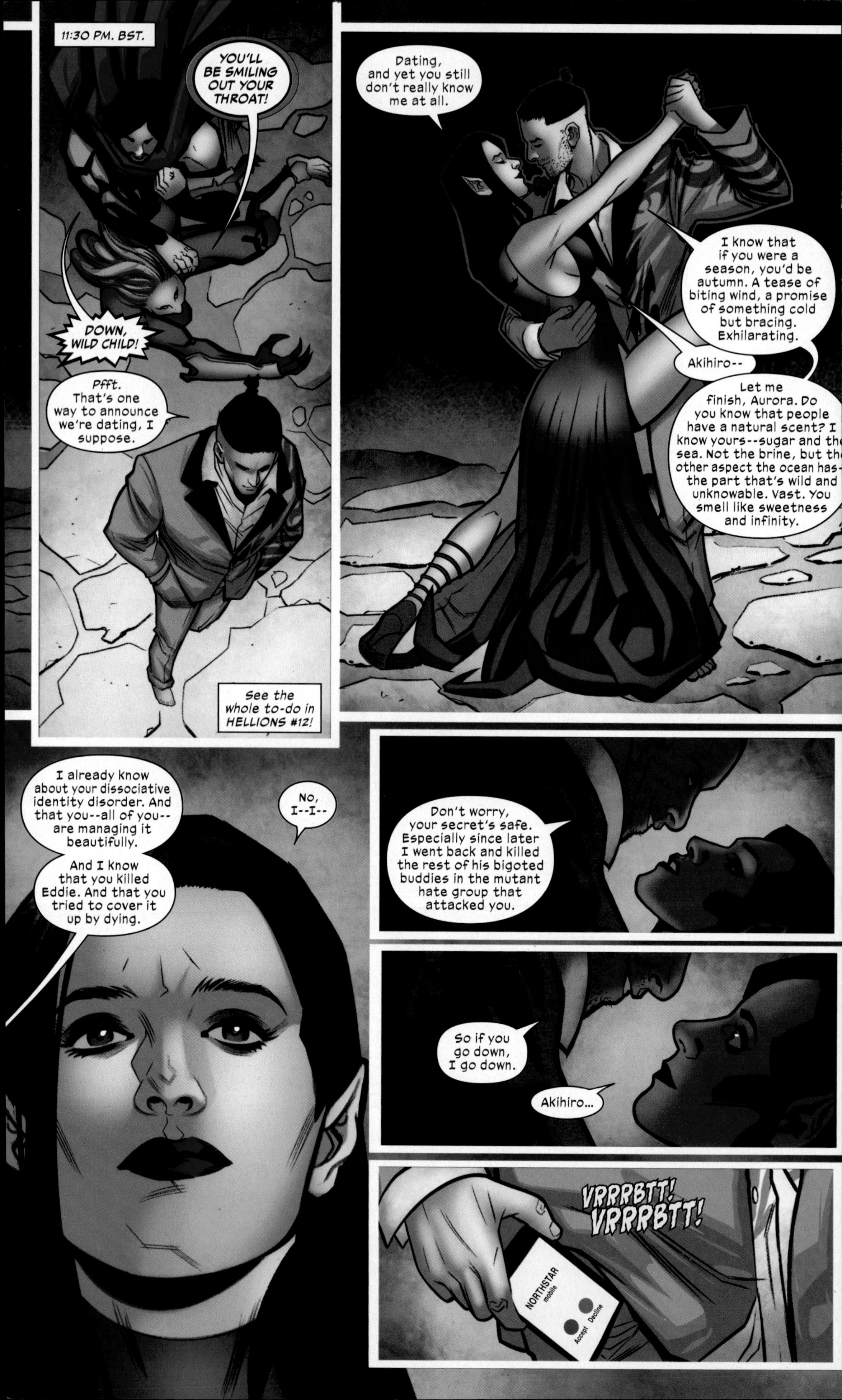
11:30 PM. BST.
YOU'LL BE SMILING OUT YOUR THROAT!
DOWN, WILD CHILD!
Pfft. That's one way to announce we're dating, I suppose.
See the whole to-do in HELLIONS #12!
Dating, and yet you still don't really know me at all.
I know that if you were a season, you'd be autumn. A tease of biting wind, a promise of something cold but bracing. Exhilarating.
Akihiro--
Let me finish, Aurora. Do you know that people have a natural scent? I know yours--sugar and the sea. Not the brine, but the other aspect the ocean has-the part that's wild and unknowable. Vast. You smell like sweetness and infinity.
I already know about your dissociative identity disorder. And that you--all of you--are managing it beautifully.
And I know that you killed Eddie. And that you tried to cover it up by dying.
No, I--I--
Don't worry, your secret's safe. Especially since later I went back and killed the rest of his bigoted buddies in the mutant hate group that attacked you.
So if you go down, I go down.
Akihiro...
VRRRBTT! VRRRBTT!
NORTHSTAR mobile
Accept Decline

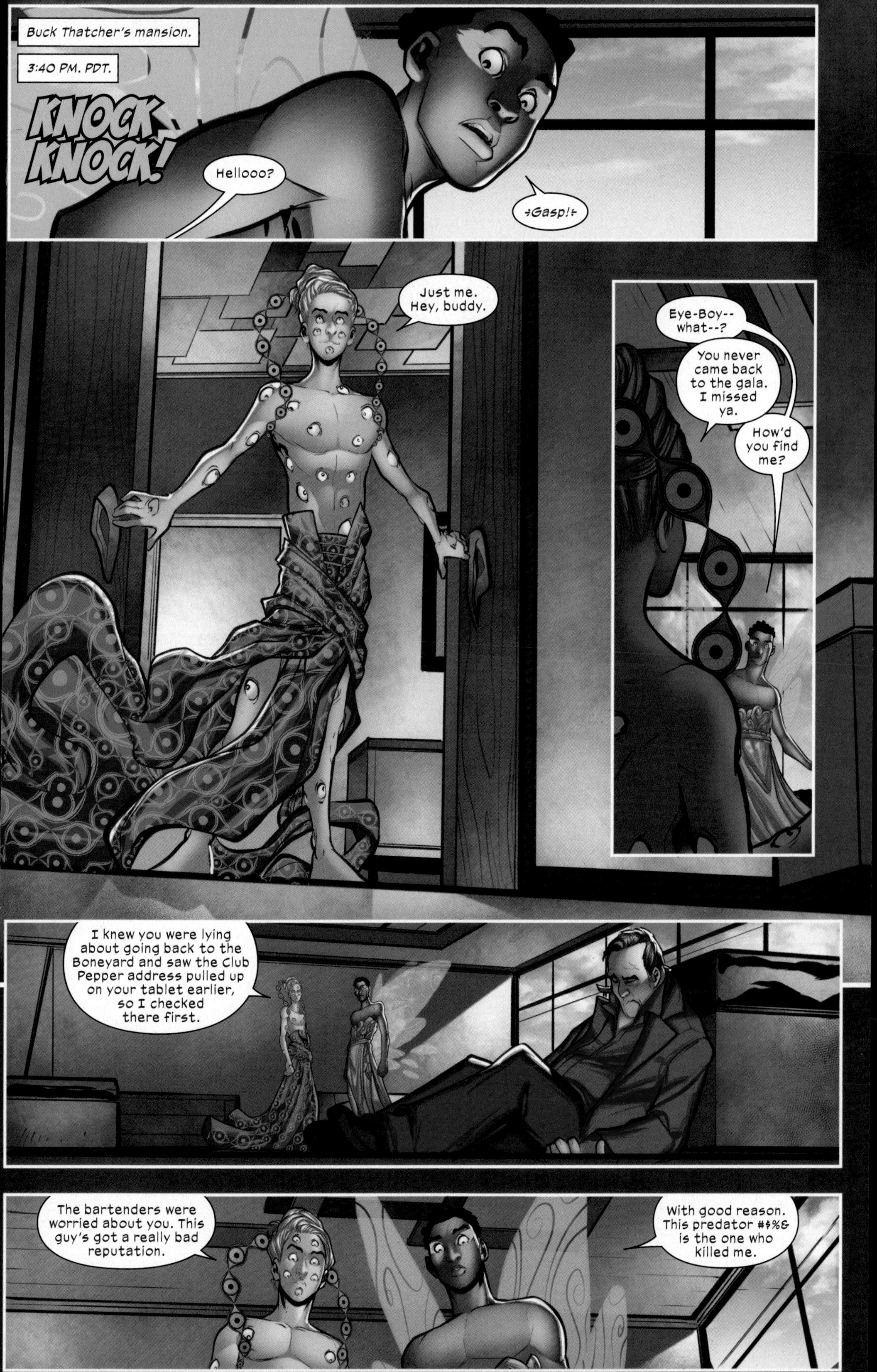

Buck Thatcher's mansion.
3:40 PM. PDT.
KNOCK KNOCK!
Hellooo?
-Gasp!-
Just me. Hey, buddy.
Eye-Boy-- what--?
You never came back to the gala. I missed ya.
How'd you find me?
I knew you were lying about going back to the Boneyard and saw the Club Pepper address pulled up on your tablet earlier, so I checked there first.
The bartenders were worried about you. This guy's got a really bad reputation.
With good reason. This predator #$%& is the one who killed me.

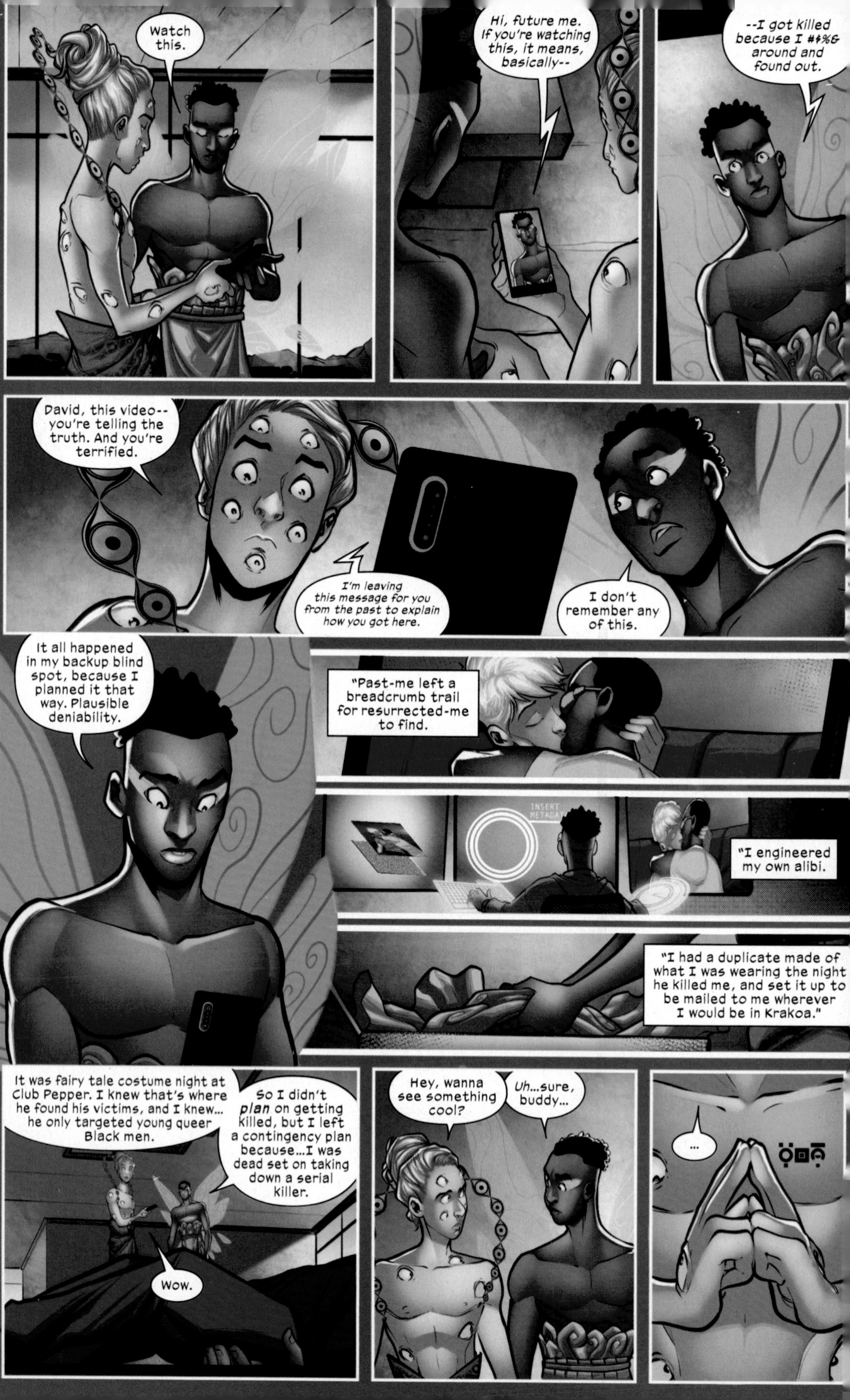
Watch this.
Hi, future me. If you're watching this, it means, basically--
--I got killed because I #$%& around and found out.
David, this video--you're telling the truth. And you're terrified.
I'm leaving this message for you from the past to explain how you got here.
I don't remember any of this.
It all happened in my backup blind spot, because I planned it that way. Plausible deniability.
"Past-me left a breadcrumb trail for resurrected-me to find.
INSERT METADATA
"I engineered my own alibi.
"I had a duplicate made of what I was wearing the night he killed me, and set it up to be mailed to me wherever I would be in Krakoa."
It was fairy tale costume night at Club Pepper. I knew that's where he found his victims, and I knew... he only targeted young queer Black men.
So I didn't *plan* on getting killed, but I left a contingency plan because...I was dead set on taking down a serial killer.
Wow.
Hey, wanna see something cool?
Uh...sure, buddy...
...

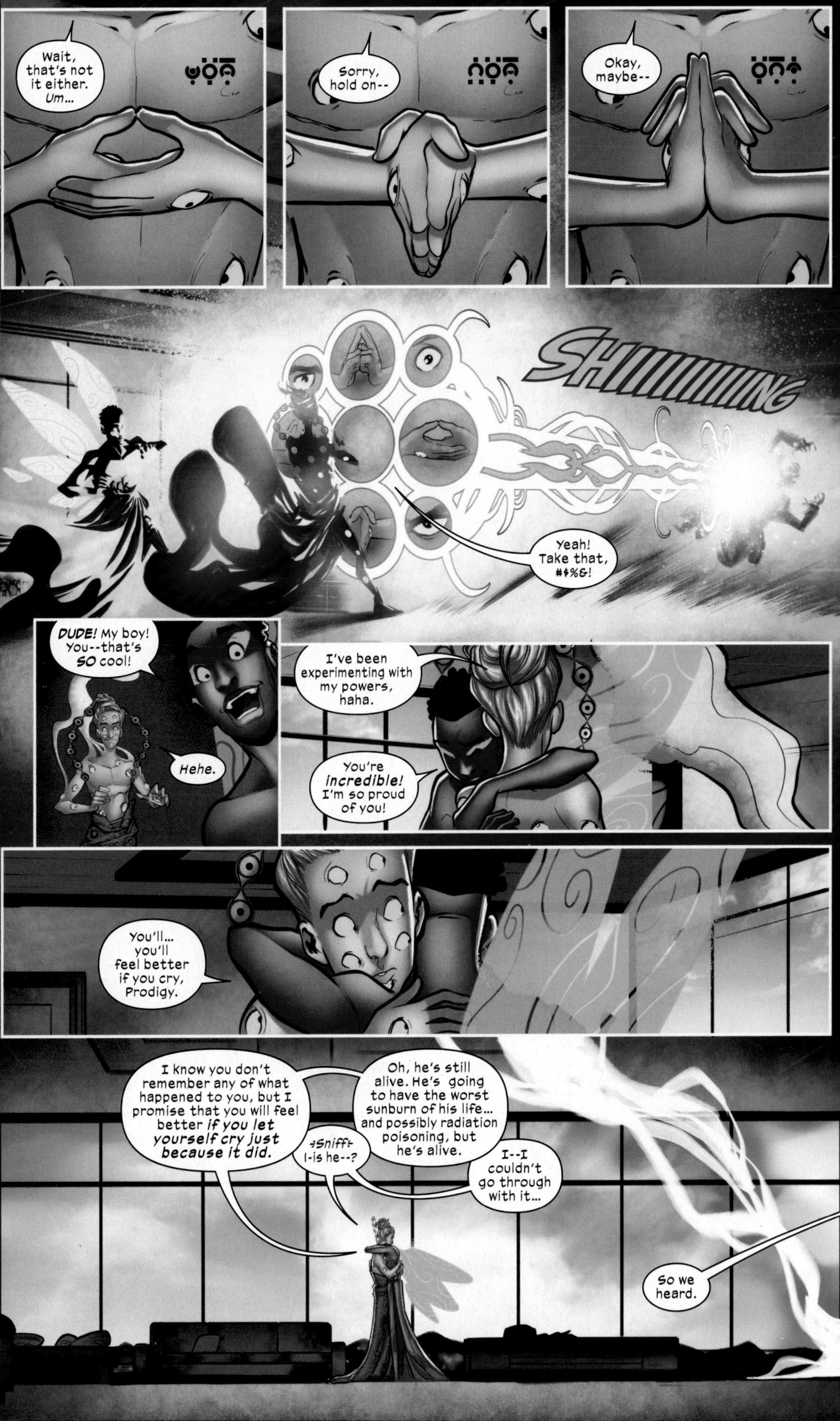
Wait, that's not it either. Um...
Sorry, hold on--
Okay, maybe--
SHIIIIIIIIIING
Yeah! Take that, #$%&!
DUDE! My boy! You--that's SO cool!
Hehe.
I've been experimenting with my powers, haha.
You're incredible! I'm so proud of you!
You'll... you'll feel better if you cry, Prodigy.
I know you don't remember any of what happened to you, but I promise that you will feel better if you let yourself cry just because it did.
Oh, he's still alive. He's going to have the worst sunburn of his life... and possibly radiation poisoning, but he's alive.
Sniff I-is he--?
I--I couldn't go through with it...
So we heard.

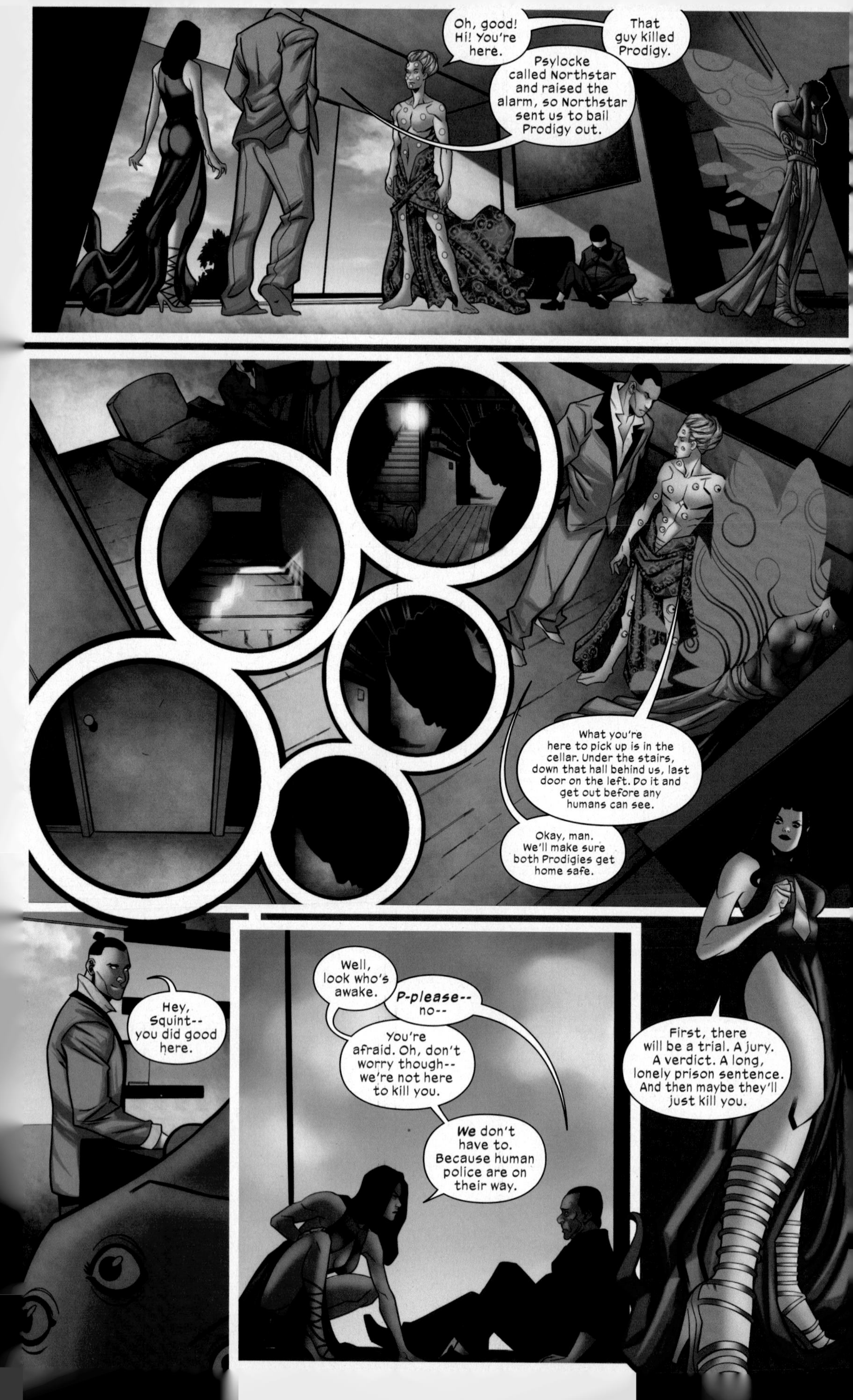
Oh, good! Hi! You're here.
That guy killed Prodigy.
Psylocke called Northstar and raised the alarm, so Northstar sent us to bail Prodigy out.
What you're here to pick up is in the cellar. Under the stairs, down that hall behind us, last door on the left. Do it and get out before any humans can see.
Okay, man. We'll make sure both Prodigies get home safe.
Hey, Squint-- you did good here.
Well, look who's awake.
P-please-- no--
You're afraid. Oh, don't worry though-- we're not here to kill you.
We don't have to. Because human police are on their way.
First, there will be a trial. A jury. A verdict. A long, lonely prison sentence. And then maybe they'll just kill you.

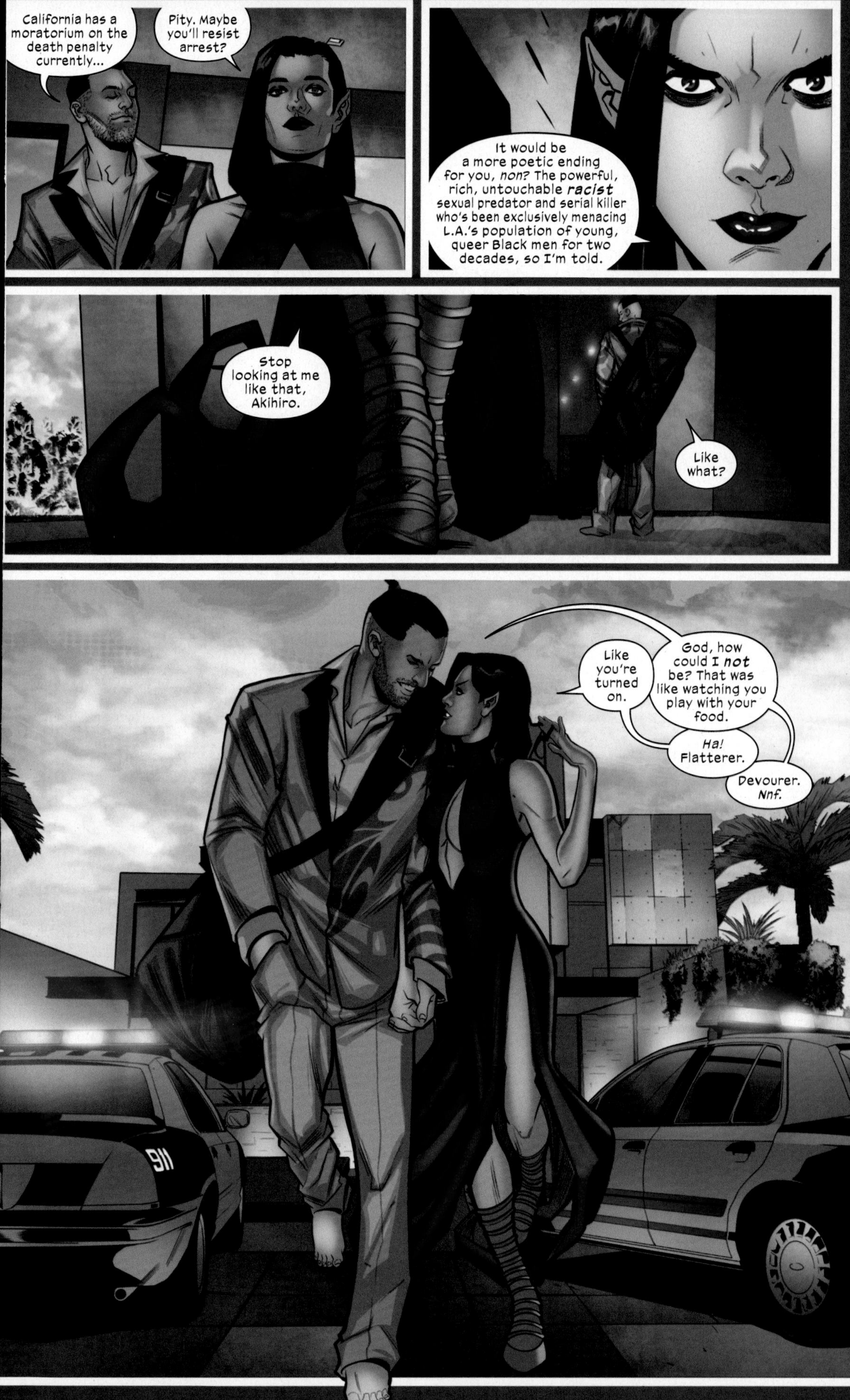
California has a moratorium on the death penalty currently...
Pity. Maybe you'll resist arrest?
It would be a more poetic ending for you, *non?* The powerful, rich, untouchable ***racist*** sexual predator and serial killer who's been exclusively menacing L.A.'s population of young, queer Black men for two decades, so I'm told.
Stop looking at me like that, Akihiro.
Like what?
Like you're turned on.
God, how could I ***not*** be? That was like watching you play with your food.
Ha! Flatterer.
Devourer. *Nnf.*
911

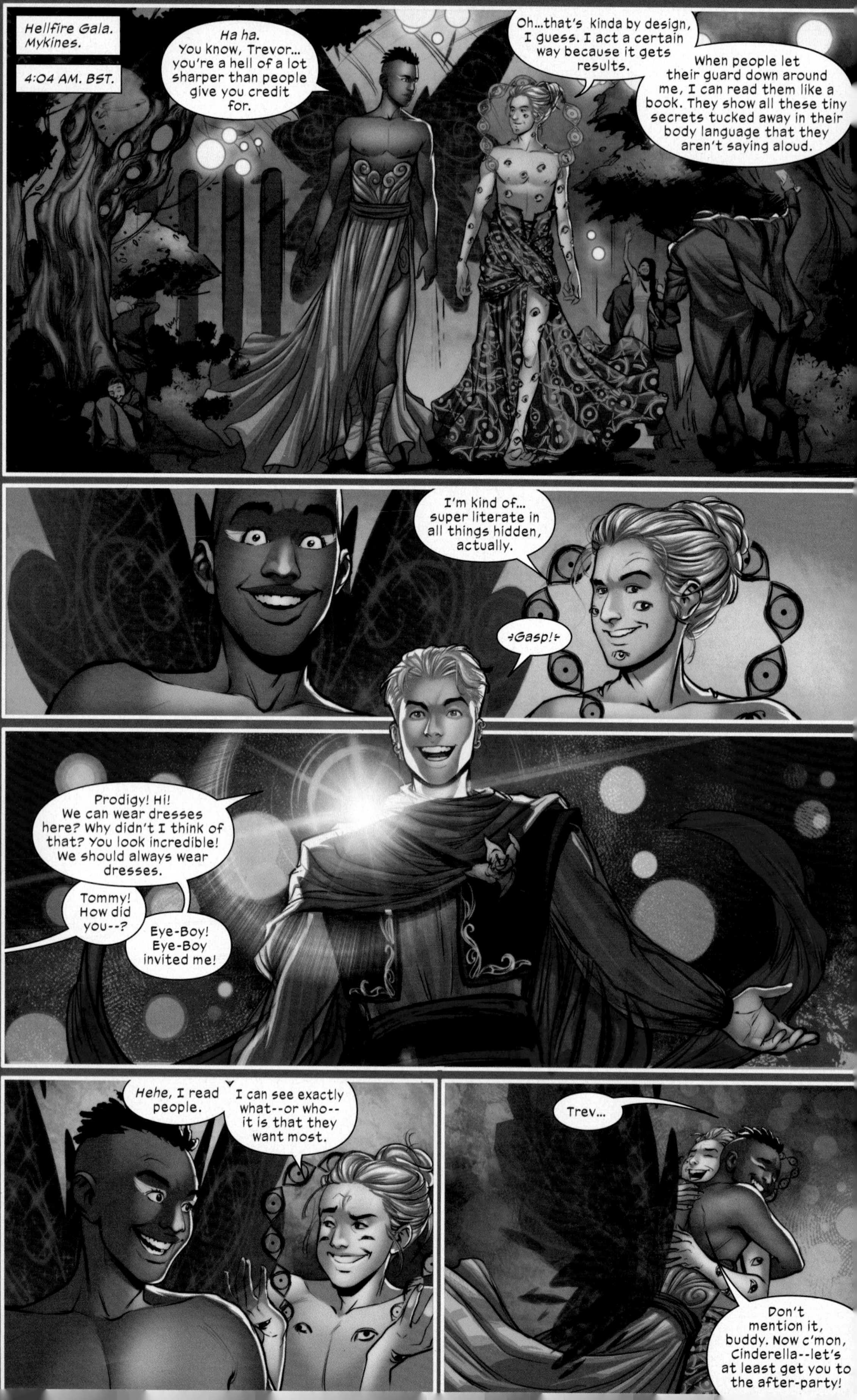
Hellfire Gala. Mykines.
4:04 AM. BST.
Ha ha. You know, Trevor... you're a hell of a lot sharper than people give you credit for.
Oh...that's kinda by design, I guess. I act a certain way because it gets results.
When people let their guard down around me, I can read them like a book. They show all these tiny secrets tucked away in their body language that they aren't saying aloud.
I'm kind of... super literate in all things hidden, actually.
‡Gasp!‡
Prodigy! Hi! We can wear dresses here? Why didn't I think of that? You look incredible! We should always wear dresses.
Tommy! How did you--?
Eye-Boy! Eye-Boy invited me!
Hehe, I read people.
I can see exactly what--or who--it is that they want most.
Trev...
Don't mention it, buddy. Now c'mon, Cinderella--let's at least get you to the after-party!

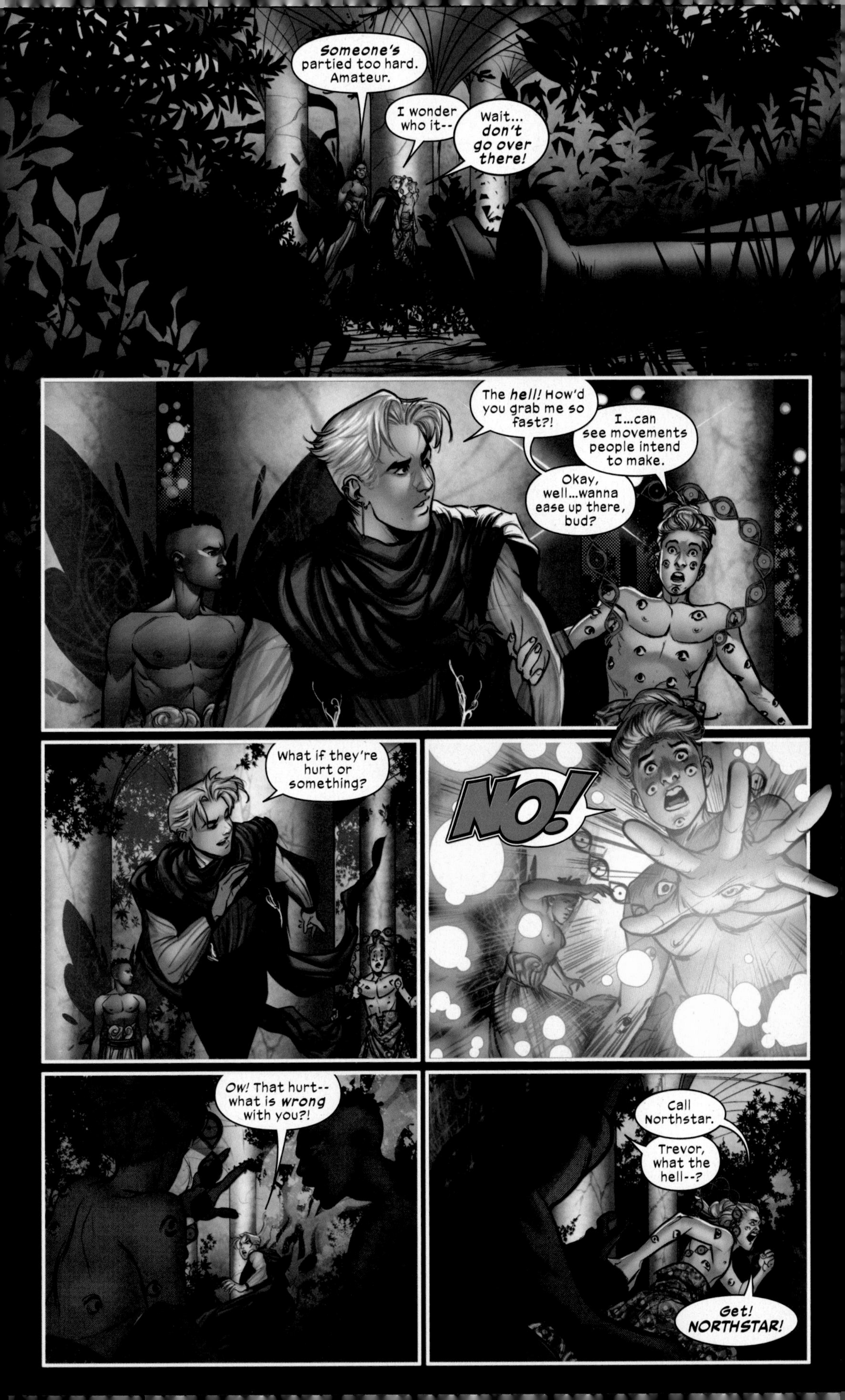
Someone's partied too hard. Amateur.
I wonder who it--
Wait... don't go over there!
The hell! How'd you grab me so fast?!
I...can see movements people intend to make.
Okay, well...wanna ease up there, bud?
What if they're hurt or something?
NO!
Ow! That hurt--what is wrong with you?!
Call Northstar.
Trevor, what the hell--?
Get! NORTHSTAR!

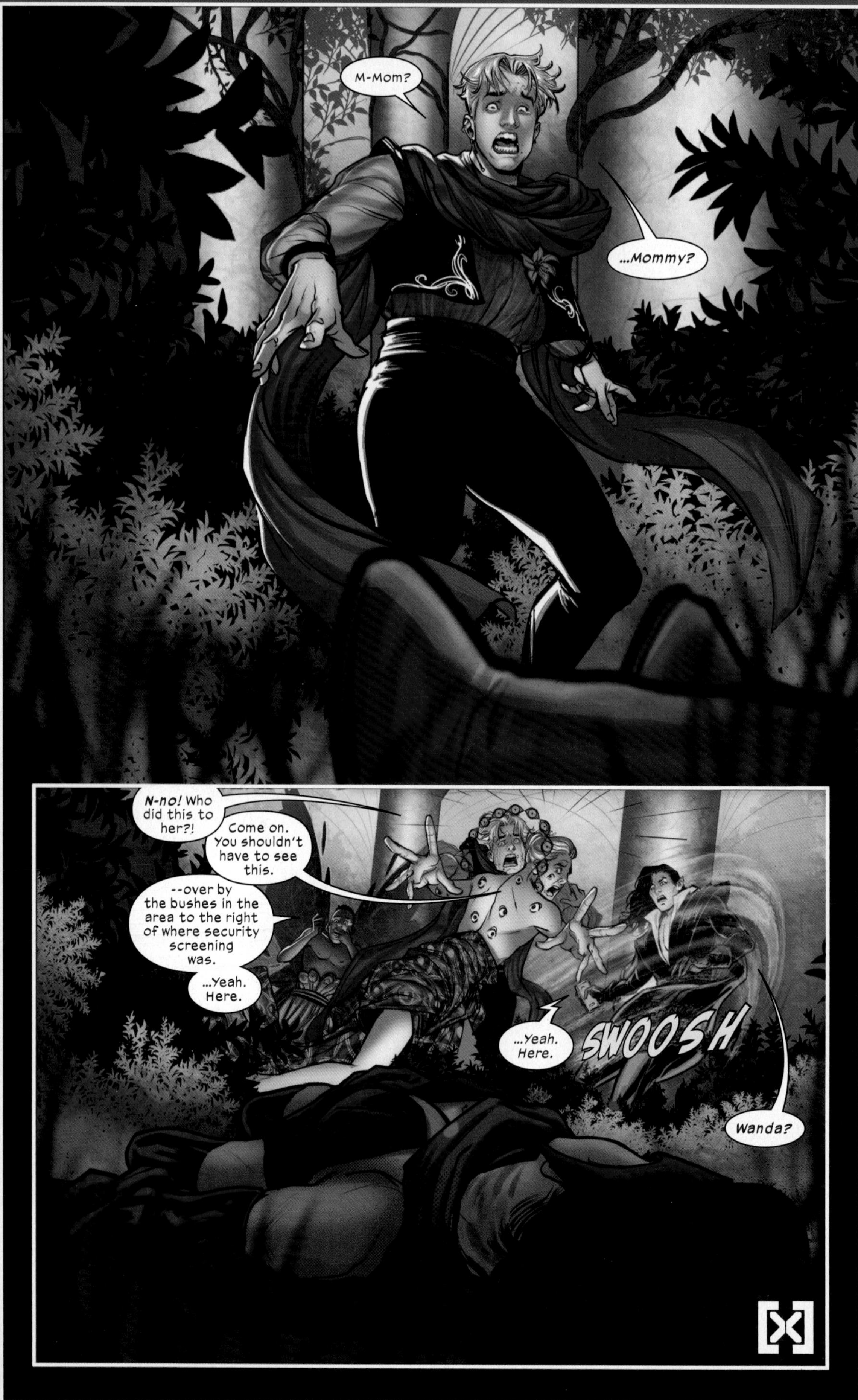
M-Mom?
...Mommy?
N-no! Who did this to her?!
Come on. You shouldn't have to see this.
--over by the bushes in the area to the right of where security screening was.
...Yeah. Here.
...Yeah. Here.
SWOOSH
Wanda?

It has been hard to say goodbye this time.

It always is. You dive deep in this job. It's a lot of hours spent with these characters. Lots of thought and energy devoted to getting to know them intimately, so you can properly convey everything that has to be told and then some. And that's okay. It's part of the job, as it is to accept the fact that the deep dive is going to end someday and eventually you're going to have to leave all these people you care for so much...no matter how much you pour into them. And believe me, it happens every time you leave a book.

But in this case...it stung a little more. These were very much our kids. It very much felt like we were holding their hands during a journey of recovery, of acceptance, of rebirth (I mean, it made sense; this is the resurrection book, right?). It's always hard. It was harder this time. And not only because we went deep with them. We could feel this story meant a lot to a lot of people out there. That it connected in a very special way. That it was not only entertainment (which is a lot to hope for in itself, honestly), but it reached a little farther. A little deeper.

I'm going to miss my X-Factor kids so much. Jean-Paul, Jeanne-Marie, Akihiro, Lorna, David, Trevor, Rachel and Amazing Baby have become such an important part of my life for the last year and a half, I've come to know them so well that it honestly feels like some family member has left and is not around anymore.

But mostly, I'm going to miss my team of partners in crime. Jordan and Annalise, Jake and Shannon, who were kind enough to invite me in to play in this sandbox and get away with so much. Joe Caramagna, who has lettered in a consistently brilliant way and has performed the impossible at least four times, by my count. Tom Muller, who is, simply put, a genius. The magician from another dimension that is Israel Silva, who has elevated every single page of this book and gave me that warm feeling that comes with knowing that, whatever I did on the page, he was going to make it look perfect.

And of course I'm going to miss Leah. So much. Her brilliance, her smarts, her beautifully emotional characters, the constant challenge to catch up with her genius. And the notes in the scripts. Seriously, guys, you don't know what you're missing. Leah has made me learn decades' worth of comic books in just a couple of years and change, all while having a blast and making a friend.

And I'm going to miss you -- all the people who have made me feel that this was, indeed, a special book. Thank you so much for that.

Yeah, it's been hard to say goodbye this time.

What a privilege.

-- David Baldeón

Dear reader,

I know some may think that X-FACTOR's end comes as a direct result of losing Polaris to the X-Men election, but here's the truth of what happened: When all of the X-office writers and editors were mulling over who would be good candidates for the first-ever X-Men team election, I suggested her. Jordan D. White, Senior X-Editor, then asked me, "Are you sure?" and I explained how we could change plans to accommodate her absence from X-Factor. And then Gerry Duggan asked me again, "Are you sure?" and I, just thinking of how good an opportunity

this would be for Lorna to shine, said yes again. No hesitation. I fully trusted that Uncle Gerry would write the hell out of her. Something the X-office excels at is pivoting and changing plans as a group -- we trust each other and take counsel with each other.

X-FACTOR was the most creatively fulfilling and rewarding endeavor of my professional career. One of the reasons for this is the community and camaraderie between all my X-office peers -- I cherish them all so much that I'm actually struggling to put into words how much my colleagues mean to me. These people are my favorite people. I feel a novel's worth of words lurking in me about that but lack the space and time here to explain. During the COVID lockdown, I got into the habit of checking the X-Slack first thing in the morning because of the grounding and encouraging conversations I'd find there upon waking. (The Brits and Gerry tend to be more active while the rest of us sleep.) Every day, I continue to find delight in how compassionate, brilliant and witty these folks are.

Eventually, I made an X-Factor slack for David Baldeón and I to start collaborating more closely -- and to move our lengthy Twitter DM conversations, where we conspire over book plans, to a less distracting venue. The X-Fac-Slack became another haven for me in 2020, and working with David has made me a better writer.

The last outing I had before the pandemic was C2E2 in March of 2020. It was such a phenomenal time -- getting to see almost the whole X-office squad, doing a panel together and then following it up with an X-summit -- that throughout the pandemic, the memory felt like a fever dream. Every couple of weeks, Tini and Vita and I would joke with each other, "Remember C2E2?" because it's the last time we saw each other or got to interact with readers.

Tini, Vita and I independently made the same picture of the three of us our tablet background screens without consulting one another. Something became very clear to us all during the pandemic -- not just me, Tini, and Vita, but also Jon, Ben, Zeb and Al -- the fact that as X-writers, we were helping by giving readers a safe place to escape to in the form of Krakoa.

That became my greatest wish in writing X-FACTOR during the pandemic and all of the turmoil the past year -- I wanted to give you all a safe place to retreat. I wanted you all to feel welcome in Krakoa and know that you belong there. I wanted you to feel the community and camaraderie that I feel with my peers and know without a doubt that you belong. I wanted to keep the gates open for you for as long as I could.

It's been an honor.

You can spot the cast of X-FACTOR in their biggest and baddest last investigation throughout TRIAL OF MAGNETO, out August 2021.

With my whole heart,

Leah Williams

#scripting-sandbox   December 4, 2020

David Baldeón (12:55AM): I've said it to you and I'll say it here again: This is the most rewarding creative experience I've ever had, and being invited into your headspace -- everyone's headspace! -- is a privilege. Can't thank you guys enough for that. 😀

Leah Williams (12:56AM): Ugh, dude, same on all counts. 😐 It feels like we're only juuuuuust getting started on creating something incredibly grand in here, and I wish we'd started working like this sooner, haha.

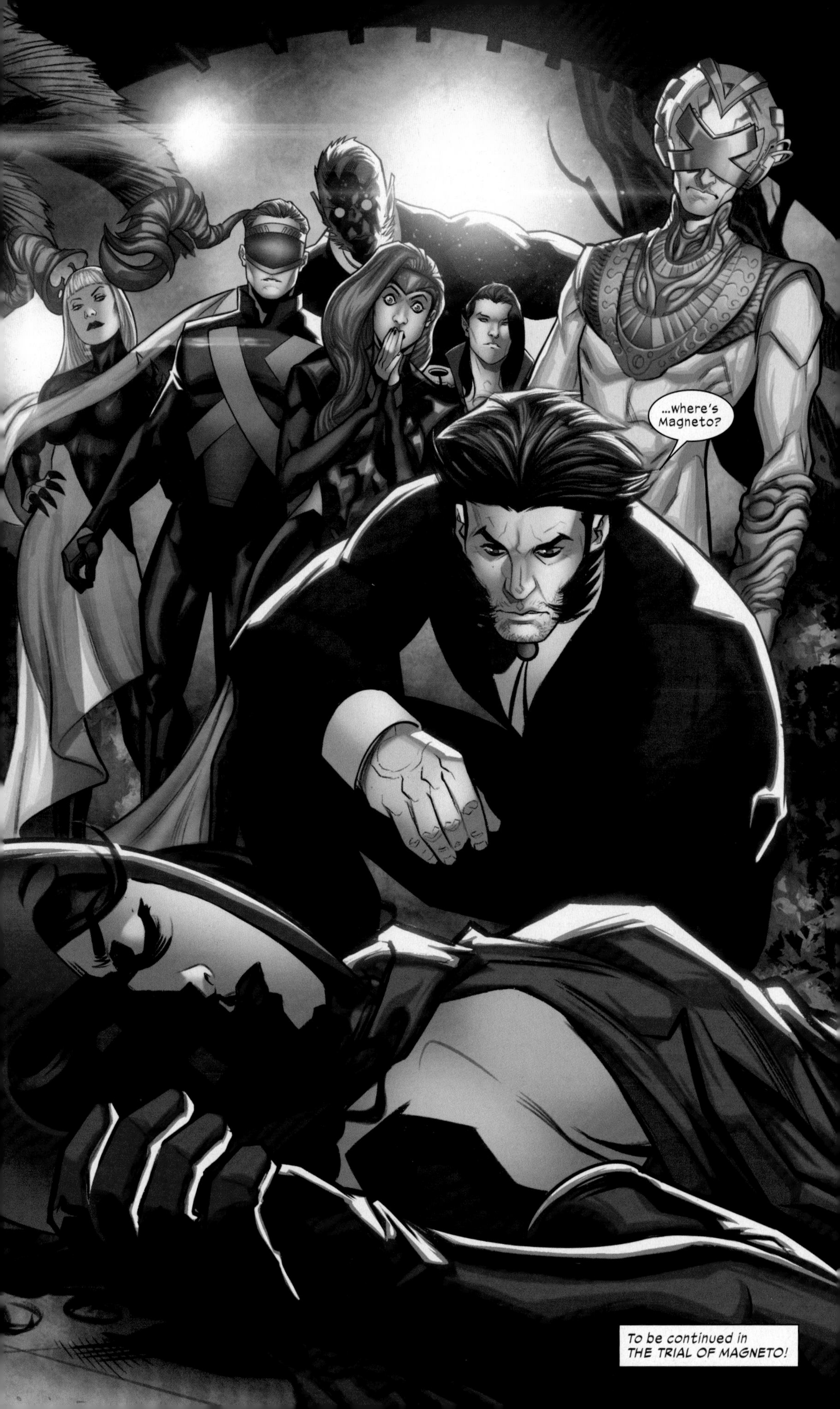

...where's Magneto?
To be continued in THE TRIAL OF MAGNETO!

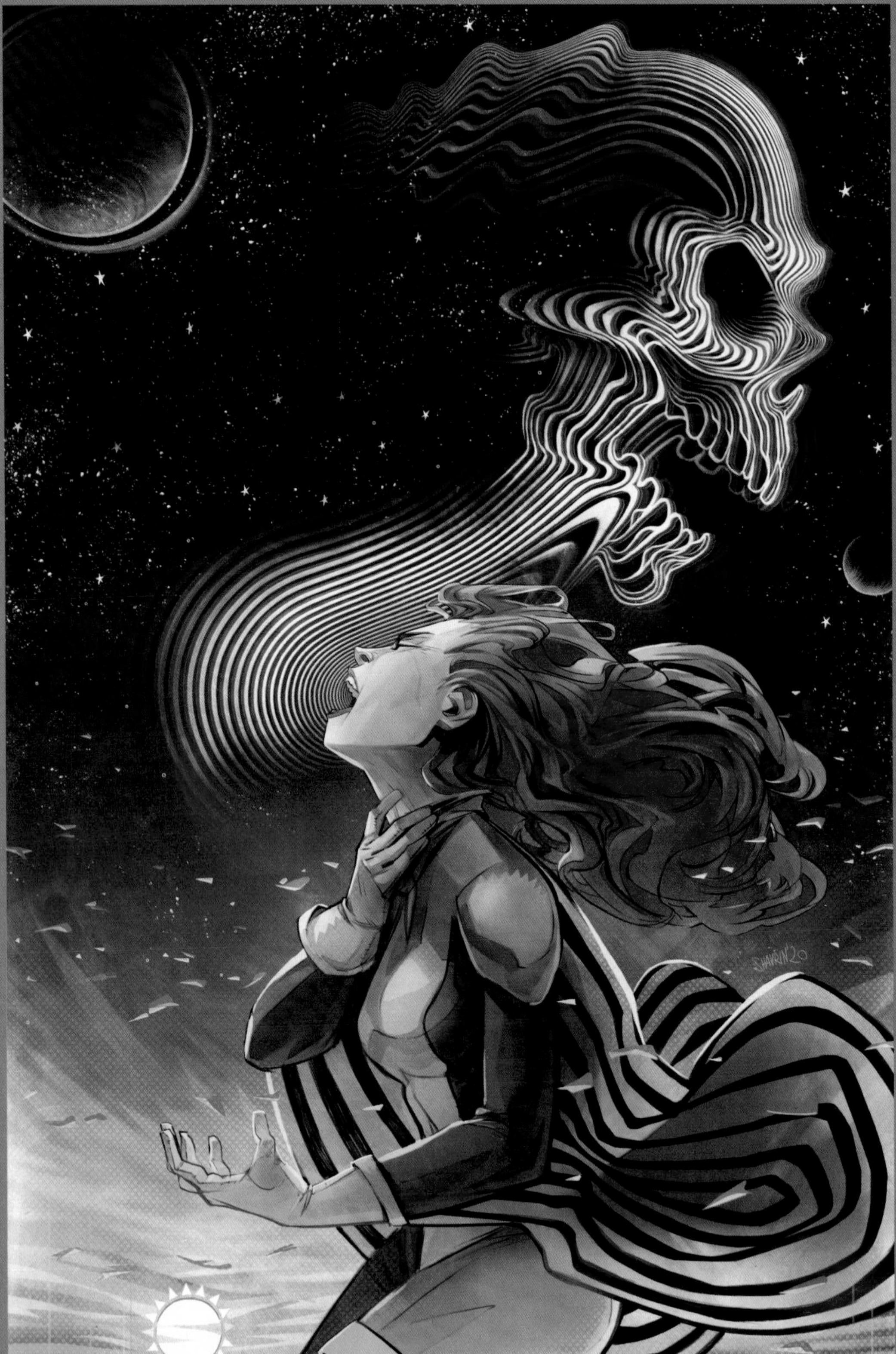
SHAVRIN'20

X-Factor #6 by Ivan Shavrin

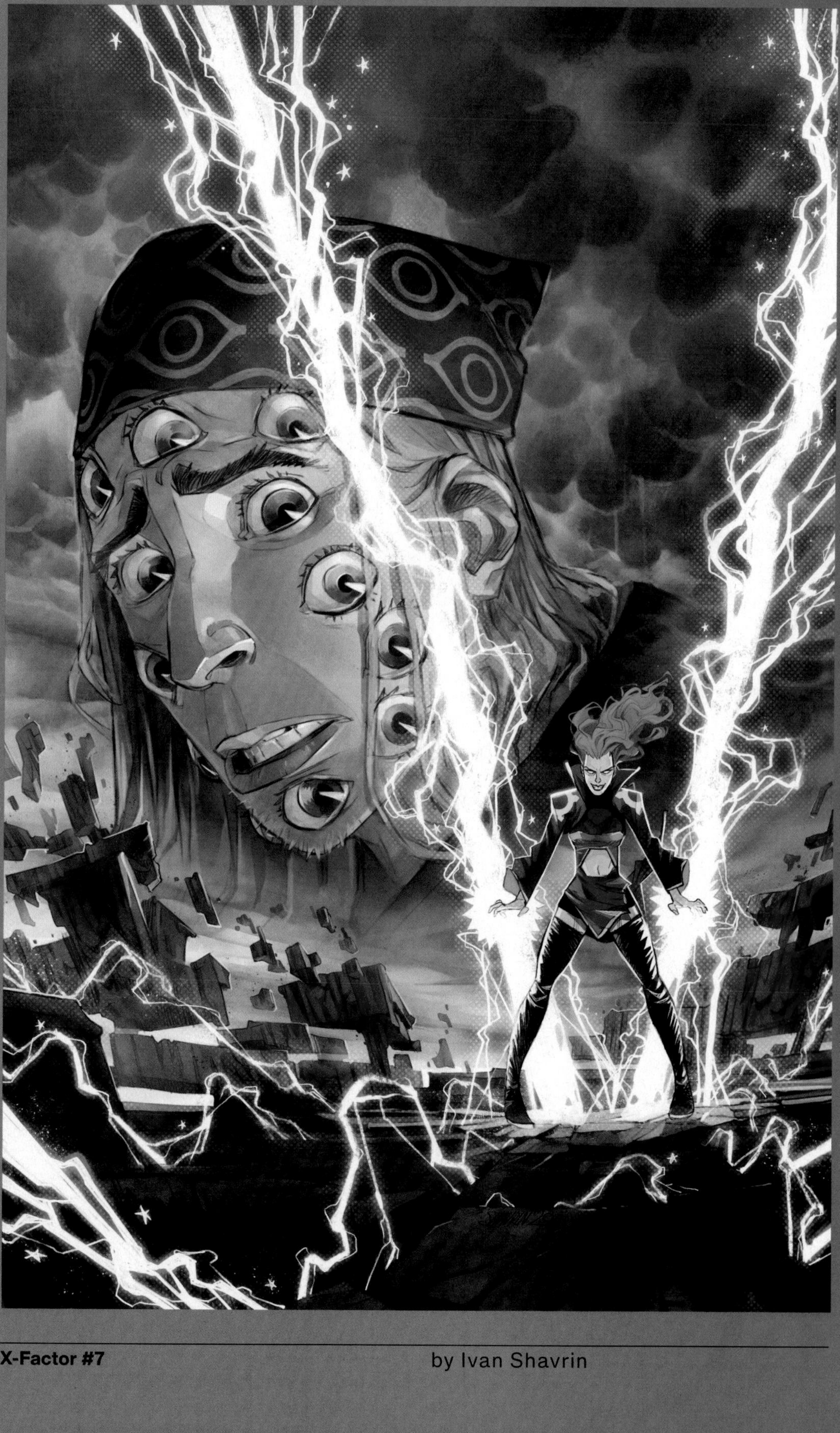

X-Factor #7 by Ivan Shavrin

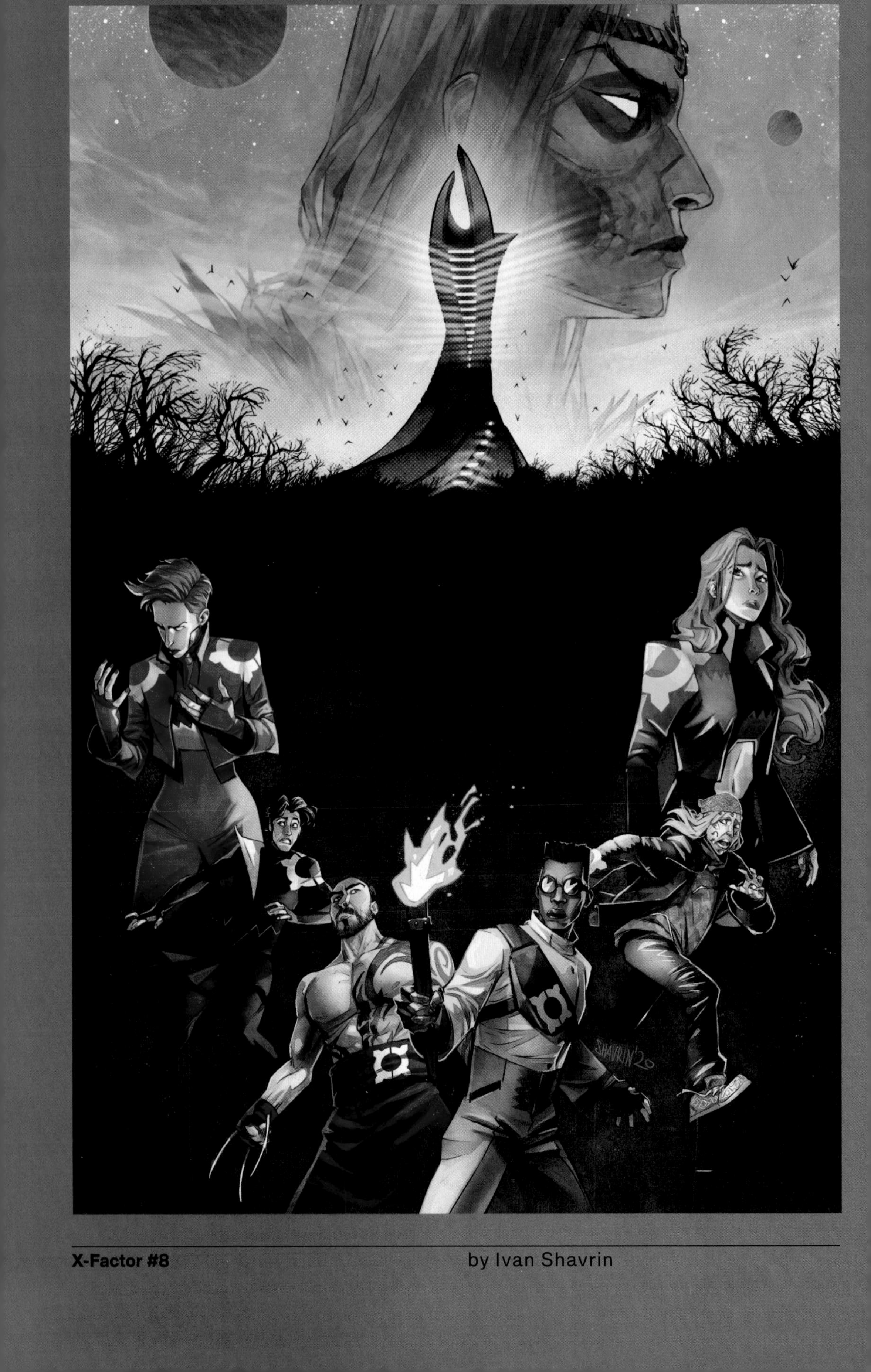
SHAVRIN'20

X-Factor #8 by Ivan Shavrin

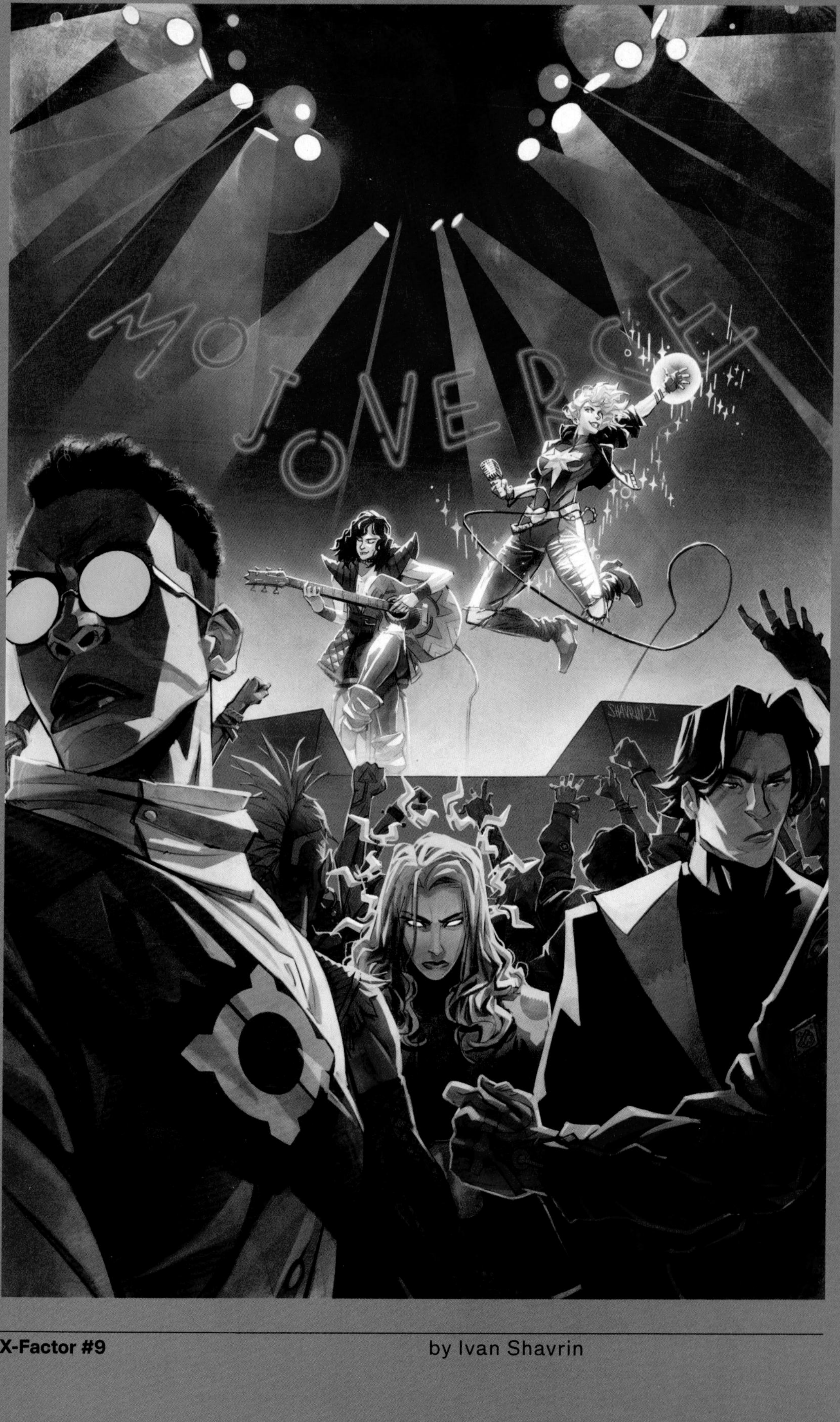
MOJOVERSE
SHAVRIN'21

X-Factor #9 by Ivan Shavrin

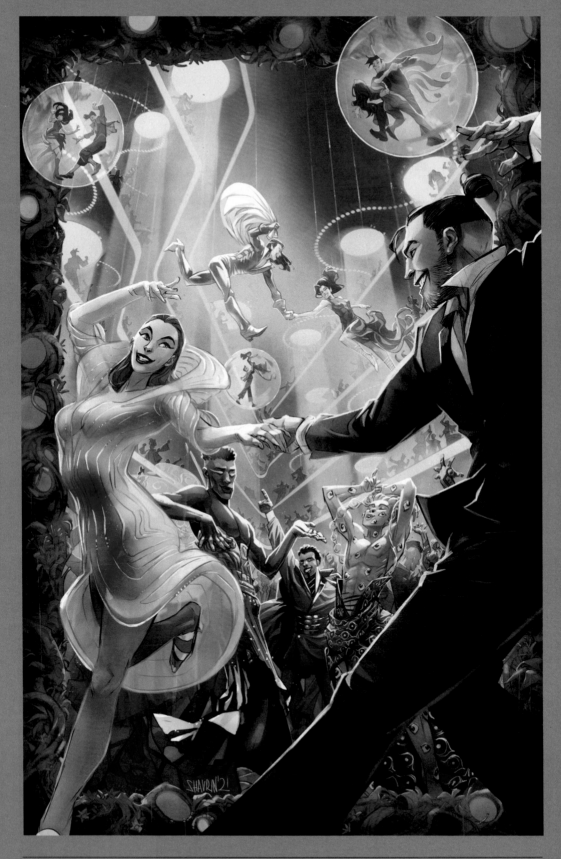

X-Factor #10 by Ivan Shavrin

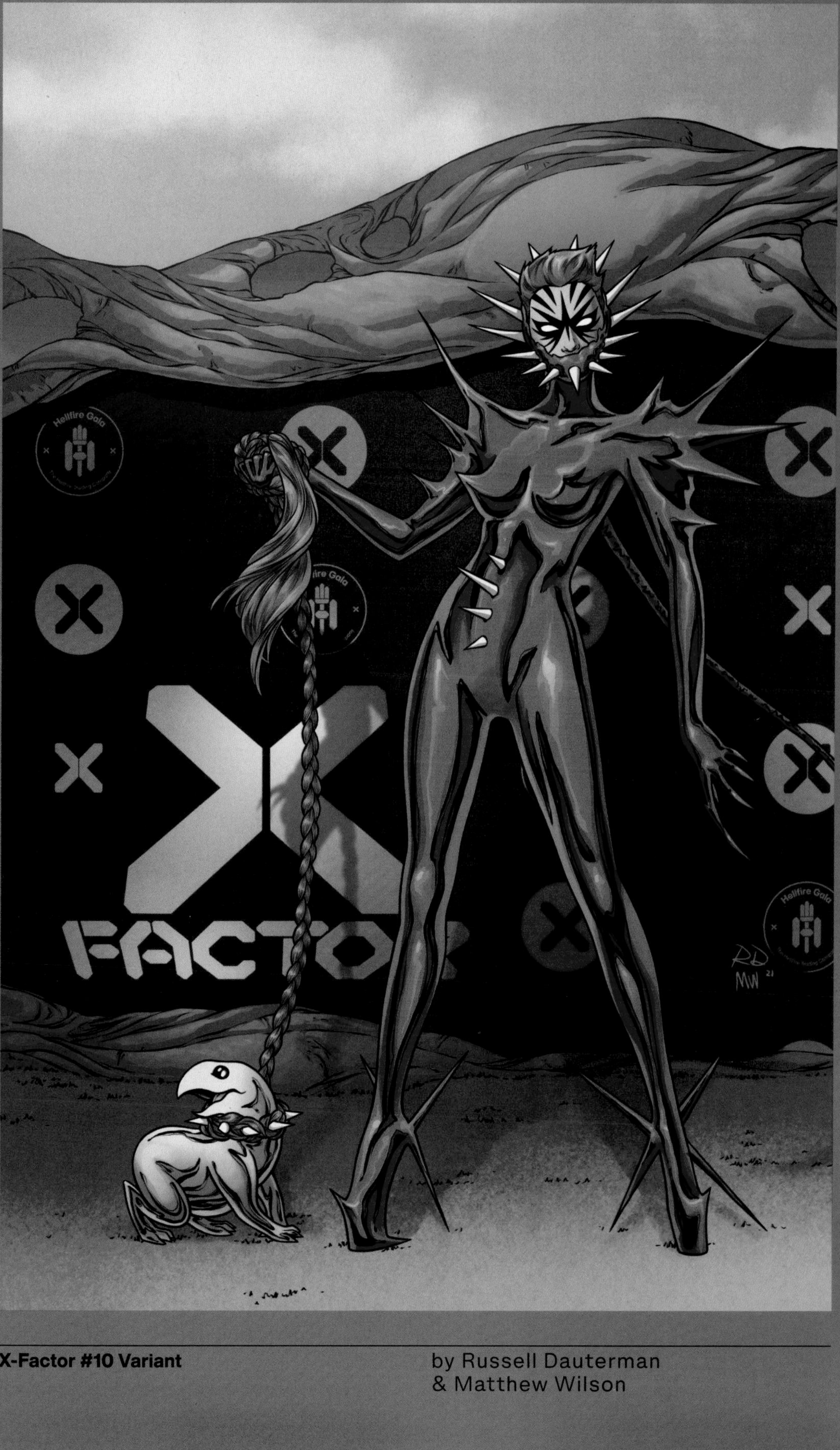
Hellfire Gala
Hellfire Gala
Hellfire Gala
X
FACTOR
RD
MW 21

X-Factor #10 Variant

by Russell Dauterman
& Matthew Wilson

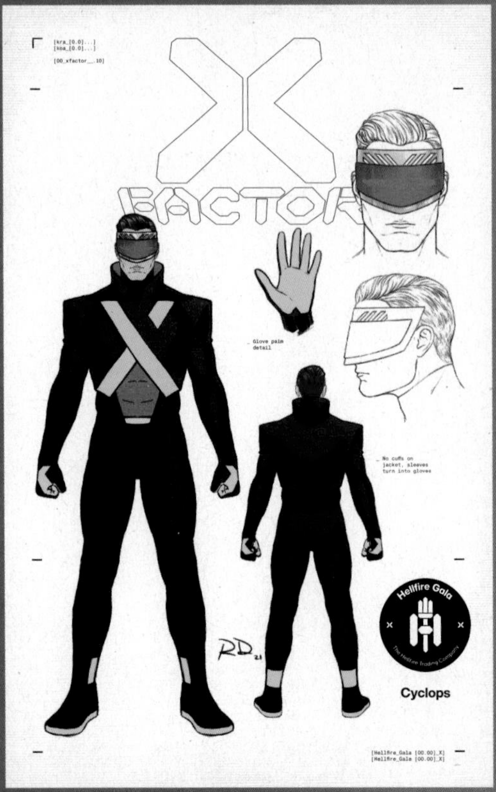
[kra_[0.0]...]
[koa_[0.0]...]
[00_xfactor__.10]
X-FACTOR
Glove palm detail
No cuffs on jacket, sleeves turn into gloves
Hellfire Gala
Cyclops
[Hellfire_Gala [00.00]_X]
[Hellfire_Gala [00.00]_X]

X-Factor #10 Cyclops Design Variant
by Russell Dauterman

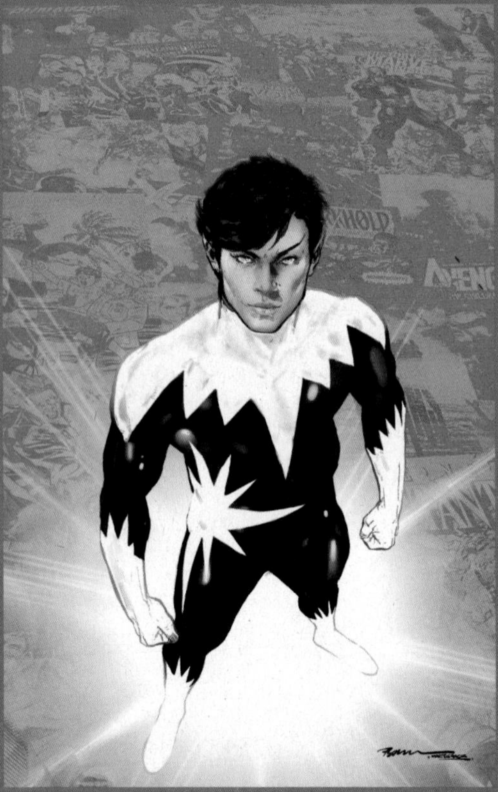

X-Men #10 Pride Month Variant
by Phil Jimenez & Marte Gracia

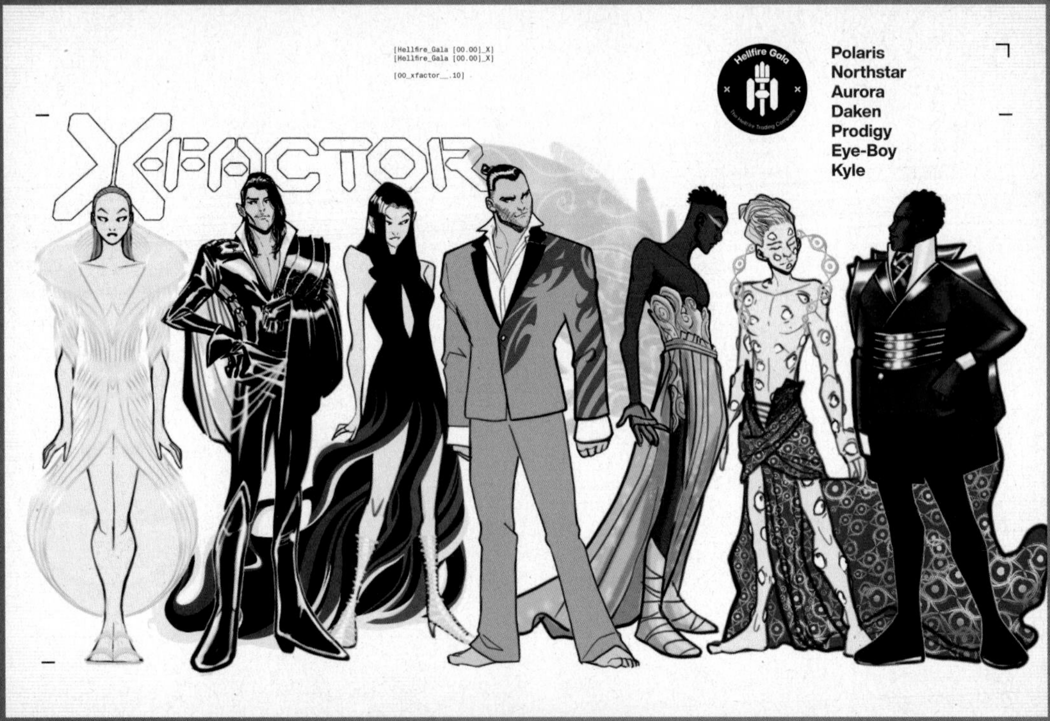
[Hellfire_Gala [00.00]_X]
[Hellfire_Gala [00.00]_X]
[00_xfactor__.10]
Hellfire Gala
X-FACTOR
Polaris
Northstar
Aurora
Daken
Prodigy
Eye-Boy
Kyle

X-Factor #10 Design Variant
by David Baldeón